Beyond the Tears

A True Survivor's Story

By

Lynn C. Tolson

ISBN: 1-4107-2416-6 (e-book)
ISBN: 1-4107-2417-4 (Paperback)

Library of Congress Control Number: 2003092018

This book is printed on acid free paper.

Printed in the United States of America
Bloomington, IN

1stBooks – rev. 03/20/03

Dedication

All my love to D.W.T., who provided the space, time, support, and unconditional love that enhanced my life, my healing and my writing.

Acknowledgements

My thanks to those who took on the task of reading early drafts and encouraged me to continue with this work: Tim Baylor, Linda Garlinger, Kelly Lock, Susan Preiss, LaVell Rucker, Pat Scott, Jill Takes. My heartfelt thanks to my counselors, Karen Edwards and Karen Martin. Thanks also to the the freelance editors who helped polish my work: Townley & Townley, Ink and Susan Ferguson.

Author's Note

The content of this book is personal memoir according to the author's experience. Most names and other identifying details have been changed to protect the privacy of the individuals involved. The counselor named in this book, Karen, is a composite character consisting of subsequent therapists, self-help books, and personal insights.

Prologue

For nearly twenty years, I engaged in careers in retail, real estate and property management. Every working day left me feeling unfulfilled, as if I was living a false life. My real life began not by changing jobs, but by putting pen to paper in journal writing sessions. Themes emerged regarding the impact of my sexual abuse, drug addiction, and suicide attempts. By using the journal to write about the problems and solutions discussed in my counseling sessions, a story of transformation evolved. My desire to share a message of healing from trauma became too strong to ignore; the book became a mission. I left the corporate environment to write my story about personal yet universal emotional issues. Although journal writing was a cathartic experience, the book was written with the courage to face my fears, with compassion for myself and others, and a conviction to tell the truth.

Sexual assault, addiction, and suicide are unsolved social problems that carry stigmas. The stigmas cast a code of silence that do not solve problems. The result from not speaking about the crime of sexual assault is too often tragic. Thus, there is a need for real stories of recovery. By bringing my dark secrets to light, it is my hope that others who have had similar events will know that they are not alone. Readers may explore their own emotions to open lines of communication, eliminate shame, and experience healing. I also hope that my book promotes understanding of the issues that cause individual suffering and plague our society.

This is our purpose: to make as meaningful as possible this life that has been bestowed upon us…to live in such a way that we may be proud of ourselves, to act in such a way that some part of us lives on.

Oswald Spengler

Pills and Prayer

Don't be afraid your life will end; be afraid it will never begin.

Grace Hansen

That night, December 20, 1978, the radio reported the most rain in Phoenix in one hundred years. Broadcasters called it the flood of the century. While I was driving, I listened to reports of accumulated rainfall and road closures. "Stay off the streets," the announcer warned. The wet pavement reflected the colored holiday lights that adorned cactus. Seasonal garlands, heavy with the weight of rainwater, drooped to the gutters. Carols interrupted newscasts, followed by the countdown: "Only four shopping days left until Christmas." I felt a pressure as intense as the rain that pounded on the windshield.

I sipped from the Michelob that rested between my legs, and then lit a cigarette. The cough of a nasty cold rattled my chest. As I passed gas stations and convenience stores, I could not decide whether or not to fill the empty gas tank. It was too dark to stop, too cold to get out, too wet to pump. My T-shirt and bra were soaked through to my skin, and the denim jacket and jeans provided no warmth. The heater vents blew warm currents of air, but I still shivered.

In a trance, I drove until the high beams of my Chevy formed a solitary tunnel of light. The roads were as dark as the thoughts driving me to an undetermined destination. The vehicle transporting me through the desolate desert was as isolated as the body that entrapped me on earth. I longed to be on the other side, in another realm.

After courting a death wish for over a decade, I thought I heard a voice that urged me to die. *Die! Die!* I imagined giving in to impulse and stabbing myself with scissors straight through the heart. *Die! Die!* Because I could no longer live with myself, self-annihilation seemed to be the only answer.

My hand shook as I reached for the glove compartment. My fingers trembled as much from fear as from the cold. The glove compartment contained vials of pain medication that my doctor had prescribed for the headaches that never ceased. I'd carefully counted and hoarded the pills: ninety Darvon Compound for mild pain, thirty Tylenol with Codeine for moderate pain, fifty Percodan for severe pain, one hundred Serax to relax me, Dalmane to sedate me, and Compazine for nausea. I planned on using this multicolored mix of tablets and capsules to put me out of my misery.

I had scripted suicide scenes for months, wondering how each setting would play out. If I killed myself in a muddy field, a cotton farmer would find a skeleton in the spring. If I committed suicide in the car along a county road, passersby would think the car had been abandoned in the mud. If the sheriff discovered my body locked inside the car, I would be considered a criminal because suicide was against the law. If I nicked a vein with a razor from my overnight bag, I would surely cringe at the first sight of blood. However, would I, could I feel any pain? Perhaps an oncoming cattle truck would veer across the yellow line, causing a head-on collision. If I spotted the bright, raised lights of a semi coming towards me, perhaps I could ever so slightly steer to the opposite lane. What if the truck driver had a family awaiting his Christmas homecoming? It would be best to stick to my original plan to take pills, leaving others out of it.

Close to midnight, I turned back toward town and pulled up to a Holiday Inn I had passed earlier. I parked in the far corner of the lot. After turning off the engine, I sat behind the wheel to think. Drops of rain were pelting the roof like pebbles: ping, ping, ping. I was trying to collect my thoughts.

I packed the collection of pills into my purse and grabbed the grocery bag of beer. As I stepped out of the car, cold currents of water washed over my leather clogs. The rustling leaves of the oleander hedge spooked me. I ran to the office. I must have looked like a breathless bag lady with wet brown hair, a soggy brown sack, and an overnight bag. As I checked in with cash, the desk clerk politely handed over a black key tag numbered 206.

In the motel room, I tugged the orange-and-green checked spread and the pillows from one bed and crawled into the other bed, fully clothed. This was the final suicide scene: checking out at the inn. Who would discover the body in the morning? Maybe the maid would think this guest was just asleep and forgot to put out the light and the do-not-disturb sign. I was still shivering, even after I'd wrapped myself in several blankets.

Sitting on the bed with legs crossed under me, I rocked back and forth. Every night I would rock away the day, rehashing the scenes that were safe to repeat and repressing the acts too intolerable to talk about. The rhythm of rocking silenced the cacophony of random thoughts. My life had been quite a dramatic production, and the curtain was finally closing.

I placed the prescription bottles around me in a semi-circle. They rattled like baby toys. I opened another beer and swallowed the Compazine first, so as not to vomit. Then, dumping the pills by handfuls into my mouth, I found they went down with an easy gulp. Soon my vision blurred and the patterns on the beds, the drapes, and the carpet floated around in geometric shapes of garish orange and green.

As I succumbed to drowsiness, I waited for death. I realized I was always waiting for some catastrophe to befall me. Why not get it over with? I gulped more pills and lay down, curled up.

I worried about the fate of my soul, if indeed I had a soul. Parochial school taught me that it was a sin to commit suicide, so I would burn in hell. Surely, my soul was unworthy of any place other than hellfire and damnation. At twenty-four years old, I deserved to die.

I sensed the presence of my deceased father. I was definitely my father's daughter, killing myself as he had killed himself. His surreal presence was neither benign nor violent, but finally, he was there for me. Was that my father whispering? *"No, Lynn, not this way."* God, please don't let my father haunt me in hell!

In case God could hear, I began to recite the Lord's Prayer: *"Our father, who art in Heaven, hallowed be Thy name, Thy kingdom come, Thy will be done, on earth as it is in Heaven."* I lost track of my place in the prayer and started over: *"Our Father, who art in Heaven, hallowed be Thy name, Thy kingdom come."* I forgot the rest and started again: *"Our Father, who art in Heaven."* How could I forget the prayer that was repeated a thousand times at Mass, in confession, during Lent and on Easter? *"Our Father, who art."*

Answer and Aftermath

Love is the only thing that we can carry with us when we go, and it makes the end so easy.

Louisa May Alcott

Suddenly, a low voice was whispering, "This way, here, over here! She checked in last night." *No! No! I checked out last night.*

An even deeper voice was counting, "one, two, three." Hands were lifting my limp body at the shoulders and ankles. Other voices were shouting from what seemed like a long distance: "Wake up, wake up!" A crisp slap to my face startled me. "Miss, open your eyes! Can you open your eyes?"

My eyes were shut tight. Even if I wanted to try, no force could open them. Fingers pried open my lids. Reluctantly, briefly, a hospital scene came into view. How did I get here, under overhead fluorescent lamps, with doctors and nurses leaning over my body? In green and white, they appeared in triplicate, like rows of cut-out paper dolls. One of the white triplets aimed a flashlight at my face. My eyes closed with leaden lids.

A voice was saying, "You are in the emergency room at Desert Community Hospital. What is your name? What did you take?"

I felt a liquid dribble down my chin as a paper cup was being shoved to my lips. An involuntary reflex made me gag as a tube was pushed into my mouth. *Please, leave me alone!* No voice came from my mouth. Pinpricks on the back of my hand made me jerk it free, but other hands held my wrist as a needle was inserted. Another tube went down my nose and throat, causing me to vomit a terrible tasting, thick, and chalky liquid.

A voice was saying, "What are these pink fragments? How many pills did you take?"

Was she examining my vomit? I told myself to give the voice a number to make her stop asking so many questions. I spit out the number "ninety."

She responded, "Did you say nineteen?"

What difference did it make? There was no point in saving my life. My inner self had already died. All that was left was a hollow outer shell.

Someone was wiping dribble from my mouth and chin. I could hear techno beeping sounds and humans whispering words as if I were eavesdropping on a telegraphed code from earth to hell. The word "why" was repeated as often as the beeps. Beep. Beep. Beep. Why. Why. Why. I could sense hands undressing my body. *Don't leave my body naked on the gurney!* The hands covered my body to the neck with a sheet, but I could not feel the contact of the cloth with my skin.

Dead. Dead. As if I were suspended from the ceiling, I looked upon my body. I saw a sad bag of bones with ghostly white skin and dark blue shadows under the eyes. I was finally dead.

Someone started using my name: "Lynn, Lynn, breathe, take a deep breath, breathe, hang in there! ECHO! STAT!" I sensed the tension as they tried to resuscitate my body. An urgent voice was shouting: "Blood pressure 60 over 40!"

Was that 40 over 60? How I wanted to tell them not to bother! I was not worth the effort. *Stop! Stop!* As much as I wanted those words to form on my lips, they remained in my brain. The body would not obey the mind, as if the body and mind were separate entities without connection. At death, I felt as powerless over my own body as I had been in life.

I heard: "I got a pulse!" It felt as though a dresser had been dropped on my chest, causing a sharp pain over my heart and a steady ache at my sternum. My head was throbbing with each heartbeat. My throat hurt with every swallow. As I breathed, I coughed. When I coughed, I vomited. My body trembled, my teeth chattered. *What went wrong?* I thought I was dead.

When I opened my eyes, I saw a wall of beeping monitors that cast a green light in the dim room. My body was shuddering uncontrollably, probably from the cold. As a nurse rolled a thermal blanket up to my chin, I noticed that I had been dressed in a hospital gown. "Your belongings are in a plastic bag under the bed," she said. The image of a bag lady came to mind again.

A dark man in a white coat said, "Welcome back. I am Dr. Fernandez." He spoke with a kind tone in a Latin accent. "How are you?"

Did he expect a response? I waited awhile, but he did not go away. Neither did the nurse, who was explaining the insertion of a catheter to empty my bladder. Apparently, not all physiological systems were receiving messages that the brain was transmitting.

"Did I die?" A hoarse sound rose from a dry well so deep below the surface that I did not recognize my own voice. The doctor looked at me. I avoided his eyes.

He answered, "Yes, you were gone for two minutes. You are in the intensive cardiac care unit. You have cardiac complications and there is a fifty/fifty chance of brain damage. You are on seizure precaution. Your condition is critical. All you can do for now is rest."

Alas, I was alive. I alternated between sleep and waking. *Please, God, let me fall asleep and never wake up*. My eyes closed.

A man's voice was softly repeating my name. The air around the voice smelled of antibacterial soap. "Lynn, Lynn?" It was Dr. Fernandez again. *Did he ever give up?* He asked, "Why did you want to die? You are so young. You have so much to live for."

His voice was gentle yet sure. But I was not comforted. I could not fathom life as anything other than a bleak descent into a blank chasm. How could anyone relate to my interminable sadness?

"Is there anything you want to talk about?" he asked.

"My head hurts," I moaned.

"I bet it does," he replied with sympathy. "But pain medication could set you back and the intravenous medications will strengthen you. We need more tests: electrocardiograms and electroencephalograms, a neurological exam and a psychiatric evaluation."

Why did he care? I didn't care about anything. However, I noticed the pleasing lilt of his accent and his accurate pronunciation of each syllable.

"Where are you from?" I dared to ask.

"I am from Honduras," Dr. Fernandez said.

"Where is that?"

"It is a country in Central America. I was fortunate to come to America to study medicine."

I was surprised by the civil and simple way that he answered, as if it were no bother to take the time to talk. He moved gracefully from monitor to monitor as he studied the peaks and valleys of white lines. "A nurse found the 'in case of emergency' card in your wallet and called the number," the doctor said.

What right did they have to search my wallet?

"We had to notify your kin of your condition," he explained, as if reading my mind.

A woman's voice was saying, "She's in and out of consciousness."

My awareness was sharpened by the smell of cheap cologne. My eyes opened to the sight of my estranged husband, Todd. I would rather be rendered unconscious than to see him seeing me. The heart monitor rapidly beeped in response to my pounding heart. As the nurse checked my blood pressure, she called Dr. Fernandez into the room. Dr. Fernandez asked, "Lynn, is this your husband?"

It took effort to nod my head as it lay on the pillow.

Todd lifted a cigarette from his shirt pocket.

"You can't smoke in here," the nurse warned.

Todd questioned the doctor as to the purpose of the machines. "What is this one for? What does that one do?" Any other husband would ask about his wife's chances of surviving. However, Todd had his own survival in mind. "You can't pin this on me," he told Dr. Fernandez.

The doctor subtly moved toward the bed and assured Todd, "No one is to blame." While they stood side by side, I studied their differences. The doctor was wearing a pressed coat and a red tie. His skin was tanned, even for an Arizona winter, and his wavy brown hair was cut to the collar of his green oxford shirt. I glanced at his brown eyes and received a look of concern in response. His bearing seemed more like a soldier than a cardiac surgeon, with his hands at his sides, ready to respond to the needs of others.

Todd was tall and slim in comparison, but Todd was slouching, and appeared small. Todd looked disheveled with his generic nylon jacket thrown over his shoulders. His skin was creased and yellow, and his salt-and-pepper beard was in need of a trim. When I looked directly at Todd, he averted his eyes; his blue eyes were like denim that had faded with age. He looked as old as he was, old enough to be my father. He kept his hands in his pockets, as if he had something to hide. Todd asked the doctor, "How about I have a moment alone with my wife?"

Dr. Fernandez watched a machine for a moment, and then walked with a smooth gait out of the room. Todd lumbered closer, bringing his smell of stale cigarettes and coffee breath to the bed. He whispered, "A spic doctor can not be trusted as far as you could throw him."

I suddenly doubted the steady compassion I thought I had experienced from Dr. Fernandez.

Todd turned to a monitor, traced a dotted graph with his finger, and said, "The nurse made it sound like you were a goner. It takes no guts to try to kill yourself." He then mumbled something about a "vegetable." He left the room, leaving me as alone as ever.

While Dr. Fernandez reentered the room and adjusted a wire over my heart, he said, "I am required by law to contact a psychiatrist after suicide attempts and gunshot wounds. I've arranged an appointment with your psychiatrist, Dr. Weingart."

"How did you know about the shrink?"

"Your mental health history is on record here at the hospital."

I thought about how I had met Dr. Weingart four months earlier, during the summer. The brutal desert heat had caused a stream of migraines and misery that literally drove me to the ground, begging for mercy. I had considered crawling on the sun-baked asphalt in front of speeding cars. Fearing for my life, I'd made an appointment with a psychologist. After evaluating me with psychological tests and consulting with a neurologist, the psychologist consulted the psychiatrist, Dr. Weingart, who had recommended a psychiatric unit. By that time, I would have done anything to relieve my suffering, so I voluntarily committed myself. Being under Dr. Weingart's care had obviously been unproductive; I was probably an uncooperative patient. I had been released from that unit only three weeks prior to the current suicide attempt.

I opened an eye to see Dr. Weingart sitting by my hospital bed. He was a puny man with a dour demeanor, and was wearing his usual dark suit and tie. After he jotted notes in a chart, he announced, “Your family should know you’re here. I will tell the nurse to call your mother. I’ll see you tomorrow.” His snappish attitude, gray goatee, and bushy eyebrows reminded me of a miniature schnauzer.

A nurse put a plate of toast beside me. The presence of food caused a round of nausea that had me retching with dry heaves. The nurse asked, “How can I help you?” as she gently popped ice chips into my mouth.

I heard my voice croaking, “What day is this?”

The nurse answered, “Why, dear, it’s the day before Christmas Eve.” Then she sat on the edge of the bed. “I called your mother.”

“My mother?”

“Yes, her name is Sophia, right? She said she couldn’t visit you because the bridge from Phoenix to Tempe was swept away by flood waters.”

That sounded like a weak excuse because the roads were built in one-mile grids, and if one road was blocked, it was simple to go to another. The real reason was that my mother would not want to see the sorry sight of her daughter in the aftermath of a suicide attempt. Her husband, my stepfather, would not be surprised if I jumped off the bridge into the turbulent waters of the Rio Grande. My father’s widow, my stepmother, had sealed my sad fate long ago with her prediction. “Mark my words,” she had warned, “You will end up a schizoid just like your father.” The family would be more comfortable attending my funeral because then I would be unlikely to tell them the real reasons for “why?”

As the nurse changed bags of fluid over the bed, she stated, “By the way, your mother said she loves you.”

“What?” My voice cracked through my parched throat. “Did my mother really say that?”

“Yes, Sophia said she loves you.”

Even after this? How could she still love me? The mere mention of love ignited an ember of emotion. Love? My father’s schizophrenia had burned my love to ashes. He had been incapable of loving me, and I believed that rendered me eternally unlovable. My mother’s message sparked a breath of life; after all, wasn't love what I really wanted?

In another two days, Dr. Fernandez was preparing me for release from the cardiac care unit to the psychiatric ward. "Your condition is stable, but you have paroxysmal Atrial tachycardia and Mitral-valve Prolapse, neither of which is life-threatening if you take care of yourself. I'm prescribing Lanoxin and Inderal to treat the symptoms of irregular heartbeat and angina. I'm also prescribing Dilantin to prevent seizures. Meanwhile, I highly recommend that you quit smoking. Be sure to make an appointment at my office for follow-up. Okay?"

I nodded. Although I was not exactly grateful to be alive, I silently thanked him for caring. Orderlies rolled me onto a stretcher as intravenous bags swayed overhead, and I was transported to the psych ward.

Recuperation and Reflections

Why is it when we talk to God, we're said to be praying; but when God talks to us, we're schizophrenic?

Lily Tomlin

A parade of nurses marched in and out of my room with needles, vials, and papers to sign. Just as I started to doze, Dr. Weingart walked into the room, his shoes striking the tile in a staccato rhythm: Tap, tap, tap.

He was peering at the chart through his bifocals. He was not big on small talk. "Your liver and kidney functions are being screened for damage because of the high level of toxicity." He raised his head, "Was this suicide attempt an act of passion or a premeditated action?"

I was tempted to say that it was a premeditated act of passion demonstrating cold revenge on an uncooperative universe. Instead, I was silent.

Dr. Weingart lectured: "I get paid whether or not you talk. If you try a stunt like that again, I will not be your doctor. I will refer your case to the state, and state institutions are worse than death. You don't want to go to the state mental hospital, do you?"

This was a threat I had to respond to with a slight turn of my head.

As he was leaving, he said, "If you refuse to talk, then think about where you are and where you are going."

I had no clue, no compass, and no map, not even a phone book. What I thought about was whether Dr. Weingart considered my case merely a risk to his reputation or if he had any concern for me as a person. It was difficult for me to determine a genuine gesture from an ulterior motive.

I thought about the group therapy sessions Weingart had prescribed during the previous confinement. The psychiatric aide leading the session would say, "Let's help Lynn increase her self-esteem." The group would chant, "I matter," expecting me to repeat it like a parrot. The words were hollow sounds; no matter how many times I had stated, "I matter" I had not *felt* like I mattered. After watching them waste their time for nearly an hour, I would ask the group, "Can you please pick on somebody else?"

I thought about the consultations that Dr. Weingart had arranged with the career counselor. Using my food tray as a desk, I'd marked "always" or "never" to hundreds of questions on personality inventories. A wide variety of interests had suggested a career as an actor or writer. I thought I just did not know what I wanted to do. The counselor had concluded that I had the ability to instill trust in people, draw them out and rally them together to pursue a common purpose. I could not catch the career counselor's assessment of "leadership abilities." Me? A leader? They had to be kidding!

The unit nurses had suggested books from the ward library such as "How To Be Your Own Best Friend." Me? My own best friend? What were they thinking?

I'd been skeptical of hug therapy, anger therapy, physical therapy, biofeedback, psychodrama, and psychobabble. I preferred my warm fuzzies full strength in a pill. Perhaps a lobotomy or shock therapy could knock some sense into me. I was supposed to recover my mental and physical strength but was out of resources, or unable to use what was available. My summer stay at psych camp had been a fiasco.

Now, on Christmas Eve morning, I wandered the same ward while wheeling an IV along like a wagon. Links of construction paper formed a red-and-green chain around the nurses' station. Patients had probably crafted the decorations during recreational therapy before being granted holiday passes. No patients I knew from my previous confinement were still on the ward.

Gone was Jose, the barefoot and robed religious zealot who thought he was the incarnation of Jesus Christ. His delusions included burning bushes and stone tablets. In a voice fit for a television preacher, he had boomed: "God spoke to me on behalf of you! Have you been saved? Have you been born again?" As I remembered his passionate pleas, I thought to myself: It took me years to descend into hell, then minutes to be dead, and now it will take forever and a day to be reborn. I could have used a miracle.

Gone was Michael, the twenty-year-old gay son of a Mormon minister, an identical twin to a straight brother. Michael's wrists had been bandaged from a run-in with razor blades after his father tried to beat and berate him into heterosexuality. Michael wanted a baby to prove he was a man and wanted me to have his baby. All I had to do was bear his child. "Once, just once, let's do it," he had begged. I had no inclination toward motherhood, surrogate or otherwise. Michael was discharged to the care of his family, only to commit suicide three days later with his whole month's supply of Elavil.

Gone was Joni, the schizophrenic lesbian twenty-two-year-old adopted daughter of Bible-belt parents. She looked tough with her cropped hair, stocky build, leather bomber jacket, and work boots. However, she composed sensitive songs on her acoustic guitar and sang aloud in the activity room: *"Come and share the rainbow, meant for only two."* Joni asked to make love to me but I was not in the mood for passion, lesbian or otherwise. The one and only time Joni had had intercourse, which was during a drunken stupor at her high school graduation, she got pregnant. Her parents gained custody of the child after a series of court cases. Joni had failed to appear in court, and then appeared intoxicated in court. That further proved that she was unfit as a mother, even as she yearned for her daughter. She tried to kill herself. She had lifted her plaid flannel shirt to show me the bullet wound; the skin folds of her belly had a sinkhole, like a second navel with jagged edges. Joni lived on Thorazine, Stelazine and Heineken, Social Security, Disability, Medicaid and legal aid. She lived in juvenile hall, detoxification units, mental hospitals, and jail. She left our shared psychiatric unit against medical advice. The last I heard, Joni was picked up by the police for being drunk and disorderly and was escorted to the state hospital.

Gone was Brenda, the manic-depressive fifty-five-year-old childless insurance executive. Unable to make peace with her choice of career over family, she longed for a baby to prove she was a natural woman. Her belly was swollen in a false pregnancy, although Brenda believed it was real. She patted her belly as it ballooned with air: "My baby, my baby!" According to her, I should have a baby before it was too late. Even after spending long evenings in her room listening to her sermon about regrets, my maternal instincts would not surface.

Brenda was sent home with lots of Lithium when her insurance no longer covered her particular condition.

Sexual orientation was a frequent topic of discussion on the mental ward. It was one way to determine identity, to classify, and/or to diagnose. No matter what the inclination, homosexual, bisexual or heterosexual, what did it matter? Since I thought it did not matter, did that make me asexual? Either way, I was indifferent.

I thought I knew better what others felt than what I felt myself. However, how well could I have known schizophrenics, depressives, and manic-depressives zoned out on psychotropic drugs? Our conversations included comparisons of prescriptions, the effects, the side effects, and the drugs to counteract the side effects. We vented how the drugs made us feel instead of expressing any actual emotions. "I feel like I'm jumping out of my skin" was a common complaint, as if it were a diagnosable ailment. I was given anti-depressants and sleeping pills. Wrapped in medications like a mummy buried alive, I felt trapped in my own flesh, even as I longed for freedom from life itself.

Instead of delving into the meanings of dreams, a patient would be given Ativan, which induced sleep without dreams. Instead of facing a repressed experience with eyes wide open, a patient might receive intravenous Sodium Amytal. The psychiatrist would question the patient, and this "truth serum" would cause the truth to surface when the patient was in a dreamlike state. Accessing the truth required time, and who had time to spare?

Sometimes, but not often, someone actually unearthed an emotion recognized from those distant days before the psychological wounds and the psychiatric establishment stole a personality. Most often, an assortment of pharmaceuticals altered the consciousness, and what needed to be known for healing remained buried in the subconscious.

While I walked around the ward on Christmas Eve, I was missing my funny farm friends. With them, I was not a misfit. A misfit does not fit anywhere except with misfits. There was something missing in me, and if only I could figure it out, I would figure it in. What would I do without my buddies? I'd been warned by psych nurses that my fascination for eccentric personalities kept me from facing my own psyche.

An older woman wearing a sleeveless housedress and bunny slippers was talking to the television, raising her arms in wild gestures, revealing armpits of hair. "Tell me child," she said when she noticed me. "Do you believe in Santa Claus?"

"Only when it snows in Phoenix," I retorted.

"But, child, it never snows in Phoenix."

I had no desire to make nice to any patients leftover for the holidays. I was without the energy to deal with their idiosyncrasies. I wandered back to my room just in time for lunch. Diana, who was my favorite psychiatric nurse, sat with me. I stabbed squishy macaroni and cheese with a plastic fork. The awful hospital food didn't fill the emptiness inside. I picked up a paper pill cup. "What are these?"

"Your midday meds," Diana said.

"I know that, but what are they?

"An anti-biotic, anti-depressant, anti-seizure, and multi-vitamin. You know, I suspected you would be back to the ward," she said.

"How could you know that?"

"You were not ready to leave the first time," Diana said. "Dr. Weingart was upset by your suicide attempt."

"Why would he be upset?"

"If the attempt was an unplanned act of passion, you might try it once. He's upset that it was calculated, and you might plan another. For now, you are on suicide watch."

I was not permitted to have matches or a lighter. When I wanted a cigarette, I asked an aide for a light. Sometimes I lit my Marlboro with a smoldering stub from a tin ashtray in the recreation room. I was not allowed a razor. If I wanted to shave, a nurse was assigned to supervise. Hairy armpits were the least of my problems, so I did not bother. A caged gorilla had more civil liberties than patients on the psych wing.

Diana sat on the bed while I bathed. She supervised without suspicion and encouraged conversation to alleviate embarrassment. "Lynn, you are very pretty. Why don't you take care of yourself?"

"Diana, you are the pretty one. You look like a Greek goddess, with your clear olive complexion, green eyes, and brunette hair. You look as though a Renaissance artist sculpted your figure. You walk like an elegant aristocrat. I wish I looked like you."

"You don't have to look like anyone but yourself. Your skin is fair, like porcelain, and you have beautiful eyes. Why not use makeup to enhance your features?"

"I don't want to appear vain. The nuns at school taught me that vanity is a sin."

"It is not vanity," Diana said. "It's about being good to yourself."

Diana unpacked a bag from a drug store: a liquid foundation called "Porcelain Beige," a tube of mascara in jet-black, and a pot of rosy red lip-gloss. Dressed in a robe, I sat next to her, pulling the hand mirror on the bed tray close to my face. Diana reached for my hair and brushed the strands away from my cheeks, saying, "Your hair is so shiny and silky! The natural red highlights give it an auburn hue."

What pretty face did Diana see? As a teen, I had mastered the technique of putting on makeup without actually looking at my face. The current crop of cystic acne and pus pimples was painful as I covered my face with foundation. The fluid sank into the pits that remained from the nights I spent popping pimples instead of primping for proms. My skin was a scrapbook of scars. When I was lonely, I applied scalding hot washcloths onto the erupting pimples. When I was angry, I squeezed blackheads until my nails left dents in the skin. I assaulted the acne with masochistic wrath, then felt a sense of release. Cosmetics were used in an effort to hide multiple facial flaws.

Diana touched my arm and said, "Try not to focus on faults only you can see."

As I slipped on the raspberry flavored lip-gloss, Diana noticed the open sore on my bottom lip. "Why do you bite your lip?"

"I don't know. Habit, I suppose."

Diana argued, "It appears to be more than a habit. I wonder what it is you are trying so hard not to tell." She did not pry any further; she must have assumed that my lips were sealed.

Diana pulled a small book from the bag. "This is a journal, or it will be when you write in it."

I flipped through the lined, blank book with the cloth cover. "But how could I write in it without ruining it?"

"Based on your description of me as a Greek goddess, I'd say you have a way with words. You should write about your experiences."

"What could I write that would be interesting?"

"If there is something you need to say but you can't quite verbalize it, you could write in the privacy of your journal."

I was wondering what I could tell Dear Diary that was not too taboo to talk about.

Diana said, "You have a lot going for you. All you have to do is to be yourself."

I was wondering who or what I was, but I was more curious about a former patient, Carol. She had been released from the earlier confinement at the same time as I. After months in the hospital, I was separated from my husband and estranged from my mother and stepfather. Rather than return to Todd, I had accepted Carol's invitation to stay at her house for three weeks. I slept on the couch, babysat her five children, and cleaned her kitchen. Carol repeatedly played the song by Anne Murray, "You Needed Me," as if it were our song.

Each evening, after the kids were in bed, Carol and her husband tried to entice me into kinky sex acts, sharing their fantasy of an Oreo cookie arrangement with my body as the creamy middle. Fending off their seductions required more energy than the making of five twin beds, two double beds, and a pull out sofa each morning. I ran from their house of pornographic nightmares. Rather than engaging in their sick escapades, I slept in my car. After a night or two in the cold rain, I checked into a motel.

"Diana, can you tell me what happened to Carol?"

"This is strictly off the record. Carol has multiple personality disorder and her husband is a known con man. You should end that friendship."

"Yeah, but, they have my things."

From my hospital bed, I dialed Carol's number.

Carol whimpered, "I knew you were going to off yourself."

Carol had talked of her own suicide attempts. We'd agreed that suicide was supposed to offer ultimate relief from unrelenting pain. Carol's use of slang insulted the serious intention.

"Could you please bring the things I left at your house to the hospital?"

"I suppose," Carol said, as if this were an imposition.

Several days later, Carol's husband dropped off a garbage bag at the nurse's station. When he did not even say hello, I figured my usefulness to them had run its course.

An orderly brought the garbage bag with my boots, books, cassettes and tape recorder into my room. Dumping the contents onto the bed, I greedily dove for the chocolate bar that landed on the pillow. My life indeed seemed reduced to that of a bag lady. I was alone with nowhere to go, so I wrote in my journal:

Loneliness envelopes my being, seals me in a tomb lacking air.
I am trapped in the darkness of my heart, all alone,
Choking and grasping to find tender loving care.

I closed my door to the forced cheer of the volunteer Christmas carolers as they made their duty bound rounds. Christmas in the psychiatric unit was far from festive.

While I sat rocking on the bed, a Neil Diamond song played on the tape recorder: *"I am, I said, to no one there, and no one heard at all, not even the chair."* My interpretation of the lyrics evolved into: I am a chair! I am an object! A memory formed as corporeal as that contained under the influence of truth serum: Could that really have been my big brother using me as an inanimate sex object? I am a chair! I am an object! I shoved the ambiguous memory down just as quickly as it had floated up. As I sat on the bed in the psych ward, I picked up a plastic potted poinsettia and hurled it into the closed door of the room.

Two night nurses who I hardly recognized rushed in: "Calm down, calm down! We're on the skeleton crew. If you do not calm down, we will have to restrain you. You don't want that, do you?"

One nurse consulted with the other, "What's the doctor's orders for when she's out of control?"

"Haldol," she replied.

Haldol? He ordered Haldol? An anti-psychotic? No way! Dr. Weingart had diagnosed anxiety/depression. I was not schizophrenic or manic-depressive. He told me he would not resort to psychotropic drugs.

After the nurse injected my buttock, she yanked up the bed rails; they made a clanging sound that put me in my place. Actually, it was a relief to go under the relaxing effect of the medication.

As I lay on my back, it appeared as though leafy, thorny live plants with long stems were hanging from the ceiling and reaching down to wrap around my neck. Even when I closed my eyes, the vision of strangling stems remained. That was unreal! The drug used as an anti-psychotic was causing psychotic hallucinations.

Suddenly, my neck went into a spasm and my head flopped to my left shoulder. I could not get my neck straight. What if it stayed this way? I would be a freak eating out of the side of my head. My face slumped and saliva slipped out from the corners of my mouth. I tried to call for a nurse but I could only groan. After what felt like hours, a nurse injected my upper arm with something to counteract the Haldol. The visions and spasm subsided. The reaction to the medication scared me more than any outburst of anger. Still, I knew no methods to control the rage that seethed under my skin.

By New Year's Eve, the nasty cough was still rattling my chest. Against medical advice, I'd smoked enough cigarettes to cultivate a case of bronchitis, which lingered long enough to lead to pneumonia. My resolution was to cure the sore throat so I could resume smoking.

Three weeks after the suicide attempt, I was discharged from Desert Community Hospital. Diana brought me to the Holiday Inn to retrieve my car. A couple of weeks earlier, I had called the motel manager. He agreed to leave my car on the lot until I was "better." I'd wondered what illness he thought I had been hospitalized for. The car contained most of my belongings, books in the back seat and clothes thrown in the trunk, as if it had served as a home.

"Where will you go?" Diana asked.

"I don't know. Back to Todd, I guess."

Diana said, "You need a solid plan. Don't forget to make appointments with Dr. Weingart. Let me know how you are doing, okay? I hope you will take care of yourself."

The words of Emily Dickinson came to mind:

"Hope is the thing with feathers that perches in the soul,
And sings the tune without the words and never stops at all."

Once, I might have experienced hope. Now, nothing filled the hole in my heart where hope used to be. The despondency was so profound that I still wanted to die. Or perhaps I just did not want to live in the way I had been living.

It was disorienting to leave the safe confinement of the hospital and enter the hazards of the real world. I sat in the car like it was the first time behind the wheel. What's first? What's next? I lifted the floor mat to get the twenty-dollar bill I had reserved, just in case. In slow motion I lit a cigarette, turned the key, and started the engine. The windshield wipers started where they had stopped, smearing mud. My heart was throwing arrhythmias in contrast to the rhythm of the wipers.

At the gas station, I avoided any eye contact and wondered if the attendant registered my brush with insanity. He barely noticed me, no one noticed me. I was anonymous to the world. Where could I go?

Olivia Newton-John sang on the radio: "*Have you never been mellow.*" As I drove, I shouted: No, I have never been mellow!

I was overwhelmed with pain. It was not the physical pain of a fractured limb, but the psychic pain of a shattered soul. The psychiatric unit had not fixed what was broken inside me or found what was missing from me. The aborted suicide attempt only added insult to a wounded spirit. I was denied death yet life was too difficult. Life had not ended as planned, and now I had to live with that fact.

In utter despair, I shook my fist at a god I did not understand: If I have to live, then guide me, God, tell me what to do and show me where to go. God, show me a sign! Perhaps a poem would impress Him:

Hear me, oh God, for I am in pain,
Hear me, oh God, yeah, it's me again.
Hear me, dear God, for I want to be free,
Hear me, dear God, please, let me be me!

Counseling and Commitment

To gain that which is worth having, it may be necessary to lose everything.

Bernadette Devlin

A January thaw had settled on the desert, and the weather was warm and sunny. On a familiar road, I noticed for the first time a house with a sign. I drove past the sign, but an interest in its words compelled me to turn the car around. I parked the car in the gravel driveway to get a closer look at the sign, "Family Counseling Center."

It was unlike me to approach any strange place. However, I surprised myself by softly knocking on the door. As I stood at the door, I started to cry. A tall woman wearing khaki pants and a blue knit cardigan answered the door. She had short, curly blonde hair, a fair complexion covered with freckles, and blue eyes that matched her sweater. She smiled with an aura of serenity and asked, "Can I help you?"

How could she help a screw-up like me? Even after clearing my throat, I could not answer through the tears. As she led me inside, she said, "My name is Karen. I'm a counselor here."

The front room of the house was sparsely furnished as an office, with only a desk and chair. I wanted to flee, but my body remained fixed to the worn carpet.

Karen offered a box of tissues, "Would you like one?"

"No, thank you."

"Go ahead, you can take a tissue."

While I wiped my eyes, Karen led me to a room with a shabby corduroy couch, a round table, and five straight-backed chairs. My eyes searched the room for anything that could catch me unaware.

"You're safe here. Please, have a seat," Karen said. "This is an agency that offers counseling. The sessions are based on a sliding scale fee system, so if someone can't afford to pay, it's covered. Okay?"

I nodded.

"Good enough," Karen said. "Now let me tell you a little about myself. I'm originally from Utah, and now live in Mesa with my husband and three young daughters. What's your name?"

"It's Lynn," I mumbled through tears and tissues.

"Lynn, is there anything else you can tell me about yourself?"

"Well, no, not really."

"You're at this counseling agency, which is a big step to take when you're hurting. There must be something you have to say."

"Well, uh, I must be crazy. Can you tell me if I'm crazy?

"Crazy is not a label I would use. I have a master's degree in marriage and family counseling. I'm also trained to offer spiritual counseling. I don't like the word crazy."

I wanted to trust this woman with the sincere smile, but I wasn't searching for religion. "Do I have to be religious to get counseling?"

"The agency does not have a religious association. But if you want to include spiritual concepts as part of a therapy process, I can help you. What makes you ask about being crazy?"

"Well, I'm scared to death of life itself."

"Please tell me more."

"I have nightmares, even during the day. Memories materialize like a movie I am living through, not acting in, but then the film fades, and I space out or run away. An impulse to do myself in comes over me. I have to get rid of the pain. I feel like I'm gong crazy, or I've already gone crazy."

"I can help," Karen offered. "You must promise not to attempt suicide."

"Well, nearly three hundred pills did not kill me, so nothing else will."

"You took three hundred pills?"

"Yeah. It's ironic."

"I don't get the irony. Please explain."

"Well, I once used uppers to feel alive. Then I used downers to die. It's also ironic that I tried to control my life by attempting death. Now I suppose I *have* to live."

"What's wrong with that?"

"Life is too hard."

"Yes, people encounter many disappointments, but not every letdown leads to despair. There are ways to allow the pain to surface without giving in to the impulse to self-destruct. You can learn to balance despair and the desire to live."

"But how can I feel better?"

"You can commit yourself to counseling."

"With you?"

"Yes."

Talk therapy? I wanted to erase my experiences, not divulge them. However, with every tentative bit of information I blurted, Karen responded with respect and concern, and that gave me the courage to continue.

"Tell me, Lynn, where are you living now?"

"I don't know. First I was in the hospital, then I was in a hotel for a couple of days."

"Where are your parents?"

"My father is dead. My mother and stepfather live in Phoenix."

"I'm sorry about your father. Why don't you stay with your mother and stepfather?"

"They disowned me."

Karen looked as if I'd used a foreign language. "What do you mean?" she asked.

"Well, I was a rebellious teenager. I guess I put them through too much. My mother said I could never go home again."

"That must be hard for you. Do you have any siblings?"

"I have a younger brother, Ryan, who lives with my parents. I have an older brother, Eric, who lives in Pennsylvania."

"Are you married?"

"Yes, sort of. We've been separated for six months."

"What's the possibility of returning to your husband?"

"I don't know."

"Let's find out. What can you tell me about your relationship?"

I told Karen about the psychiatric unit that past summer, and the one therapy session that had included Todd. My psychiatrist, Dr. Weingart, had insisted on meeting my husband. The doctor indicated that it was necessary for him to evaluate all factors that led to my "condition." Dr. Weingart's assistant repeatedly made calls to arrange marriage-counseling sessions for Todd and me. Apparently, several alternative appointment times had been offered to Todd but he claimed each one was an inconvenience. Finally, in the third month of my hospitalization, Todd agreed to an appointment.

As if poised for a circus act, I waited with Dr. Weingart for Todd to show up for the appointment. The anticipation was as protracted as a trapeze artist performing without a net. After arriving late, Todd refused to take a seat and shouted: "You shrinks are just out to milk my insurance. *She* is not *my* problem. I don't give a damn if she rots in this money-grubbing hellhole." He threw his wedding band on the floor, stormed out of the room, and slammed the door.

Dr. Weingart called security to escort Todd out of the building. For a psychiatrist who had probably seen everything, he seemed stunned.

"What's a woman like you doing with a jerk like that?" Weingart asked.

"I don't know."

"Don't you think Todd's performance seemed rehearsed? He was too ready to demonstrate with the ring as a prop. Throwing the ring indicated that the marriage does not mean much to Todd."

"I wouldn't know."

"Todd is twice your age yet he acts like a juvenile. Why would you want to be married to a man so much older and far less mature than you?"

"I honestly don't know."

"I'll tell you why! You have a passive-aggressive personality disorder. You are searching for a satisfying father figure to rely on for security. Yet, Todd is dependent on you for his own ego gratification. When he thinks you are fulfilling his needs, his ego is satisfied. Furthermore, to reinforce his ego, Todd treats you like an infant. So the security you're seeking is unattainable."

I was too shaken to decipher the doctor's Freudian theories. I cradled my head in my hands, trying to hush what sounded like bowling pins being knocked about in my brain.

"As your therapist, I will not support efforts to save the marriage. There is no love and no trust. You must make a life separate from

Todd. For that, you need independent living skills. I insist that you participate in the assertiveness training sessions."

I was trying to ignore the ring on the carpet. The silver band, inlaid with turquoise, seemed to mock me with its symbolic insignificance. Todd had haggled with a dealer at a swap meet for the cheap piece of jewelry. The wedding band wasn't worth the effort it took to bend over and pick it up.

In the assertiveness training sessions, I learned that I was indeed passive-aggressive, allowing emotions to simmer until they exploded like an untended pressure-cooker. An assertive personality considers everyone's rights while striking a balance between compliance and resistance. I learned that "no" is an acceptable answer all by itself. No. No. No. I had the right to say no, and the right not to feel guilty about saying no.

I learned how body language conveys messages. The psychiatric aide pointed out that I usually stood with my arms folded across my chest, as if to hold myself together. Or I sat on a couch with a pillow over my abdomen, as if to protect myself. In the assertiveness class, the aide encouraged me to practice standing in an upright posture that demonstrated control of my surroundings.

Karen had been listening as I talked about that particular session with Dr. Weingart and the subsequent assertiveness training classes. All the while I was waiting for her to tell me to quit whining. Instead, she said, "You learned a lot in a short period of time. What insights do you have that would relate to the here and now?"

"It seems inconceivable to return to Todd. At the same time, I desperately need a place. Perhaps if I'm assertive with Todd we can get along until I get my act together."

"As long as you'll be safe," Karen said.

"Beats the streets!"

From an office at the center, I called Todd for reconciliation.

"Todd?"

"Oh, it's the prodigal wife," he said. "I'm getting ready for work. I took an extra mid shift. What do you want?"

"I'm out of the hospital."

"It's about time. Where do you think you're going next?"

"Actually, I was hoping we could give our marriage another chance."

"Is that right?"

"Yeah. You were right. I can't live without you. I need you."

"Woman, you are a nut-case. What exactly is it that you want?"

"I want to come home."

"I told you so."

After I hung up the phone, I told Karen, "I can't tell Todd about counseling."

"I got that," Karen said. "It seems like he would try to sabotage your treatment. Remember, anything you tell me is confidential. Here's my home number. Promise me you'll be here tomorrow morning."

"But, what if I can't make it?"

"You can. Promise."

"All right, I promise."

Todd readily accepted my return because he thought he had won a contest. I was a mere trophy to him, and the prize was to get to tell me: "I told you so."

Foreign and Familiar

It is worse than folly...not to recognize the truth, for in it lies the tinder for tomorrow.

Pearl. S. Buck

My heart skipped beats and raced along as I entered the apartment I had left over four months earlier. Immediately, I noticed that my houseplants were dead. Even the philodendrons, which were able to live with low light and little water, were wilted and brown from neglect. Todd, already working the late shift, had not exactly planned a welcome home party.

I unpacked overnight bags and garbage bags, arranging bras and panties in the top drawer of the dresser as unobtrusively as possible. It felt as though I were intruding upon Todd's space, although I was the one who had turned this generic one-bedroom unit into a home. In order to earn my keep, I washed and ironed his hopsack trousers and pearl-buttoned shirts, lugging baskets up and down the stairs to the laundry machines. How had he managed these tasks without a maid? He never helped with the chores he considered "woman's work." I rolled each pair of his socks into a ball, and folded his briefs in thirds. As I placed them in the second drawer of the dresser, I uncovered a picture of a young, brunette woman, with a local address and number. This was no house-cleaner. This was a mistress. What did it matter? It was my fault, wasn't it? After all, Todd had asked, "What am I supposed to do while you're locked up in a loony bin?"

Late into the night, I unwrapped a bar of Todd's deodorant soap and took a sudsy, unsupervised shower. After using Todd's shaving cream and steel razor, I replaced the blade so he would not nick his cheeks while carving his beard. As I dried my body with a fluffy towel fresh from the laundry, I made a list of necessary items: toilet paper, deodorant, toothpaste, and toothbrush, reminding myself to ask him if he needed anything.

When Todd returned from work the next morning, he asked, "Pumpkin, what did you do all night?" He never used my name. When he was in a good mood, he referred to me as "pumpkin" or "sweet pea" or some other vegetable that lowered my link on the food chain. When he was in a bad mood, he did not hesitate to call me a bitch.

I listed what I had accomplished: The kitchen and bath were cleaned until they sparkled, the carpet was vacuumed with the nap raised in rows, and the wood furniture was dusted and polished. Being of service made me valuable.

I neglected to list my missing items. The one bottle of drug store perfume he had bought me was gone along with a pewter pendant my grandmother had given me. I assumed he had given them to his girlfriend. I also failed to tell him that I'd found the crystal wine glasses that my mother had given me under the bed, of all places. Had Todd intended to toast the New Year with his girlfriend? I avoided confronting him about the disappearance of my rock-and-roll albums. I figured he had thrown them in the dumpster since he liked only country music. I was grateful, though, that my clothes were still in the closet. Probably, the round-faced woman in the picture could not fit into size 4 slacks.

While Todd slept for the day, I summoned my weak courage and went to see Karen. It was the first promise I kept in a long time. Driving up to the counseling center, I could see her on the porch. She welcomed me with genuine warmth that melted my heart.

"Hi Lynn! How are you?"

My thoughts spun around like a blurred black-and-white kaleidoscope, words tumbling like tiny shards of broken glass, none of the parts fitting to make a whole.

"Lynn, there are no right or wrong answers."

Karen led me outside, and we sat on a blanket in the grass. After weeks without fresh air, the sun dazzled me as it warmed my cheeks.

"Nice weather for winter," Karen said.

I was rummaging through my purse for sunglasses and cigarettes.

"How did it go with Todd?"

"It was all right."

"Tell me, how did you meet him? When?"

I looked at my watch. How could I tell the whole story in a fifty-minute session?

"Don't worry about the time. I have all the time you need to tell your story," Karen offered.

I told Karen that I'd met Todd about four years earlier, when I was nineteen. I was a waitress at a Howard Johnson's in Phoenix. As a server, I was forced to overcome a tendency to be shy. Not only was it my job to be friendly with the customers, but also I tried to be friendly with my co-workers, which included many Mexican-Americans. When the roaches scurried out from under the coffee station, I sang: *"La Cucaracha, La Cucaracha.*" The dishwashers laughed at the song, and called me "bonita" for pretty and "amiga" for friend. Todd sat at the counter, which was my station, every morning. Todd warned me not to be too friendly with the Mexicans because, he said, "They should all be lined up and shot one by one with a rifle." I was disturbed by his prejudice, but dismissed it rather than respond.

Todd resembled the rugged Marlboro man on the billboards complete with the pack of cigarettes he carried in his shirt pocket. He wore cowboy boots and a cowboy hat and a silver belt buckle with turquoise stones that spelled his name. His black beard and mustache were streaked with gray, and his angular features and denim blue eyes made him almost handsome. His smile was a slim slit that revealed even white teeth. The macho package intrigued and flustered me at the same time.

While I served him breakfast, he teased me about the clothes I wore to and from work. "Are you one of those hippies?"

I must have looked like a flower child, wearing peasant blouses with colorful trim and bell-bottom jeans embroidered with flowers. Beaded earrings dangled through my long hair, which was parted in the middle and tucked behind my ears.

Todd seemed amused by how I pronounced "saw" as "soar" and "idea" as "idear." I let him know that I was born in north New Jersey and raised in rural Pennsylvania, and now I lived near my mother and stepfather in Phoenix. According to Todd, that made me a "cute-as-a-button country pumpkin."

"What nationality are you?" he asked.

"Nationality? I'm American."

Todd chuckled, "What I meant was, where are your ancestors from?"

"Italy."

"You're Italian? Well, that explains why you're built like a brick shit-house."

"What?"

"You are one hot tomato," he winked and made a wavy gesture. "Curvaceous."

I turned my back.

"I'm just trying to give a gal a compliment," he said. "Can't you take a compliment?"

The morning conversations became more about me offending him for not graciously accepting what he considered compliments that were offensive to me. I was increasingly uncomfortable and tried to avoid him, but he was a customer demanding attention.

Smiling his narrow smile, he would say, "How about another cup of coffee, sugar? Stick around a while, why don't you? I'm not going to bite you. I'm a meat and potatoes man," he said as he speared a greasy sausage link.

I had not eaten meat in years, and his plate of fried eggs covered with catsup turned my stomach.

Todd volunteered personal bits and pieces. He was thirty-eight years old, of German descent, and a jet mechanic. He left his home state of Colorado after a divorce. "My ex-wife was a mental case. She tried to kill herself with a bottle of aspirin." I was taken aback by how readily he revealed private information. I had been raised to be more reserved.

I usually rode my bicycle the few blocks from my studio apartment to work. During an evening shift I had added to my workweek, it started to rain. Riding my bike home in the rain would not have been a problem except that my bike had been stolen from the side of the restaurant. Only the padlock was left where my bike had been chained.

Todd happened to be off that night, and sat at the counter drinking black coffee, as if he had nowhere to go. He had so much to say on the subject that for a moment I suspected that he had stolen my bike.

"It was some spic that stole your bike," Todd accused. "Didn't I tell you to watch out for them? They are all alike and not to be trusted. It's blacker than a well digger's asshole out there. They saw their opportunity and wasted no time. Better watch out getting home. The roads are slicker than snot on a doorknob."

Looking out the window again, it became obvious to me that Todd was not exaggerating about the weather. Maybe I could call my mother and stepfather who lived only four blocks from the restaurant. They were probably all warm and cozy by the fireplace, watching sit-coms. It would be best not to bother them. I might as well borrow an umbrella and walk home.

Miss Barkley, the manager, offered to take me home after closing. She was an efficient manager with a matronly manner. She had recently asked me why I called in sick whenever I was scheduled to work the breakfast counter. How could I say that I was avoiding a customer? It never occurred to me to request a change of stations or shifts. Now it looked as though that unwanted guest spoiled even the night shifts.

Todd got into the action. "Hey, honey, it would be my pleasure to give you a ride home. A nice gal like you shouldn't be walking the streets. You could be mistaken for a lady-of-the-night."

When I hesitated to accept his offer, Miss Barkley asked if I'd like to wait until she closed the restaurant. "It won't be until midnight," she said, "but I'll give you a ride."

Todd took this as a challenge. "Don't you trust me to give a damsel in distress a ride home?"

I was in the middle of a controversy centered on a perceived inability to take care of myself. I accepted Todd's offer in an effort to stop the trouble I was causing.

Todd opened the passenger door to his Dodge Charger. I'd often seen him holding the restaurant doors open for females, in a show of chivalry.

I asked, "Please stay on the main roads."

Todd slapped his thigh and echoed, "stay on the main roads," as if I had said something hilarious. He grinned and rubbed his beard.

I saw the black revolver under the front seat. I hated guns. He reached over to turn on country music. I hated country twang. I spotted a serpent tattoo on his forearm. I hated snakes.

As we drew closer to the apartment complex, Todd asked, "What number do you live in?"

Ignoring the question, I asked, "Please pull up to the clubhouse. Thanks for the ride!"

In the rain, I ran through the entrance gate and turned right, not left, toward my apartment, because I knew that Todd was watching. I dashed down the cement stairs to the level of subterranean units called "garden" apartments. As I opened the second door in a row of ten, the lamppost outside let in a streak of light on the green shag carpet. Quickly, I shut the door behind me, sliding the brass lock and securing the dead bolt.

Day or night, the apartment with brick walls was dark, except when car lights flashed through the kitchenette window, which was flush with the parking lot. A fixture shaped like an upside-down basket hung over the dinette area, casting light to the whole apartment. After I poured a whiskey and soda, I turned on the radio to hear Elton John's "Rocket Man" and flopped with relief on the stiff mattress. A bright bedroom in my mother's four-bedroom house would have been more comfortable. However, she set one room up with her sewing machine, and she never sewed a stitch. The other room was set up for guests that never came. My younger half-brother had his own room. My dim apartment suited my current disposition just fine.

Karen was interrupting this recall, asking, "How did you feel when you met Todd?"

"Everything about him was foreign yet familiar."

"In what ways?" Karen asked.

As I was responding to my counselor, I recognized the connection between my real father and my husband. There were obvious similarities between my father and Todd: My father liked country music, guns, and unfiltered cigarettes. There were also subtle similarities: Todd teased me like my father had and stirred sensations in the pit of my stomach, just like my father had. I was confused by

Todd's attention even as I craved affection, the same as with my father.

Only a few weeks before I met Todd, my stepfather, Frank, told me what had happened to my father. I had been in my apartment having a drink and listening to the rock-and-roll station, when there was a knock on the door. Frank was standing implacably, like an arresting officer, telling me to get my purse and get in the car. This was his only visit to my place. Alarms rang through my body like a jammed, blaring car horn.

"What's wrong?" I asked.

"I'll tell you when we get to the house."

There was no conversation on the short drive to their house, only the officious silence of my stepfather on a secret mission. I felt like I had been summoned for an execution with me as the intended target.

My mother, who I hadn't seen in several weeks, was on the couch with pillows propped behind her back. She was wearing a turquoise sweat suit with an Aztec design, and her auburn hair was set beauty-salon style.

"Hi Mom. How are you?"

She pursed her lips. "I'm fine, considering the circumstances."

"Do you want me to tell her?" Frank asked my mother.

"Would you? I'm not up to it," she responded.

"Just tell me what's wrong," I said. "Did somebody die?"

"There's no easy way to tell you," Frank said. "Your father is dead. He shot himself. He finally did us all a favor."

"Is that any way to tell her?" my mother asked. "If I had known you were going to be so blunt, I would have told her myself."

My father had faked his death before and I was suspicious that this was another hoax my father had arranged. "How did you find out?" I asked Frank.

Apparently, my father's brother, Henry, found my father, Manny, dead in an apartment in New Jersey. My uncle Henry, who was my godfather, called my stepmother, Holly, who was divorced from Manny. Holly called my older brother Eric, who lived with my grandmother in Pennsylvania. My brother called my mother in Phoenix, who told my stepfather, who came to pick me up and bring me to my mother so he could tell me. The chain of communication was as convoluted as ever.

"You know," Mom said, "his death is for the best, so we can all rest in peace."

How did she know what was for the best? My mother hadn't had contact with my father since their children were grown. I reflected on my parent's early relationship. My mother had met my father when they were in high school. She'd said that he once had charisma, able to charm the girls with a wink of his striking blue eyes. He'd been a handsome football hero, with a solid six-foot physique. Although he had a rugged complexion, pockmarked from adolescent acne, she said he could draw people to him if and when he smiled. If and when he worked, whether as a waiter or a bartender, he would wear a sedate suit and tie. By the time I was in high school, my father was a different man, repelling people with about as much charm as a snake.

My father had frightened me. He'd had Bell's palsy in his twenties, which caused his cheek and brow to droop on one side, making his mouth crooked. What went into his mouth was a river of Pabst beer, and what came out were streams of swear words. He wore tattered T-shirts with splashes of foodstuff; the tank tops barely covered his fat stomach. But a beer belly and partial paralysis could not contain his frenetic presence. He was like an exploding stick of dynamite that was shooting hot sparks around the room. Afraid of being burned by the ashes of his psyche, I'd ended my association with my father long before the bullet killed him.

I was slow to respond to the news of his suicide, but finally I repeated, "It's for the best." After all, his death could not hurt me more than his life had.

"How are you feeling?" Mom asked. "Do you want to stay here for the night?"

"I'm fine," I said. "I need to get back home. I have an early shift tomorrow." I'd left a drink on my table, and I couldn't wait to wash away the mix of relief and regret with the whiskey and soda.

Later I learned that my father left no suicide note. Even if he had, who would have recognized his handwriting? He never wrote a letter or signed a card. What he left was unfinished business, a mess of blood and brain matter for his brother Henry to mop up and emotional debris for the family to sort through.

I never wanted to see him again, dead or alive, so I refused to attend the funeral. Besides, how does an adolescent daughter eulogize her schizophrenic father? My brother Eric made the arrangements. It was too much of a traumatic task to ask of a twenty-two-year-old son. To bury his own father, a suicide, seemed cruel and unusual punishment for a son who had been subjected to the vast violence of this madman his entire life.

Karen was speaking, "Lynn, you're wandering into someone else's psyche, which diverts attention from your own therapy. Let's stay on track. The relationship with your father remains unresolved. People often seek a life-partner who serves to resolve issues of the past."

"I wasn't looking for Todd," I replied.

"No, not consciously. We sometimes operate on an unconscious level, which may lead to repetition of unhealthy patterns. When we examine our motives, we make better choices," Karen explained.

"So, if I know why I did what I did, I might do it better next time?"

"Right! Please tell me more about your marriage."

I recalled the events that led to my marriage to Todd. I had enrolled in college full-time, quit the job as a waitress, and moved to an apartment closer to campus. I also thought I had distanced myself from Todd.

When I applied for the apartment, the leasing agent noted that I was unemployed. With a condescending attitude, she asked, "How do you expect to pay the rent?" I replied that a college trust fund covered the costs, and I offered to pay six months rent in advance. That settled it. My grandmother, who had established the trust fund, arranged for the money to transfer. I presumed that money was power, and the trust fund was a source of security for a young woman in an insecure world.

The apartment community was within walking distance to the campus and the grocery store. My second-floor apartment was a furnished studio with a balcony for cacti in clay pots. The kitchen was so efficient that a cabinet and the oven could not both be opened at the same time. Cinder blocks provided shelving for Kahlil Gibran and Herman Hesse books and my rock-and-roll albums, arranged from Allman Brothers to Led Zeppelin. A cool bedspread was created with fabric from the import store, and strands of beads divided the living room from the sleeping area. Having an apartment, a college schedule, a backpack, a new bike, and a checking account all seemed so “normal.” Normal seemed like a state of being I ought to achieve, like wearing a costume to a masquerade ball. I felt as if I was merely conforming to society. If I let go of those standards, my perfect normal might lie bare naked, and unwanted by others.

College and Court Orders

I believe that we are solely responsible for our choices, and we have to accept the consequences of every deed, word, and thought throughout our lifetime.

Elisabeth Kubler-Ross

"In what way did you think that conforming to college had a negative connotation?" Karen asked.

"Well, I had a court order that required me to stay in college."

"Tell me about the court order. Don't leave anything out."

I told Karen that shortly after my high school graduation in Pennsylvania, my cousin Annie, who was about my age and my best friend, introduced me to one of her boyfriends, Peter. Like the other teenage boys, Peter had hair that reached his broad shoulders. Boys with blonde hair and blue eyes were hard to resist, as was my cute cousin Annie. She had curly blonde hair, light olive skin, and a thin body built for tank tops and mini-skirts. We'd been taking drugs for some time, and Annie said she and Peter had a plan to get the buzz of a lifetime. The only problem was that they needed my help.

"Lynnie, will you *please* take a prescription in to be filled?" Annie had asked.

"Why can't you drop it off?" I'd retorted.

"All the pharmacists know me from having prescriptions filled for myself or my mother."

It was true that my aunt or my cousin was always at the doctor for accidents, asthma, allergies, and attention. A doctor's visit would not be complete unless pills were prescribed.

"Why can't Peter take it in?"

"You know how this town gets spooked by guys with hair below the ears," Annie explained. "Please, Lynnie, please. Just get this one prescription filled."

When Peter handed me a prescription I said, "I recognize the doctor's name. He was at a party. What's up?"

Peter shrugged, “Maybe he’s a shady dude.”

Although Peter had a cool, convertible Karmann Ghia, he insisted that we use my Chevy Nova to drive to the pharmacy. He put other prescriptions into my glove box. The always-reliable Chevy suddenly stalled along the way, but Peter opened the hood and restarted it. “Just a loose spark-plug,” he reported. Then he directed me to a specific corner drug store.

“What am I supposed to say?” I asked as I drove toward town.

“Tell the pharmacist it’s for a sick and elderly grandmother.”

“What is she supposed to be sick with?”

“Tell them she has epilepsy.”

“Should I cruise the aisles first?”

“Yeah, pick up some aspirin.”

Peter waited in the car while I went into the drug store.

The pharmacist stood behind the counter in his white lab coat, peering through his black-rimmed glasses. “Who is this for?” he asked.

I mumbled something about a grandmother.

“Your grandmother? What’s her name?”

“No, not my grandmother. A friend’s grandmother.”

“I can’t make out this address.”

“I don’t know my friend’s grandmother’s address.”

The pharmacist was stalling to avoid filling the prescription. “Dilaudid is a narcotic that we don’t keep in stock,” he said. “I have to call the hospital pharmacy. Do you want to wait?” He left the counter before I had a chance to decide.

Should I wait? I stood in the aisle for what seemed like a long while. I decided to leave without the prescription, even if Annie and Peter got mad.

As I turned to leave, two uniformed police officers walked up the aisle. With a touch to my elbow, one officer indicated that they were there to escort me out of the pharmacy. When the cops asked to search my car, I did not resist. Evidently, the pharmacist had noticed that the doctor’s signature was spelled incorrectly. I was arrested for forgery, fraud, intent to illegally obtain a narcotic prescription, and theft of a prescription pad. “Do you understand your rights as I have read them to you?” *No, I don’t understand anything.* I nodded. While he sat in the back seat of the police car with me, Peter denied any involvement and demanded to know why he was arrested, too.

I could not control my crying while enduring fingerprints, mug shots, a shower, which included an antibacterial scrub down, and a strip search. The warden kept saying, "It's okay, stop crying, I'm not going to hurt you." I hadn't been concerned about physical pain; what hurt was the humiliation of being used by my cousin.

Using the allowable phone call, I telephoned my mother in Phoenix, who put my stepfather on the line. He said he certainly could not bail me out, since he was in Arizona, I was in Pennsylvania, and "whether or not it's one hundred dollars bail or one million dollars bond," he did not have the money. He promised to call my rich uncle, Tony, who co-owned a resort in Pennsylvania with my grandmother. Meanwhile, I cried on a cot in a holding cell, watching the afternoon fade, the sun set, and the night fall through a narrow window with iron bars.

My uncle used a farm he owned as bond and I was released to his recognizance. He looked respectable in his suit and tie as I gathered my personal belongings from a manila envelope. The desk clerk dumped my watch, my license, and a bottle of legally prescribed Darvon Compound on the counter. While my uncle was driving me to my grandmother's house, he told me to tell him every detail. I failed to mention his daughter's involvement.

It was close to midnight when my grandmother greeted me and tried to make me comfortable. "Oh, Lynnie, are you all right? Do you want something to eat? It's too late to call your mother. Call her first thing in the morning. It's in times like this that family has to stick together."

The next day, telephone in hand, I heard my mother's judgment crackling through the long-distance wires. "How could you embarrass your poor mother this way? What is the matter with you?" She had already found me guilty. Accepting full responsibility was more heat than I could handle, so I told her that Annie was an accomplice. "Oh, spare me your self-pity," my mother responded. "You are no angel. Granted, Annie is no angel, either. However, your uncle is a prominent businessman with a reputation to uphold. Don't implicate his daughter in this crime." It seemed easier to take the rap myself, especially if my own mother was not about to support me.

My stepfather flew in from Phoenix to attend the hearing, carrying his opinion along with his baggage. "Let me give you some advice. You better keep your nose clean and your mouth shut."

At the arraignment, my lawyer, the pharmacist, the doctor whose name had been forged, his lawyer, and a judge were present. The only other woman was the court reporter. Nothing intimidated me more than being in a room with men who wore the suits and ties that represented authority. Their implied power rendered me impotent in the pursuit of what was fair and true.

The lawyer interrogated me: "Did you ever see this doctor before?" The doctor was twitchy, like Al Capone facing an interview with the FBI. I thought I had seen him at a party, wearing jeans and a brown suede fringed jacket. However, I knew that it was too hard to prove which party, and a respectable doctor would not attend that kind of party. The doctor could accuse me of being too loaded at the party for accurate testimony at the hearing.

I said, "No," raising the vowel like a question.

As if he knew something I did not know, my lawyer asked, "Are you sure? Take your time before answering."

I stated with conviction, "Yes, I am sure I never saw the doctor before."

"If that's the way you want it," the judge said, "then you need to be available for a court appearance."

After the arraignment, my uncle, my stepfather, and I gathered at my grandmother's. My stepfather announced his contempt for courts and crime: "There is no sense in wasting any more of my time waiting for Lynn's day in court. I'm going home on the first flight out of here."

"Family should stick together at a time like this," Grandma said.

"Family? I have a wife and son in Phoenix," Frank said.

"I hope the heavy chip on your shoulder doesn't weigh the plane down and keep it from taking off," she said.

"This is not the time to air differences," my uncle said. "We have to put our heads together to clean up this situation."

My older brother Eric, who worked for our uncle and grandmother, walked in on the scene.

"How about you go to court with your sister?" Uncle Tony suggested.

Eric coached me on courtroom etiquette, advising me to wear a dress and address the judge as "Your Honor." In this case, image was important, and Eric knew all about appearances. Our relatives had forced us together over a crisis. I felt uncomfortable with my brother, who could cover his feelings with a neutral attitude.

I felt small and scared as I stood before the judge in the courtroom. I had no control over my fate, my future. Fortunately, the judge didn't take long to review the case before admonishing me: "You are lucky that I am not sentencing you to the women's state prison in Muncie, Indiana."

"Yes, Your Honor."

"Young lady, I am aware that you were a National Honor Society student, college funds are available to you, and your mother and stepfather live in Phoenix. You are ordered to enroll in college, not in Pennsylvania, but far from your party chums and near your parents in Arizona. You are full of potential. Don't waste it."

"Yes, Your Honor."

The judge assigned me to a meeting with a probation officer, and Eric went along. The officer informed us that Peter was a juvenile delinquent with a rap sheet and the doctor was disreputable. The probation officer said that it was a "setup" and I was a "patsy." Obviously, I was not the criminal who stole the prescription pad and forged the doctor's signature. The judge expunged the record.

In a matter of days, I got a one-way ticket to Arizona from a travel agency, as if I were leaving Pennsylvania for a vacation. Eric drove me to the nearest airport, Newark International. Newark was an old factory town with air pollution that smelled like sulphur. The airport was a city unto itself. Convoys of busses and taxis waited with engines running, international drivers waiting for international travelers. Eric walked me through the terminal and loaded my trunk of albums on the baggage belt. I was sure he was relieved to be rid of me. I went to live with my mother, stepfather, and younger brother, Rusty.

Invitations and Obligations

We are free up to the point of choice, then the choice controls the chooser.

Mary Crowley

Karen was sitting in front of me, following the story with an interested expression on her face. “Please go on,” she invited. “Tell me what led to the marriage to Todd.”

“I’d started college and was diligent with studies. I never missed class. I walked home to watch soap operas at lunch, and then researched in the library at night. My name was on the Dean’s Honor List.”

Karen said, “That must have made you proud.”

“I did not think of academics as achievement. I believed that if ability came easy, it did not count as an accomplishment. School was the only activity I could succeed at without fail.”

“So studying was an acceptable method of withdrawal,” Karen stated.

“Maybe I filled my mind with facts to recall, rather than to remember.”

“Remember what?”

“I don’t know.”

“How was Todd involved with your college career?”

I explained that one afternoon Todd had shown up on campus, which was as surprising as the spring storm that sprang up during class. How did he know I would exit the psychology building at precisely 12:50 p.m.? He looked old and out of place in his cowboy hat and boots among students in rock-concert T-shirts. I was tempted to ignore him as he walked toward me but was afraid he would make a scene. Todd justified that he followed me because, he said, “I think the world of you. I miss you. Let me take you to the Sizzler for dinner.”

“I don’t eat meat.”

"There's your trouble. You need to put some meat on your bones."

"I need to study."

"Woman, you think too much."

"I have tests tomorrow."

My excuses were irrelevant to him. He made up my mind for me: "You need a change of pace from sticking your nose in that gibberish." He took my backpack, saying, "You're too smart for your own good."

Todd seemed to envy my mind, competing against it for attention. Or perhaps he sensed that I did not know my own mind, and he tried to take advantage of that. With a strange yet familiar feeling of obligation, I yielded to his invitation. I must have been out of my mind.

As I was talking to Karen, I was beginning to connect the links on the chain of reenactments of the past in the present.

My father would suddenly show up after long absences, saying, "I missed you. How's Daddy's little girl?" How I was did not matter to him; before I could tell him, he would tell me. "You missed me, didn't you?" Then he would quiz me about my mother. "How is your mother? What is she doing? Did she miss me? Did she say anything about me? What did she say?" It was not *me* he was interested in but a fantasy reunion with the woman who had rejected him. Nevertheless, I felt obliged to get closer to my father even as I doubted his love.

My father also disparaged my interests. After reading the encyclopedia's entries about horses and dogs, I memorized the characteristics of each breed. My father called me a "bookworm" and scolded, "Go outside and play like a normal kid," implying that I was not normal. Instead of appreciating my intelligence, he was afraid of it. Perhaps he was afraid that I would figure him out for the phony he was. Like counterfeit money, I did not know how deceiving he could be until I was emotionally bankrupt.

A week after Todd had invited me to the steak house, he surprised me again while I was watching *Days of Our Lives*. I was taken aback not only because Todd knew my schedule well enough to find me, but also because he brought me a puppy. Todd took it upon himself to provide protection in the form of a German shepherd, as if I needed it.

My father had often brought pets home for my mother to care for, then disposed of them when their behavior mimicked the chaos in the family.

I named the puppy Todd gave me "Louie." As my affection for the dog increased, so did contact with Todd. I thought the puppy was a present, but there were strings attached. Todd used the dog to create a tie between us and discussed its shenanigans as if we shared the pet.

That dog was more trouble than it was worth, especially since it was already oversized for an apartment. While I studied on campus, Louie munched on toilet paper and tin foil right from the rolls, protesting his long hours alone. In order to keep the dog from tearing the place apart, I spent more time in the apartment.

On Sunday afternoons, I would call my mother from the pay phone. Although we lived only twenty miles apart, we connected via telephone. Our conversations were about characters on soap operas. Sticking to superficial story lines was simpler than keeping my own life straight. One spring Sunday, my mother offered to take me to Denny's for pie during the week to celebrate my birthday.

How could I tell her about Todd? What would I tell her about the dog? My stepfather had often accused me of lying by omission because I avoided confrontation by consciously leaving out certain key elements. I had to clear the apartment to ward off any questions. I hid the dog food and chew toys.

"Todd, will you kindly keep the dog away for a day?"

"Sure, sweet potato, but why?"

"My mother is coming and everything is so complicated!"

"Why can't you just tell her you have a boyfriend who bought you a dog?"

That was not the way it really was, was it?

Consumed by curiosity, Todd kept close to the apartment.

When my mother came to my door, she immediately commented, "There's a man playing with a big puppy on the grass. He said hello to me. Do you know him?"

"No." I quickly closed the door. Then we heard a scratching sound.

"Lynnie, do you hear a scratching sound?"

"No."

"I do, I hear a scratching at your door." She opened the door and Louie leaped inside, licked my face, and sniffed around. "Lynnie, this dog seems to know you," my mother said as she filled a cereal bowl with water. "Are you sure you don't know the man the dog was with?"

Looking out the window, down the stairs, I saw Todd sprawled out on the lawn. With his shaggy gray and black hair and glassy blue eyes, he looked like an Australian shepherd. "I've seen him around," I admitted, but failed to say more.

Being pinned between my mother and Todd was a familiar position. I'd been pitted between my father and my mother. Besides, I was used to men telling me they would do one thing, and then doing another, as if my wishes did not matter. These attitudes were unavoidable, like an arranged marriage or custom not to be questioned.

On my birthday, Todd gave me an unwrapped box from Wards with a polyester shirtwaist dress inside. The dress was meant for a housewife, not for a twenty-year-old college student. Todd emphasized that he bought it special, just for me, but it was two sizes too big, and boring beige. What with all the colorful beads and bright bedspreads in my apartment, couldn't he see that I hated beige?

"Why won't you wear it for me?" he whined.

"All right, already." I tried on the ugly dress, which was unlike anything I ever wore. How could I wear it for him?

The following Sunday, I told my mother how I met Todd, how he had followed me, how he brought me a puppy and bought me a dress. "Mom, what should I do?"

"You are already attached to the dog. However, you have to give the dress back. If you accept the dress, you accept a relationship with that man and the role he intends for you to play. You don't want any part of that, do you?"

I was not assertive enough to return a new toaster that wouldn't pop to a department store. How could I give a dress back to a man who intimidated me?

My mother invited me to join her, my stepfather, and my younger brother for an Easter buffet. Having a meal with my family, even with tension stifling our conversation, was better than eating a frozen dinner alone. "Lynnie, we'll pick you up. Wear a dress, but not *that* dress. By the way, did you end it with that man?"

"Yeah, well, maybe."

When I told Todd about my plans with my parents, he objected. "Will you be tied to your mother's apron strings for the rest of your life? It's time you grew up. I thought you'd at least spend the day with me. I'll take you to a holiday dinner, just the two of us. Why don't you wear the dress I gave you?"

Todd was standing in my apartment with his back against a wall but I was unable to stand up to him.

I called my mother. "I'm sorry, Mom, but I can't make it to the buffet."

"Why not?"

"I have to study for mid-terms."

I envisioned how my mother would look in a spring outfit, complete with white pumps that matched her purse. Whether she wore a pleated skirt or a pantsuit, it would be altered to fit her petite form. Her brunette hair would be styled by the hairdresser, as it was every week, cut short in the back with slightly teased, tapered bangs across her forehead. Her lips would be colored with coral to compliment her complexion. She would wear a tailored fashion and a poised expression, even if she was facing a physical ailment or a failing family.

I should have faced the fact that Todd was moving in on me. He moved into a two-bedroom apartment with a roommate, in my complex. A month later, Todd complained about his roommate, and moved out of the two-bedroom into the vacant studio next door to me. Todd claimed he needed privacy.

A single, working mother named Susan lived with her little girl in a studio across from Todd. Susan and I were acquainted enough to share *Glamour* magazines and makeup tips. Susan, who was separated from her husband, struggled to pay the rent and day care. According to her, it was romantic for an older man to "court" a younger woman. Not much of a matchmaker, I introduced Todd and Susan in the hopes that he would like her enough to leave me alone.

Susan swooned to me, "Oh, he's so nice and handsome, and he makes a good living."

Todd complained to me, "Her little rug rat runs up and down the stairs and keeps me awake." Susan overheard Todd and was offended enough to discontinue our acquaintance.

One evening, hauling clothes down the stairs to the laundry room, I was unaware that I had dropped a bra. As I went back up the stairs, a young man was waiting by my door, holding up a bra, and asking, "Is this yours?"

I stammered with embarrassment. "No, well, maybe."

He grinned, "It must be yours because it is unfortunately not a size my wife wears, and you two are the only women on this floor. I will put it in your laundry basket and you can figure it out later. I'm Scott."

A young woman stepped out of the studio across the hall.

"This is my wife, Cathy."

As the weeks went by, we bopped back and forth between our apartments, sharing pots and pans. They often invited me over for dinner and while we prepared a salad or casserole, we listened to our rock-and-roll collections. Scott was a budding artist and sketched portraits of his wife.

"You should see my husband's drawings!" Cathy said.

When they showed me his sketchbook of charcoal nudes, I felt my face flush.

"Don't be embarrassed. This is art!"

Cathy was enrolled in a medical assistant curriculum and struggled to get average grades, so I helped her study for terminology tests. "Look, Cathy, anything that ends with 'itis' is an inflammation."

We watched *The Six Million Dollar Man*, commenting on the mysteries of bionics and how even the six million dollar woman was afflicted with split ends and bad hair days. There was comfort in the company of friends of the same age and interests.

As the months went by, I tried to release myself from Todd's grip to spend time with my friends. He demanded that I give him equal time. Todd became possessive because, he said, he loved me. He slammed my door and his door to demonstrate. The stucco landing of the apartments shook like an earthquake in California. There had to be a rational explanation for Todd's conduct.

"He's just jealous," Scott said.

"Yeah, he must love you a lot," Cathy said.

I ached to be loved. So I mistook the outbursts for love, the same way I accepted my father's explosive behavior for the sake of love.

When Scott and Cathy invited me to have Thanksgiving dinner with them, they said that I could bring Todd if I wanted, but I wanted my friends to myself. The day before Thanksgiving, Todd called Cathy a "pain-in-the-ass broad" and said Scott just "wants a piece." Todd insisted that I eat at a holiday buffet with him. I was afraid of another door-slamming scene, so I declined Cathy's offer.

As we walked past their apartment, Cathy cheerfully waved, "Happy Thanksgiving." Scott commented, "You look like a model in that dress. The green matches your eyes."

Todd gritted his teeth: "I told you so! He just wants to get in your pants." Then he grabbed my elbow to steer me toward the inside of the sidewalk. "Never walk on the outside. That means you're for sale." Was he a pimp? Was I a prostitute? It seemed like I had sold out something, in some way.

At the holiday buffet, the servers smiled as they dished out mashed potatoes, gravy, and corn. I selected the sliced turkey breast and Todd piled on the rare roast beef. While we ate, I surveyed the other diners, fine families of four or five, as if from afar; I felt so alien from their normal American holiday that I might as well been watching from Jupiter or Mars. What were they so happy about?

While I studied, Todd invited himself into my apartment to watch *The Price Is Right* and *JEOPARDY*! He fantasized about winning a "shitload of money." He was curious about the trust fund that afforded me financial ease but I shrugged off the questions. I tried to ignore him as I compiled statistics on a cohabitation survey for Sociology 101. It was nearly impossible to concentrate on studies with Todd around, but it was equally impossible to say no to him. When I tried to be assertive with Todd, he'd shoot my words back like an errant boomerang until what I thought I said did not sound like what he said I said.

Todd wanted my body, telling me: "Some men love legs, but I'm a tits man." He blatantly ogled voluptuous women: "Wow! Look at them hooters!"

When I used lack of birth control as a reason to avoid sex, Todd boasted that he was sterile from a vasectomy. Intrigued that an older man wanted sex with me, I let it happen, albeit apprehensively. Sex with Todd was perfunctory, and fortunately, did not last long. He grabbed my body like I was a slab of sirloin steak, and groped and groaned about loving a woman with meat on her bones. I stared at the ceiling rather than at the wrinkled man. My body felt flat except for a sickening sensation that spread through my psyche, as if I had been in this position before. We'd made love; did that mean he loved me? My eyes closed with a regret that crept across my consciousness, leaving me hungry for love.

Todd acted as though he owned me once we had sex. He convinced me that I could not live without him and that I was nothing without him. It was true that I felt worthless enough. He warned me that no one could take care of me like he could. Although I had my own apartment, I felt incapable. He also said that no one would love me like he did. I was sure that was true too; I felt unlovable. I was afraid of being rejected, and afraid of rejecting him. Todd swore that he could not live without me, saying, "If you don't marry me, I'll kill myself!"

My mind flashed to his .357 Magnum. I imagined Todd putting the barrel to his head and pulling the trigger. How could I deal with the responsibility of Todd killing himself? My life was already obscured by visions of death, including wondering about my father's suicide and pondering my own.

I must be dreaming. *A funeral wreath surrounds Todd. With vacuous blue eyes, he stares through a ring of flowers and candles. It's as if his dead spirit is showing itself.* I awoke afraid that it was already too late. Was the image an omen that Todd would indeed kill himself if I did not marry him?

On my way to class the next day, Todd stopped me as he pulled into the parking lot. He handed over a small, unwrapped box from Service Merchandise. Inside was an inexpensive star-sapphire ring with a diamond chip.

"Thank you. But what's the occasion?" I asked.

"That's your engagement ring."

I was disappointed by the unromantic gesture, so unlike a passionate proposal in a soap opera, but I figured it was all I deserved. Within a year of meeting, Todd had maneuvered me nearer to him and farther from my parents. Weary from the battle, I surrendered. I never decided on a college major, but I chose to marry Todd.

My mother and stepfather pleaded with me not to marry him. In a letter, my mother stated that she could not condone my choice to participate in an inappropriate and potentially harmful marriage. Her words were grenades about to detonate and blow my heart to bits. I tore her handwriting into vertical strips, then horizontal, and burned the shreds in an ashtray.

When I told Todd that my mother sent a devastating letter stating her disapproval, he nonchalantly commented: "No big deal. Who needs her, anyway? I don't need a mother-in-law meddling in my affairs!"

I dreaded the required blood test for the marriage license. When I used an aversion to needles as an excuse to delay a wedding date, Todd sneered, "Stop that belly aching."

During the appointment for the blood test, the nurse noticed black-and-blue marks on my upper arm. "Where did you get that nasty hematoma?"

"I don't know." I silently recalled that Todd had punched my arm during an argument.

"We should let the doctor examine it," the nurse suggested.

"No, it's okay."

The nurse offered pills to alleviate the bruise; I wanted pills to obliterate my life. I deliberately diverted her attention from the bruises to my splitting headache. "Could I have something for the pain, please?"

If I got the marriage over with, I could divorce him sooner rather than later. At least I would fulfill my obligation by marrying him and preventing him from killing himself. Unfortunately, I forgot to fulfill my own purpose.

On the wedding day, I was filled with inner conflict and utter confusion, along with the excruciating pain of a migraine. My face hurt. First one side hurt, then the other, over the right eye, then over the left. I shoved my fist under the brow to release the pressure of the pain. My whole head hurt, back and front, from the nape of the neck to the top of the nose. My head throbbed with the beat of my heart. When I bent over, I was dizzy. When I stood up, I practically fainted. My body involuntarily alternated from the cold sweats to hot flashes to dry heaves. I numbed my aching head and nervous tension with painkillers. Even as I swallowed a pill or two, I knew it was useless, because with a sip of water I threw up the pills whole. The migraine gave me something else to focus on besides the civil ceremony. The ride to the courthouse, the noise of the traffic, and the hundred-degree heat increased the pain. When I shut my eyes to block the glaring sun, there were flashes of light, as if the flash bulb of a camera went off repeatedly behind my lids.

Todd strutted like a stallion stalking an unsuspecting mare; he must have thought he was quite the stud. Assembled in the judge's chamber, the justice of the peace said, "If anyone objects to this marriage, come forward." I wondered if that included the bride. Slipping a silver and turquoise band purchased from the swap meet on Todd's finger, I contemplated the vow, "Till death do us part." To show what a nice guy he thought he was, Todd stood in as a witness for the next couple on the civil ceremony calendar. I stood outside in the lobby, smoking, staring at the closed carved wood doors of the judge's chambers and thought: Oh, my God, what have I done?

Investments and Afflictions

Invest in the human soul. Who knows, it might be a diamond in the rough.

Mary McLeod Bethune

Not long after that fateful ceremony, I turned twenty-one. Todd celebrated by asking me to use my trust fund to buy land in Chandler, Arizona. Past the dairy farm and the rodeo arena, there were alfalfa fields newly zoned for mobile homes. He said we could get rich quick on the land while living cheap in a trailer. Whenever I objected to moving out of town, Todd threw a fit, until it seemed easier to comply with his wishes than to confront his temper.

I called my grandmother and asked her to release the remainder of the trust fund to buy a plot of unimproved desert. My grandmother said she was happy that I'd found a man to "take care of" me. According to her, college was just something for a young woman to "fall back on." She readily helped me financially because, as she often said, "families must stick together." She considered land ownership a sound investment, as it had been for generations of Italians. The mass migration of Italians during the late 1800's had been a flee from oppression. The peasants, descendents of Roman slaves and medieval serfs, had labored in poverty, farming tomatoes, peppers, and grapes for the ruling class. Therefore, land ownership represented liberty, whether it was a city lot in New Jersey, five hundred acres in the mountains of Pennsylvania, or two acres of desert tumbleweed. On their own land, immigrant families stuck together against hostility from other races and classes.

After installing a well, a septic tank, and a fence, I rationalized the benefit of the deal by buying a horse. The gentle Pinto gelding, named Jack, behaved more like a puppy than a pony, nudging my butt as he followed me around the pasture. He would stick his head through an open patio door, watching and whinnying. Todd bought a used saddle and bridle from a farm and feed co-op store. Although I loved the clop-clop of hooves on the firm desert floor, I did not ride often. What if we encountered a rattlesnake or scorpion, and the horse spooked and ran amuck?

Besides, it was too hot: one hundred degrees by 9 a.m., one hundred ten by noon. Even the weather forecasters spread rumors to make desert dwellers feel cooler in hundred-fifteen degree weather: "It's a dry heat, with low humidity, so you barely feel it. You get used to it." You have got to be kidding! When I fed the horse or got the mail, the scorching sun bit my skin as if I had collided with a prickly pear cactus. At the same time, residents were asked to avoid using excessive water to prevent drought conditions. Even after a short shower, perspiration poured from overburdened sweat glands.

To open windows was to allow the sour odor of urine and manure from the dairy farm to drift in. The neighbor's chickens, crossing under the chain link fence for horse feed, caused yet another stench. So I applied sun-shield film to the panes, closed the drapes with their sun-repellent lining, and holed up in the trailer cave. The ineffective swamp cooler churned its clanging blades while spraying a mist of warm water.

In an effort to conserve my low energy reserves, I watched *Good Morning America* and *Days of Our Lives*, and read Jackie Collins' "Valley of the Dolls" and Sidney Sheldon's "Stranger in the Mirror." I was indeed a stranger unto myself, sitting and smoking, and choking back tears. I missed the real challenge of college and the fantasy of rescue. I wasn't a strong heroine able to flee from inner demons and Todd was no knight in shining armor slaying dragons.

Any independence I may have had all but vanished as I became isolated in a singlewide trailer south of Phoenix. "You're scared of your own shadow, aren't you?" Todd said. "You even sleep with clenched fists."

Nights were fraught with fears of creatures lurking behind a curtain of consciousness, waiting to capture me. Nightmares would awaken me with their shrewd yet senseless messages; the nightmares lingered long into the days. In all my childhood daydreams, I never imagined a life like I was living. Years of untold loss, unfinished business, and unfulfilled promises were taking their toll. I was paying a high price for accumulated grief by sinking lower into depression.

I wasn't motivated to tend to domestic duties. The waterbed remained disheveled because I was often dozing to dodge the endless days. Toilet tissue unraveled from wayward rolls on the floor. It was beneath Todd to replace toilet paper and too much trouble for me; the spring would not catch or the roll would not unwind. Todd dug at his teeth with toothpicks and left the used toothpicks where they landed. He refused to clean up after himself, since he regarded me as his maid. When Todd chided, "Get off your lazy ass," I resentfully managed to do a load of laundry in the ancient, inefficient, stacked washer/dryer.

When Todd was scheduled to work graveyard shifts, we watched television in the evenings. According to the ratings, *Three's Company* and *Happy Days* wildly amused the viewing public. What did we know about a happy face? Todd stared at sit-coms without smiling. I asked him why he never laughed.

"I do laugh," he said, "I laugh inside."

When I laughed out loud, Todd mocked me, "You think that's funny?"

So, I started staring at sit-coms also, outwardly acting as if I was not seeing anything entertaining. The urge to chuckle became a thoughtful process: Was that funny? Should I laugh? I lost spontaneity along with a sense of humor.

Afternoons were spent driving in my air-conditioned Chevy Cavalier to wait in an air-conditioned doctor's office. Dr. Hammel was a former minor league ball player turned general practitioner. He had good looks and a good bedside manner, offering me the tender loving care unavailable from my husband. The doctor treated me for bronchitis, vaginitis, gastritis, duodenitis, conjunctivitis, sinus infections, yeast infections, impetigo, insomnia, and migraines.

For months, I either woke up with a migraine or a migraine woke me up, each migraine more miserable than the last. I was forever frozen in a solid block of ice-pick pain. Desperate to relieve the pain, I gingerly pulled Todd's gun out from under the bed and placed it on the night table. Sweating and staring at the shiny revolver, I was anticipating its usefulness in alleviating pain. When Todd came home, he casually challenged, "Why don't you do me a favor and get it over with?"

"I want to, I really do."

"They shoot horses, don't they? Do you want me to do the job for you?"

"How considerate of you to offer!"

While I tossed, turned, writhed and worried, Todd was as inconsiderate as ever with his uncivilized noises. He cleared his throat and spat in the sink, slurped, belched and farted.

I called from the bedroom, "Do you have to be so noisy?"

"Noisy? It's like a funeral parlor in here. And you look like death warmed over."

His callous comments felt like a quick kick with spurs on a high-strung racehorse. Full-blown anxiety galloped out of the gate. "God. Todd. Can you please help? My head hurts so bad I think I'm dying." Finally, he loaded me into his Ford pick-up and drove the sixty miles to Doctor's Hospital, where Dr. Hammel had orders of Demerol injections ready for me. I thanked Todd for rushing me to the emergency room. At least in the swift ride to the hospital he'd been Prince Charming.

By the first wedding anniversary, I'd lost more weight than I had on any crash diet or juice fast. Although I heated cans of corn and fried potatoes and round steak for Todd, I could not eat much more than cold cereal for lunch and ice cream for dinner. I became less and less of a body as I felt less than human. My periods had ceased for the last two years. The feminine cycles were mirroring my mind, and I was becoming less of a woman. Even as I was eating, food ran through my system without assimilating. Cramps and incontinence caused me to double over in colon spasms while my bowels rumbled. Often, I ran to the bathroom with diarrhea. Along the way to anywhere, I carried rolls of toilet paper in case of a roadside emergency. Sometimes, I frantically searched for a ladies room. If a restroom was not available, I ran right back home.

Dr. Hammel was alarmed when I reached ninety-eight pounds. I was hospitalized to determine the cause of "chronic and acute intestinal distress." As I was wheeled on a cot back and forth from x-ray and labs, I felt old, alone, and in the way. The technicians conducted barium enemas, diabetes, and hypoglycemic tests. There were needles in my arms to draw fluid out and needles in my hands to pump nutrients in, and Mylanta and Tagamet by the bed. The doctor speculated about an eating disorder or a stress disorder.

The diagnosis was ulcerative colitis. Dr. Hammel informed me that the colitis was so severe that a colostomy was indicated, and he illustrated the procedure: The colon would be removed and replaced by a bag I would wear around my waist. The body waste would bypass the colon and empty into the bag that could be concealed by clothing. The bag would be emptied several times a day. However, the doctor was reluctant to perform the procedure on "one so young." He suggested a regime of medications to ease the symptoms. Over the next few months, he prescribed Compazine and Combid for nausea relief, Librax and Librium for stress reduction, and Lomatil and Cantil for diarrhea.

My body had been revolting against a heavy dose of unhappiness, explosively discharging unbearable inner tension. Besides radical surgery, I hoped there was another way to cure what was eating me. Those hours spent reading magazines in waiting rooms proved useful. A profile of a doctor who prescribed visualization techniques to his cancer patients caught my eye. According to the article, relaxation causes a physiological response that reduces the symptoms of stress. The patients were instructed to relax and see with their minds' eye the good cells attacking the bad cells. The doctor advised patients to imagine themselves in good health, free from pain.

My daydreams as a child had been methods of escape and wishful thinking. Now, I was learning to use imagination to direct my life. The idea was to focus on an image that represented the desired result and use positive adjectives to describe the achievement in the present tense.

With that article, I caught a glimpse of the connection of the body to the mind. Alone, at home, I attempted the healing method. As I tried to relax, every area of my body tensed with rigid muscles. Fluttering eyelids, a rumbling stomach, and shallow breathing made it difficult to concentrate. It was easier to visualize a treatment than an outcome, so I imagined the pink liquid of antacid traveling through the stomach and intestines, coating and soothing the lining. Even as I actually lay in the fetal position from colon spasms, I visualized standing up straight instead of doubled over with pain. Perhaps a combination of determination and intention could repair my ripped insides.

Frequently, my friends from the apartment community, Scott and Cathy, telephoned to say they wanted to visit. I made excuses: "It's not a good day. Todd worked later than usual last night. He's still sleeping." "It's not a good time. I have to go to the doctor." "It's not a good year. I am very, very busy." I was not avoiding seeing them; I was avoiding them seeing me.

It had been nearly a year since we'd last seen each other. One afternoon Cathy called and insisted on visiting. Despite my excuses, they were not about to let a desert monsoon keep them away. Scott and Cathy pulled up in their Honda while a dust storm was developing. As I stood outside, hollering "hello" above the noise of the rattling aluminum awning, a gust of wind literally blew me down.

"Lynn, you're as thin as a reed!"

The wind flipped my shorts like a sail, revealing the bruises on my thigh.

Scott asked, "Are you all right?"

"Well, no, yeah, I'm all right."

We made small talk while watching dust devils that looked like tiny tornadoes flitting across the terra firma. Cathy and Scott were saying goodbye. "We're moving to Utah. We'll write." As Cathy moved toward me, I stepped back, resisting her outstretched arms because my body experienced pain with an embrace. Todd had swatted me often enough that my body no longer recognized the difference between a hard hit and a warm hug. "Lynn, you take care of yourself, okay?"

"Yeah, sure." I was sure that another friendship bit the dust.

I still had my horse, my rationalization for living in the wicked desert heat for two eternal summers. One muggy morning, as I was leading Jack around the pasture, I noticed that his hooves buckled under. Jack regularly got new shoes from the blacksmith but he was hobbling on his knuckles. I curry combed his soft white and rust-colored rump, brushed his mane and tail, raked the stall, and called the vet.

"This animal has muscular dystrophy," the vet said. "Sorry, hon. You've got no choice but to put him down."

The next day, the vet arranged to haul my dear Jack to horse heaven. When I lost my horse, I had nothing to gain by keeping myself captive on a couple of acres of abandoned pasture. "Hey Todd, can we move to Tempe?"

"We who? You got a mouse in your pocket? We are not going anywhere. If you think you got someplace to go, you are on your own. You can bet your bottom dollar that will not last long since you got no common sense. I'm parking my butt right where it's at."

The property had been purchased with my trust fund. But it never occurred to me to tell Todd to get lost in a crevice of the Superstition Mountains.

When Todd agreed to sell the land a few weeks later, I assumed he had some self-serving agenda. We consulted the broker who had initially sold us the property. The broker told us that if he could buy the land himself, he would. However, interest rates had soared to seventeen percent, bringing the market to a standstill. Even as he took the listing, the broker suggested that we wait to sell. Apparently, Phoenix would spread to the south within a couple of years. A new Coca-Cola plant would employ thousands, and two-lane Riggs Road would expand to a four-lane freeway. A developer was planning to purchase surrounding acres for subdividing, and my land would be worth a fortune. Todd was snide with the broker, "Yeah, and your commission will be higher so you can buy the adjacent lots for yourself." The contradictory advice of the broker and the sarcasm of my husband served only to confuse me. I decided to take a chance, stay in the boondocks, and wait for the real estate boom.

Waiting for a potential pay-off was not my forte. When Todd found a buyer among his co-workers, a young man who was gleeful about his good fortune, I decided to sell. With the proceeds from the sale, I paid off our credit card debts. After accounting for the depreciation of the trailer, there was only a thousand dollars left over. I couldn't have been in my right mind; I'd relinquished my inheritance for naught.

Transitions and Improvements

If we keep on doing what we always done, we'll keep on getting what we always got.

Barbara Lyons

"What happened when you left Chandler?" Karen asked.

"Todd and I moved to Tempe."

"What were your plans?"

"Plans? I hoped that someday I would return to college at Arizona State University."

"What were your more immediate goals?"

"To get through the day."

"What was your daily routine like?"

I told Karen that the relationship was like a passing acquaintance. Communication from Todd was further reduced to a series of nagging questions regarding dinner. "What's for dinner? Is dinner ready? When are you going to get dinner ready? How am I supposed to eat this crap?" I never promised him pasta primavera. Perhaps I could toss poisonous oleander leaves into his salad.

Cooking was not my strong suit, though kitchen duty was in my genes. My maternal great-grandmother had migrated from Italy to America. In her small cottage in New Jersey, she sewed an apron for me when I was only six years old. The apron symbolized my responsibility to prepare meals because the value of an Italian woman was based on her ability to feed her family. The more able-bodied the men, the more money they could earn, so the peasant women in old Italy served feasts fit for kings. Eating with family and friends represented the peasant's triumph over poverty.

Subsequent generations used food as the center of celebrations. In my family, a birthday party or wedding anniversary began with a Chianti toast: *Salute!* An antipasto followed, with platters full of olives, anchovies, celery hearts, sliced Roma tomatoes, and provolone drizzled with olive oil. My grandmother prepared chicken cacciatore or calamari with macaroni and Parmesan. We finished with spumoni, which was an iced cream filled with fruit bits, and the dessert liquor that tasted like licorice, Anisette. *Ciao!*

I'd learned at seven years old that grown men mattered more than little girls. When celebrating my First Holy Communion with my family, I reached for the celery hearts on the platter. My grandmother slightly slapped my hand, saying, "Those are Uncle Tony's favorite. Wait until he eats what he wants, and you can have what he leaves."

When I was a pre-teen, my mother tried to teach me the secret unwritten recipe for marinara sauce: whole tomatoes, plum tomatoes, tomato paste, oregano, fennel, and garlic galore. However, I had no desire to cook, which was a character flaw for a female in my family. To be a good girl, I scrubbed the pots and pans. My specialty was cleaning.

When I cooked for Todd, my recipe was runny sauce from a jar dumped over thickets of spaghetti. Once, when I was fed up with Todd calling the meals "pathetic," I lifted the pot off the stove and threw the boiling pasta at him. My aim was way off, and spaghetti al dente clung to the cabinets. This outburst surprised us both, and he backed off. On my hands and knees, I scraped clumps of sticky, gooey pasta from the kitchen. My specialty in cleaning came in handy in the aftermath of heated arguments, when no more words were spoken to resolve an issue.

Since I was raised to believe that women are subservient to men, I accepted what Todd gave me. He had nothing to give but bossy orders: "Give me a cigarette! Pass me the lighter! Get me a cup of coffee!" He snapped his fingers, "And hurry up, why don't you?"

Karen remarked, "You're becoming more aware of patterns that pertained to your husband and family. It's not unusual to do things as we saw them done."

"Oh, I get it," I responded. "Todd was the perfect pick for perpetuating passivity."

"That's one way of putting it," Karen said. "What else went on in Tempe?"

I continued to tell Karen about the relationship with Todd. I'd remember an event like a fragment of a dream and analyze the part to understand the whole.

I told Karen about one afternoon when I had been washing and ironing slacks to wear to an appointment at the university admissions office. I noticed then that none of my clothes fit, so I called a phone number posted in the laundry room which advertised tailoring by "Sally the Seamstress." When she came over to pin the alterations, we saw we were about the same age. She looked healthy, with rosy cheeks, glossy dark hair, and a plump figure. She had majored in home economics and loved to cook and sew.

"Would you like to come to my place and try my cinnamon snicker-doodle cookies?" she invited.

"Maybe later. I'll have to tell my husband."

When Todd walked in, I introduced them, Sally smiling "hello" through the straight pins in her mouth. As if I were not in the room, Todd stated, "She wouldn't need her clothes mended if she wasn't such a scrawny broad."

Sally spit the pins. "How could you talk about your wife like that?"

Todd snuffled, "Ah, she's a piece of work."

"From what I can see, your wife is a wonderful woman and you're a lucky man."

Me, wonderful? Todd, lucky? She had to be kidding! Sally was so outspoken! Todd was as dumfounded as I.

"Worthless women," he griped, slamming the door on his way out.

"Sally, it's all right, he talks like that all the time."

"It's not all right. You deserve better."

"No, I don't."

"Lynn, don't put yourself down."

Sally paused, and then asked, "Does Todd hurt you in other ways?"

"No, well, maybe." Todd smacked me when we passed in the hall or as he walked by my chair. When I complained, he would say. "That was just a love tap."

I was raised to think that affection hurt. In greeting, my uncles twisted my cheek or my nose. When I complained to my mother and asked her to make Uncle Sal, Uncle Tony, or Uncle Vic *stop*, she would say, "It's a love pat. That's how men show affection."

Apparently, women did not tell men when to stop because men were strong and women were weak.

Todd bullied me: "I ought-a wup you upside the head" or "I ought-a haul off and kick you in the ass," and sometimes he did just that. He grabbed my arm, squeezed it hard, and twisted both his hands around it, until I bruised. "If you weren't such a skinny runt, you wouldn't bruise so easy," he would justify.

Sally told me, "Todd's abusing you."

"No, he never beat me with a broom or broke a bone."

"It's abuse, plain and simple."

As I was telling this to Karen, she confirmed the abuse: "Putdowns, name calling and threatening behavior, as well as hitting you, then denying that he hurt you, are all forms of abuse."

I recognized a frame of reference regarding my family. My father was like a jack-in-the-box, ready to spring without warning. I was all wound up, ready to strike in defense. According to my father, *I* was the one who was high-strung. I did not know where his tension ended and mine began. When I was around him, I was on guard, watching for his next move. My older brother imitated our father; Eric bullied me by shoving me back, pushing me forward, staring me down, and kicking me under the table. The exact scenarios applied to Todd.

Karen was interrupting my long recall. "Lynn, listen. Are you listening?"

"Sure," I said as I searched for some tissue to tear, some gum to chew, or some nails to spit.

"The isolation from friends and family was emotional abuse. Goading you into marriage and coercion of your college funds to obtain community property were also forms of abuse."

"Karen, why do I continually make mistakes?"

"Your experiences were not mere mistakes, but life lessons. Human experiences pertain not just to suffering but also to personal development and soul growth."

Evidently, I had a lot to learn.

"Karen, I've been around abusive men my whole life. Why I am so stupid to let myself to be abused?"

"You perceive yourself as a victim and are led into circumstances that continue the victim role. The inner resources to defend your self were eroded by the myth that men are a force to fear. The fact is that men and women are equal in the emotional and spiritual levels. It's possible to transform from a vulnerable target to an empowered woman, but you need to develop the strength and skills required to be independent. Change your way of living by changing your way of thinking."

"How can I do that?"

"You can replace negative self-talk with optimistic thoughts," Karen said. "It is possible to change a negative perspective on life into a positive life force if you keep a sense of proportion."

"Oh, so not every minor inconvenience leads to a major catastrophe."

"Exactly. It's up to you to make the conscious choices that bring about a better future. Find new methods to deal with old routines. You have to take charge of your life, to be accountable to yourself and responsible toward others."

I couldn't count on myself. I could not make up my mind or I would change my mind, or anyone could change it for me. As unpredictable as my father, I imitated the exact behavior that irked me. I changed plans, habitually procrastinated, and invented excuses: a headache, a stomachache, it was too early or it was too far, or the weather was too terrible for whatever it was that I was avoiding.

Karen was encouraging change but I was paralyzed with ambivalence. My desire to change was in conflict with the fear of change, and I resisted change even as I risked change. If only change could occur overnight, by osmosis, or at least if I could leave well enough alone. In a poem I wrote after that counseling session, I pleaded with the universe to cooperate:

Now travel, Time, no more delays,
Propel me now to future days.
To days of good, new days unfold,
Now faster, Time, before I am old.

Karen started the next session by teaching me the concrete steps to making a change: Be aware of the behavior needing change, examine the reasons for developing the behavior in the first place, have compassion for the choices made under the circumstances, find new ways to meet the needs, and get support. Set goals in small timeframes, one day, one week, one month, and break down the larger goals into smaller ones. Get rewards along the way.

"What if I fail?" I asked Karen. I realized that I failed to try anything that I could not do perfectly and all I could do perfectly was clean house. I thought about trying other things but never got around to it. I made a mental note: *"To think and think and think about a thing and never to accomplish it at all."*

Karen responded by saying, "Use failures as a learning experience and try again. It's a waste of time to wait to do everything perfectly. In order to grow, it's necessary to attempt new skills. Let go of the limiting controls of perfectionism! To make mistakes is to be human and everyone makes mistakes. Besides, the power to change is already within you, ready to be discovered, with God to guide you."

Karen's straightforward introduction of God took me off guard. I'd put up walls to defend myself against a God that had abandoned me.

"I just don't understand. What does God have to do with it?"

"Knowing that God's love remains constant can serve as a foundation when making changes in life."

Pausing to comprehend Karen's comments, I realized I needed to change my physical condition. After years of letting my body literally waste away, I could not even run for my life. If I were to live, I wanted to have a healthy body. As I was lighting a cigarette, I cried, "I wish I could quit."

"You can," Karen encouraged. "Think of the body as a temple for the spirit, and take care of your body."

It never occurred to me to stop smoking to enhance my health, but I made the decision to quit. I enrolled in behavior modification classes at the hospital's wellness center. At a series of aversion therapy sessions, posters of lungs deformed by nicotine hung on the walls. Smokers were encouraged to remove habit triggers such as ashtrays and lighters from their environments. After only a week, I quit smoking and hacking, and was intoxicated by fresh air and fresh starts.

Sally had been my cheerleader while I quit smoking. Then she asked me to join her in a fitness class.

"I can't," I whined.

"You can," she insisted.

At first, I endured only five minutes before falling to the floor from exhaustion. Gradually, I was able to get through fifteen minutes, then thirty minutes. Exercise goals were measured not by the scale but by the increase in stamina. After completing a sixty-minute low-impact aerobics class, Sally and I treated ourselves to frozen yogurt.

While I was incorporating healthy changes into my life, I was in transition, no longer the person I was and not the person I was yet to be.

Karen asked, "How does it feel to achieve goals?"

I shrugged my shoulders, which was not an acceptable answer to her.

"Try not to minimize triumphs but appreciate the steps toward self-improvement," she suggested. "Now tell me, how does it feel to set a goal and meet it?"

"It feels like a victory, like winning a ribbon in a horse show."

To increase self-confidence, I peeked into the mirror each morning and repeated: "I can, I can, I can." Once, I would have considered this a corny gimmick, but now I viewed it as a tool to get myself together. Prior to using this "believing mirror" technique, I would only glance in the mirror, afraid to face the image of shame, guilt, anger, and regret that reflected back.

Karen said, "You don't see yourself as others see you."

Afraid of the answer, I asked, "How do others see me?"

"I see a bright, beautiful woman with talent. You have paid too much attention to negative traits while neglecting your positive qualities. Try accepting all aspects of your identity, both your strengths and weaknesses. You are greater than the sum of all parts. Let's consider the concept of self-love."

"Self-love? Isn't that conceited?"

"Conceit is a result of the ego, and a selfish point of view. However, self-esteem and self-love originate in the soul, which is the essence of love."

"I was considered stuck-up in school, when in fact I was shy."

"Shyness is a symptom of fear," Karen said. "What are you afraid of?"

"I don't know." Perhaps it was the pervasive apprehension that cast an ominous shadow on my world.

"You are strong," Karen said. "As your fears recede, courage will emerge. Love was locked inside, shielded by fear. When the darkness of fear disappears, the light of love appears. You built walls around yourself to block out bad feelings, so you also blocked out any good that could come your way. You perpetuate pain by locking up feelings. When you excavate and explore emotions, you allow the fear to fade."

It was essential to bridge the gap between fear and love, but there was a roadblock. I envisioned myself teetering at the top of an open drawbridge, over a river, about to fall into the empty space where the road ends, afraid to leap to the other side, yet afraid to jump into the water. The qualities of self-esteem, self-acceptance, and self-love were necessary to close the drawbridge and move forward on the road.

"Lynn, you understand in your head, but you need to *feel* in your heart. Transformation requires more than rationalization. Healing transpires from fully feeling emotions, and then taking necessary action."

"But!"

Karen held my hands: "You have hurt very deeply for a very long time, and you need a very long time for that to heal."

I cried with relief that someone understood. Still, I was afraid to unlock my heart and uncover emotions. If I felt a bona fide feeling, I would surely go insane.

"The depression used to cover up emotions becomes a permanent part of the personality," Karen explained. "Actually, emotions are transitory. Try to determine the cause of an emotion, identify the feeling, and acknowledge its presence. Honor an emotion in the moment; just be with it, and that is more like going sane."

"Okay."

"Lynn, what are you feeling?"

"I don't know."

"You must be feeling something."

"No, nothing."

"Please, tell me what it feels like."

"I don't know."

"Yes you do."

"I feel like my life was a mistake of the universe and I am an unnecessary burden on the planet."

"What brought that on?"

I told Karen that I swear I witnessed my father's mental illness and my mother's emotional distress from the womb. My father's anger and my mother's anguish made me feel unwelcome. My father treated my pregnant mother like a venomous black-widow spider about to hatch a billion eggs.

My mother told me she had not wanted another child until *after* she had me. She also told me about the day I was born. She was in labor as my father was driving in heavy traffic, and the drawbridge over the Passaic River was scheduled to open. He used his obnoxious voice and car horn to hail a police escort, and our car was the last over the bridge. They were racing to the hospital accompanied by a siren while the drawbridge opened and cargo ships passed through.

"Karen, why was it that I came into the world with bells and whistles, and still did not feel welcome?"

"Don't think of yourself just as the daughter of your biological parents. Your parent's suffering need not be a blueprint for your own. There is no need to attach your identity only to them. You are the daughter of a loving father, God. You can claim your birthright as a child of God. There is a diversity of creatures on this planet, and each of us is celebrated as a child of God."

"But God made a mistake with me."

"No one is a mistake of God's creation. Everyone is necessary on earth. Simply by being born, you belong on earth as a rightful member of the human family. We are all children of God, so all human beings are inter-connected. We all play a purposeful part in each other's lives. Everything and everyone we encounter is for a purpose."

"Why didn't I die?"

"Life is a gift from God and what we do with our lives is a gift back. The greatest gift of all is love. There is a purpose to life, which is as simple as experiencing love and extending that love. All that is encountered is a part of that divine plan."

"It's not like I do anything special."

"The love of God is not reserved for special people who perform certain acts. Love is not a matter of deserving. No list of accomplishments is needed to earn love. For example, I love my own children as they are, before they were even born, without saying a word or doing a thing. It's like that with God's love: unconditional."

"But!"

Karen asked a candid question: "Do you believe in God?"

I was fidgeting, fumbling, searching for lip-balm, anything to stall.

"Lynn, this is not a problem to be solved with intellect, but a question to be answered with heart and soul. I'd like to give you a homework assignment. Write about whatever vision of God comes to mind."

I had to see it in black and white, so I consulted dictionary definitions of the words that came to mind.

> *"Atheist: one who denies the existence of God."*
> *"Agnostic: one who doubts the existence of God."*

I recalled my family's versions of God: Manny was an atheist, Holly was a pagan, Frank was agnostic, Eric wanted scientific proof, Rusty went with the flow, Grandma went to Italy to visit the Pope, and Sophia gave up on God altogether. I wrote a few cynical words that expressed my belief: "God hates me therefore God punishes me." I prayed that Karen was not serious about the homework assignment.

Mishaps and Mind games

Some truths are moral illnesses.

Marilyn French

Summer comes to the desert before Memorial Day, arriving like a freight train with a blast of hot steam. Like a sleeping passenger, I'd closed my eyes to the scenery of spring and let the season pass by me. Now, on a May afternoon that was too hot for its time, I was walking to the mailroom at the apartment complex.

I realized that Todd and I had settled into a symbiotic relationship. We fed from each other like parasites, leeching what we needed to exist. I earned my keep and he paid the bills. I slept while he worked at night; he slept during the day while I cleaned. We'd encounter each other for brief periods in the morning and evening to talk about mundane matters. After the suicide attempt, all my energy was spent on survival, with none to spare for moving on. And then I got the mail.

Among the bills was a square envelope addressed to Mr. and Mrs. The return address was from a woman with the same last name as Todd, my married name. After deciding not to open the envelope, I practiced assertiveness skills, and then confronted Todd.

"Todd, who is this from?"

"Mind your p's and q's, woman." Todd tore open the envelope, which contained an invitation.

"Todd, who is it from?"

"It's from my daughter. She's graduating high school."

"You have children?"

"Yessiree. Four: Debra, Denise, Dorothy, and Donald."

"Four? Four?"

"They're from my first marriage, to Dottie."

"First marriage? How many marriages were there?"

"Well, let's see. You're number eight. And you know what? I loved all my women."

Loved? How well could he get to know an individual woman in a series of short-term marriages?

Todd named the wives in chronological order, counting twice one wife that he had married, divorced, and remarried. He admitted that he had been arrested for bigamy when he forgot to get divorced between his first and second marriages. The parents of the second wife sued him for fraud and misrepresentation, and had the marriage annulled.

"Her parents kept me from ever seeing my second wife again," Todd whined.

"When was the last time you saw your children?"

"It's been years. Dottie kept me from seeing them after I left her."

The news of his numerous marriages came as a moment of truth: I had married a menace to society. How I could be so stupid? Stupid! Stupid! Stupid! I tried to deny that I had not discovered Todd's deceit. Perhaps he did not really have six or seven previous wives. Perhaps if I pretended long and hard enough, it would all go away. Go away!

I was wary that Karen would turn on me if she knew that I was so stupid. I needed a therapist to pull me from the deep waters of insanity to the shallow shore of sanity. Karen had extended herself like a lifeline and I was afraid to break the bond. So, one day in session, instead of revealing Todd's serial monogamy, I blurted to her: "Men are not to be trusted."

"What makes you say that?"

"Not trusting men began with my father. He manipulated my mother with false vows to change and disappointed me with his broken promises."

"That sounds so intellectual. What are you feeling?"

"I don't know."

"Let's go with memory. What do you remember from when you were three or four years old?"

"I hate to remember that age. I don't want to remember my childhood."

Remembering was like watching a movie that's flat on the screen without projecting emotion. Feeling was like viewing a stage play from the orchestra seats, a live act vibrating with intensity. I could remember but I could not feel. Perhaps I couldn't afford to feel the emotions that might wipe me out like a cyclone levels a community.

"I'll be with you the whole time," Karen responded. "You're safe here. Go slow."

Memories began to eke out from the recesses of my mind. When I was three years old, we lived in a small house in suburban New Jersey. The houses stood side-by-side and back-to-back, divided by chain link fences. The yards were large enough for clotheslines and swing sets. The front door of our house led directly to the living room. The bathroom was adjacent to the kitchen/dining area, and outside the back door were steps leading down to the driveway. Mommy and Daddy had one bedroom; my brother Eric and I each had our own room. When playing cowboys and Indians, my brother and I chased each other through the front door, through the house, and through the back door in a split-second, without disturbing anything.

It was best not to disturb anything after Mom had put everything in its place. She liked the house clean and neat, and I liked knowing where everything was supposed to be. At dinnertime, Mom set the table with placemats; the seating arrangement never changed, whether or not my father showed up. Mom made the best meatloaf, mashed potatoes, and green-bean salad. If Daddy came home late after drinking with the guys, she would make him a cold meatloaf sandwich while he watched television.

The house was a different place when my father was home. He'd get things out of place. After reading the evening newspaper, he left the sports page in the bathroom and the want ads in the living room. He smoked and drank in his chair, by the lamp shaped like a mermaid, and left empty bottles and overflowing ashtrays.

Eric could beat me at cowboys and Indians because his big feet ran very fast. But he was left-handed, so our father claimed Eric had been born "defective" and Daddy said that using the left hand was "not natural." Our father criticized Eric for not taking to sports. "What are you? Some kind of sissy? It's high time you learn to fight. It's for your own good. Put your dukes up, boy, jab right, jab left, knock 'em dead, boy! Right, no left!" Mom and I watched as Daddy and Eric went around each other like boxers in the ring on TV, but it was not Eric's nature to fight with his father.

On the other hand, Eric was rough with me, especially when no one was looking. When we were alone, he would push and shove and kick. When we were with Mom, he would share, and she would say, "Eric, you are such a good boy to share with your sister."

When our father was around, my brother did not talk much. Eric had a speech impediment. The more our father yelled, the more my brother stuttered. When the speech therapist made house calls, I listened in, hearing Eric practice. "Wocket, wocket, wocket, rrrrrrocket, rrocket!" I was so proud of him when he got it right! Although I was three years younger, I spoke more clearly than my brother, although my mother complained that my voice was whiney. I just hoped I wouldn't say anything wrong.

While Eric was at school and Daddy was away, Mom would clean the house spick and span. First she would ask me to amuse myself in my room, then she would ask me to clean up my room. Crayons and coloring books belonged in the toy chest, Candyland got stacked with the games, and storybooks went upright on the shelf. During the day I felt safe in my room, as if I were in a palace for a princess.

At night I felt scared in my room, as if I were in a creepy dungeon. I would lie and wait for the shadows. Or I would sit and rock in my bed, which had wheels and railings. No matter how hard I tried to stay awake, I'd fall asleep.

The slight sound of shuffling on the kitchen floor wakes me. My door is open a little, and light from the kitchen leaks into my room. Just outside my door, I see shadows the shape of a large man's legs. The shadows move forward and backward. The shadow sidesteps toward my brother's room. Why would the shadow go into my brother's room? He is supposed to be sleeping. I try not to fall asleep. I hope the shadow does not come into my room. I wait. Maybe I fall asleep.

My door is opening. My eyes blink, blink, blink to black out the beam of light. A dark figure is coming into my room. The door closes to complete darkness. Somebody, turn on a light. Somebody, pinch me so I can see if I am sleeping. The dark figure leans over my crib. It has a voice whispering, "Let's play a game." Nighttime is not for games. I am supposed to be sleeping. The voice whispers, "You will not remember a thing." What is happening?

In the morning, my crib was not against the wall, like it was supposed to be.

"Lynnie, your room doesn't look right," Mom said. "How did your crib get to the middle of the room?"

"I don't know."

"You must have been rocking so hard the bed rolled across the hardwood floor."

I couldn't remember rocking myself to sleep, but something felt wrong.

When I was four years old, I was listening from my room one night while my mother and father tossed insults at each other.

"You're a lousy excuse for a human being," I heard my mother say.

"Well, excuse the hell out of me for living," my father said.

Their phrases flew through the air like a Ping-Pong ball, paddled back and forth over a net. I was like the net, suspended by two poles, waiting to catch and contain the last word. If only they could stop fighting, then they could love each other, love me, and love my brother. They continued their torrent.

"I wish you were dead."

"I hope you drop dead."

"I'm gonna kill you if it's the last thing I do, so help me God."

"Over my dead body."

"Get out of my life."

"You think you can get away with murder, don't you?"

I was scared to death. While I waited for the fight to end, I held my breath and my pee. Barefoot, in my pajamas, I tiptoed from the bed to the door, and peeked out of my room. My brother Eric opened his door too. He stood in the doorway in his Superman pajamas long enough to stick his tongue out at me, and then he went back inside his room. How could he sleep with that racket? My mother and father were standing by the kitchen sink, facing each other. She was in her nightgown and robe, and in tears. He was wearing his boxer shorts, his flabby and hairy belly in full view. I looked past them toward the bathroom. Could I sneak by my parents to the toilet without them noticing?

"You're such a bitch," my father said.

"You're a son of a bitch," she responded.

My father opened a kitchen drawer and pulled out a knife. That's the knife my mother used to cut bones from chicken. He was holding the knife over his head with the sharp blade aimed at my mother. She looked so small compared to his large body, and his rage was larger than life. My father noticed me long enough to stop killing my mother.

"What the hell do you want?" my father yelled.

My voice squeaked like Minnie Mouse: "I have to go to the bathroom."

"Go to the bathroom and get back to bed," my mother snapped. "Go ahead. It's okay."

While I went to the bathroom, I heard my mother whisper, "Get out! Get out of my sight!" Although I knew she was telling my father to leave, I wondered what I'd done wrong. Then, my mother was knocking at the bathroom door, asking me, "Do you need any help?"

"No," I called out as I nearly fell in the toilet because I'd forgotten to put the booster seat onto the potty. When my mother led me back to my bedroom, I didn't see the knife or my father, but I could see her wearing worry on her face like a heavy layer of cold cream that had dried and caked.

I was used to my family's expressions of final moments and had one of my own. Kneeling by my bed, I prayed: *"If I should die before I wake, I pray the Lord my soul to take.*" My mother was kneeling beside me, rubbing her fingers on her forehead.

"Thank God Eric is sleeping like a log," she said. "Can you go back to sleep now?"

"Okay, Mommy." I loved my mother more than anything in the whole wide world, and I'd do anything for her. I'd even tell a fib if I had to, or make believe to make her happy.

We heard the back door slam. Slam! The fighting always ended with my father slamming the door as he fled the scene. Would my father ever come back? I was afraid that he would and afraid that he would not. Either way, my mother would be sad, my brother would hide, and I'd mix up love and fear until I didn't know the difference.

My father would deliberately build me up to the height of excitement only to let me down into the depths of disappointment. By the time I got to the treasure chest, it was not worth the effort to open the lid for fake gems from my father.

When I was about five years old, my father decided to paint my bedroom pink, for a girl. "Please, Daddy, please, may I have blue, like the sky?"

"Blue is for boys. You're not a tomboy, are you? No little girl of mine is going to be a tomboy. Girls are supposed to be sugar and spice and everything nice."

The pink in the paint can looked like melted strawberry ice cream, a color I could savor. I decided that Daddy knew best. When my father bent over to load the brush, the crack of his butt showed above his boxer shorts. "Droopy drawers," I giggled. While he painted, I explored the caves that the sheets formed, draped over the bed and onto the floor. Under the bed, I spotted the biggest spider ever. I stared at the spider until I got the guts to come out, keeping an eye on the spider and bumping my head.

"Look, Daddy, look at that spider!"

Sensing some fun for him, my father lifted a sheet and peered under the bed. "Are you afraid of that spider? It won't hurt you. Watch, I'll prove it to you." He plucked the spider out from under the bed, saying, "It's just a daddy long legs." He dangled the spider by one thin leg while the round body squirmed. "See, it won't hurt you. See? Are you watching? Watch out, here it comes!" In one swift motion, he threw the spider at me and I ran screaming from my room. I had no place to go, but I knew that anywhere else would be better than with my father.

After that, I did not want to sleep in my own room, even with the blue-and-pink chenille bedspread on my twin bed. Afraid to lie down under the sheets in case the roving spider crawled up my leg, I rocked on my bed in the dark for as long as I could keep my eyes open. When I lay down to sleep, I curled my legs up so the spider could not snatch me from the foot of the bed.

Rather than protect me from childhood fears, my father instilled even greater fears until I was never able to feel safe. Any innocuous event contained an undercurrent of deliberate hurt.

My father's favorite game was to tickle me. His fingers felt like an octopus on my tummy, twisting my insides into knots. "Are you ticklish? Are you? Huh? Huh?" He knew I was ticklish, and not strong enough to fight his fingers. He wrestled with me on the floor, on the bed, on the couch.

"Please, Daddy, please stop!"

"You want me to stop? Say uncle!"

"Uncle!" Hiccup, breath. "Uncle!" Hiccup, breath. "It hurts, Daddy."

"Say uncle!"

"Uncle!"

That never made him stop.

"You love this, don't you? I know you do!"

"No, I don't. Please stop!"

"Don't ever say "no" to your father! You hear me?"

"Yes, Daddy." I felt as helpless as Dorothy in *The Wizard of Oz*, caught in the whirlwind of a twister, unable to flee the force field that was my father.

At night, the radiator hissed like a snake. *I am dreaming that the curves of the covers are slithering serpents. The squirming snakes are different sizes, some long and menacing, some short and sneaking. The snakes glare with moist, beady snake eyes.* When I awoke, I thought I could still see coiled snakes raising their heads to strike and inject the venom that could kill. I left the bed cautiously, one leg sliding off the mattress at a time, so as not to disturb them.

In the dark, I flattened my palm against the wall to feel my way into my parents' room. I was afraid to wake them because they might yell at each other or me. Curling up on the rug by their bed, I reminded myself to return to my room by dawn.

One morning, I watched as my mother kept busy after another argument with my father the night before. Cleaning was her way of maintaining control, so she picked up ashtrays and mopped up spilled beer. She put the remains of the mermaid lamp into the garbage; the lamp had sailed through the air and landed at a wall. I felt so sad for my mother. Her heart was broken, but she swept those pieces under the rug. This time, she put a letter on the kitchen table and the white paper reflected in the shine of the dark wood.

My mother was packing a suitcase. We were about to leave New Jersey to see my mother's mother in Pennsylvania. I was wearing the cowgirl outfit I'd received for my fifth birthday.

"Mom, can I have boots to go with?"

"Ask your father?"

"Mom, who is the note for?"

"Your father."

"What does it say?"

"It says we are leaving your father."

"Where are we going?"

"To live with your grandma."

"How come?"

"I have my reasons."

"Does Eric have to go with us?"

"Of course. Now be a good girl and stop asking so many questions."

I watched through the screen door as my mother loaded luggage into the trunk. Whatever her reasons, I put all my trust in my mother, the one parent I could count on to take care of me.

Sandy the dog put his head in my lap. "Mommy, are we bringing the dog?"

"Yes, we have to take Sandy. Otherwise he's liable to starve to death waiting for your father to feed him."

Was my father *so* bad that he could starve our pet? I was remembering when my father brought the Golden Retriever puppy home that year. My mother liked dogs, but she was upset that he had not consulted her.

"This dog will be more trouble than it's worth," she had complained. "Can't you see I'm busy enough with two kids, a house, the laundry, and you to pick up after?"

"Please, Mom, please can we keep the doggie?" My brother and I had pleaded in harmony.

My father latched onto that. "See, the kids want the dog. You want to make the kids happy, don't you?"

If she refused, she would look bad, so she gave in. Mom, Eric, and I loved to chase our dog Sandy around and around the table, an endless circle of fur and tail, brother and sister and mother, until it was not clear who was chasing whom. When Sandy grew tired, he'd lap water from a cereal bowl turned doggie dish. He'd pant with a pink lolling tongue, and then moisten my face with thick, sloppy licks that made me giggle with pleasure. Although Sandy and I stood nose to nose, he didn't scare me one bit. Mom had called the dog "a gentle giant."

The day we were leaving my father, we picked up Eric from school and the dog slept between us in the big back seat of the Buick. Whenever we drove from Jersey to Pennsylvania, we usually sang, *"She'll be coming round the mountain when she comes."* This time, Mom had some explaining to do: "Lynnie, you'll be going to a new kindergarten. Eric, you will be attending a different elementary school. And you won't be seeing your father for a while."

My brother did not have much to say about leaving our father. Eric sat up straight while our mother drove, barely glancing my way as he stared out the window. The houses got fewer and farther between and the trees blurred as my mother was driving. It was okay with me that we were going to my grandmother's without my father. When he went there, or anywhere, he always caused a commotion.

I was remembering the last time we were at my grandmother's. My father had nearly killed me. He had held me up over his shoulders and tossed me in the air. The black-and-white linoleum floor swirled below. He caught me. Then my father sat me on his shoulders with my ankles crossed around his neck, my hands cupped under his chin.

"Please, Daddy, please let me down!"

My mother looked up at us. "Let Lynnie down. You're over-stimulating her."

"She loves this," my father insisted. "Hold on tight, Lynnie!"

What could I hold on to? His whiskers prickled my fingers, so I put my hands on his head, but they slipped from the styling cream on his hair. His hands released my ankles and I fell backwards. Black and white stars swirled around as I hit the concrete floor.

Next thing I knew, I was lying on the back seat of the car. As we sped along, my mother and father were fighting in the front seat.

"It's your fault. This should not have happened. You could have killed her!"

"She's the one who let go," he snarled.

It was not my fault, was it? I did not fall on purpose! Was it his fault? For a second I thought my father might have deliberately dropped me. What did I do to deserve that? Before I could give it another thought, I dozed off.

I woke up in a crib in a hospital to see my mother smiling over the bed rails. I was so happy to see her, to hear her talking to me, to have her all to myself.

"How's my pretty little girl? The doctor said you have a boo-boo on your brain. You can come home in a couple of days."

"Where's Daddy?"

"He's back in New Jersey. He can't come to see you."

I was so mad at him. He could hurt me, and he could not make the hurt go away. He wouldn't even try.

Kidnap and Courage

You gain strength, courage, and confidence by every experience in which you really stop to look fear in the face...You must do the thing which you think you cannot do.

Eleanor Roosevelt

So, I was glad to be going to Grandma's without my father. My grandmother's place was a resort named Tanglewood Falls. My grandma and grandpa had purchased a lodge in the Pocono Mountains during the late 1940's. Residents of New Jersey and New York drove from the city to the Pennsylvania mountains for rest and relaxation. By the early 1950's, Tanglewood Falls was a honeymoon haven with heart-shaped tubs in rooms lined with red velvet.

Just as my grandparents were making their first million, the mountain creeks flooded the resort. My grandmother said she watched from the attic window as the water rose to the eaves. My mother said that we huddled in the attic with the bats. My mother and grandmother had to climb onto the roof with me, four-year-old Eric, Aunt Ruthie, and her infant Annie so that a helicopter could rescue us. Tanglewood Falls was ruined but the state government gave my grandparents a grant to rebuild. As they were making their second million, my grandfather died of a heart attack.

After that, my grandmother lived with weather-related phobias, complaining that it was too hot or too cold or too dry and too wet or too windy. "When the weather is bad, the business is worse," she would say. She watched the weather forecasts like a religious ritual, so she could complain in advance. Even when the meteorologists predicted rapture in a glorious spring day, my grandmother would say that the weather was terrible.

Now that we were living at Tanglewood Falls for good, my mother and my brother and I stayed in the family's private quarters, upstairs. My grandmother lived in her apartment downstairs, next to my mother's brother, Tony, his wife Ruthie, and my cousin Annie.

Tanglewood Falls was my favorite place. At five years old, I thought that living there was a dream come true. But even here, nightmares soon mingled with dreams, sometimes during the day.

Thinking back now, I recalled several scenes that replayed in my mind and caused me to lose sleep.

Once, when I was about five years old, I heard my younger cousin Annie crying as I was walking toward Ruthie and Tony's apartment.

"Annie, I want you to eat this," Ruthie ordered.

"No! I don't want to!"

"You're my daughter and you'll do as I say!"

As I walked closer, I could see that Ruthie was standing over Annie, who was sitting in a booster seat. Ruthie used the heel of her hand to push Annie's forehead backward. The back of Annie's head hit the wall behind the chair. Then, Ruthie was shoving a hotdog into Annie's mouth and Annie was kicking. Seeing my aunt force-feeding Annie frightened me, but my aunt was acting like nothing was amiss.

Ruthie saw me, "Oh, we have a guest. Lynnie, come on in."

I guessed it was polite to pretend.

"Annie, you better be on your best behavior by the time your father gets home," Ruthie warned.

A few minutes later, Tony raced into his apartment with a gait as brisk as a Thoroughbred. He tweaked my cheek. "Well, look who's here." I rubbed the place he had pinched. It hurt.

"Lunch is almost ready," Ruthie said. The smell of her Chanel perfume followed her around the cozy kitchen. "You better do something about your daughter. She's acting like a spoiled brat."

"I thought I told you to have lunch ready by 12:30. It's past 1:00," Tony said. He tweaked Annie's cheek. "What's the matter with you, acting like a brat? You been a cry-baby today?"

"No need to fawn over her," Ruthie said. "She's going to play with Lynnie."

Tony sat with his gut spilling over his lap and ate a plate of ziti and sausage. His brown eyes darted about, "I have a meeting with the vacation bureau tonight, so I'll be home late. Have a plate ready, will you? You two girls go play nice."

Annie was a year younger than me. At four years old, she looked like a chubby cherub plucked from a stained glass window in church.

Her curly blonde hair and blue eyes elicited an "Oh, how adorable!" from absolutely everybody. I would have traded my straight brown hair and long skinny legs for that child-star look of Annie's any day.

Ruthie was like a stage mother, ushering Annie to dance lessons and piano recitals. As though Annie were in show business, Ruthie routinely took Annie to photography studios. The modeling sessions were a big production. Ruthie would brush Annie's wild, curly hair while Annie wriggled like a puppy with a collar. My aunt would dust Annie's face with a powder puff, fold the ankle socks just so, and fluff her newest chiffon dress. The pictures were mounted in fancy frames for her father's office or our grandmother's dresser. Annie was a superstar destined for fame and fortune. Maybe she'd be Miss America some day.

My mother had to use home permanents to put a bend in my hair. At bedtime, she wound hunks of hair around pink sponge rollers. The acidic smell of the solution and a fitful sleep on twenty rods was the price to pay for curls. The next morning, my hair looked like a dirty wad of cotton candy.

"No matter what I do to your hair, it's still straight as a stick," my mother complained. Objecting to my hair was a family hobby. My father would gripe: "Her hair sticks up in tufts like Alfalfa on *The Little Rascals*. I do not want my daughter looking like some kid character. Can't you do something with her hair?"

"Mommy, why can't I have ringlets like Annie?"

"It sounds like you are forming an inferiority complex."

"What's that?"

"You feel second best to your cousin, don't you? There's no reason for that. I hate to say this, but Annie's rather homely. Her hair is frizzy and her teeth are yellow from all that medicine her mother gives her. Annie chews her fingernails to the quick, and with that bump, she will need a nose job someday."

"But Mom, everyone says she's so cute!"

"Her father is a prominent businessman. His cronies butter him up about his daughter to stay on his good side. Remember, sweetheart, beauty is in the eye of the beholder, and I think you are beautiful."

Mothers were supposed to say stuff like that. Still, I felt like an ugly duckling next to Annie. Even Annie's name sounded so much prettier than just plain Lynn.

Although Annie had all the toys and games in the world, we mostly explored the outdoors together. In the spring, we laid back on the ground that was cushioned with pine needles, and searched for shapes in the drifting clouds. We shared the images in the harmony of friendship.

"Lynnie, what do you think that cloud looks like?"

"It looks like an angel."

In the winter, we dropped our bodies backwards onto freshly fallen snow, and waved our arms. Pulling herself up and looking down, Annie said, "Look, we made snow angels."

In the summer, we pricked our index fingers with a pin and pressed bloody finger to bloody finger. "Lynnie, this means that we'll be best friends forever."

"Okay, but we have to say 'Cross my heart and hope to die'."

Year round, Annie and I were as close as sisters, and our relatives said we were inseparable. Sometimes, my aunt took me along on her shopping sprees. She usually ran late on outings, and rushed through her day at the last minute. One afternoon, she put Annie and I in the back seat of the Lincoln and started the car.

"Oops," Aunt Ruthie said, "I forgot the credit card." She stopped the car as it headed down the hill, jumped out, and ran into the house. Oops, she forgot to put the gearshift in park. The car began to roll down the hill, straight toward the lake. I imagined plunging into cold pond scum, face to face with frogs and slimy catfish. Annie and I started yelling for help.

A kitchen employee sprinted to the car, half hopped in, and stomped on the brake pedal. We were rescued by Denny the dishwasher. That was what I would call helpful, even though my grandmother frequently complained: "You can't get good help these days."

When my uncle heard what had happened, Ruthie was in trouble. In the back of the hotel kitchen, in front of the cooks, Tony shrieked at his wife, "Are you some kind of nut, out to kill your own daughter and goddaughter? I ought to take the keys from you!"

"Look, the children are fine, everything's fine," Ruthie said. I had a sore throat from screaming at the top of my lungs, but we went on our outing anyway, as if shopping were a cure.

When Annie wasn't around, I checked on my brother. Since our mother was divorcing our father, our relatives often said to Eric, "Guess you are the man of the family now." Although he was only eight years old, he liked to do what he had seen our father do, which was to tinker with the hammers and nails in the maintenance garage. One afternoon, when I wandered over to the workbench, Eric noticed that I was as tall as the table saw.

"Come on, Lynnie, put your forehead up against the table."

Seeing rusty nails and grease spots, I stood back.

"Closer, Lynnie, get closer. I'm conducting an experiment."

I was wary but wanted to trust that my brother would not hurt me for the sake of science.

"Stand against the table," he said. "I want to see how this works."

Quick and sharp, the serrated blade of the table saw crossed my forehead and cut the skin. I started hopping on one foot, grasping my head with my hand. "Ouch! Ouch! Ouch! You made me bleed!"

Eric grabbed an oily shop towel and pressed it on the blood spilling over my eye. "I'm sorry, it was an accident! Please don't tell! Promise you won't be a tattle-tale." He smoothed my bangs across my forehead to hide the cut.

My mother noticed the cut when she was detangling my bangs. "How did you get that?"

"I don't know."

"It's a jagged cut, like your skin was sliced with a bread knife."

As she dabbed iodine on it, I shrugged my shoulders and bit my lower lip. I did not want to get Eric in trouble because he already had no friends, and I didn't want to make us enemies.

On Saturdays, Eric and I explored the woods surrounding Tanglewood Falls. We were searching for the origin of the waterfalls, named "Weddingbell Falls" to attract the honeymooners. Once a week, the resort's social director would announce the activities through the public-address system. The horns blared, "Attention love-birds! Meet at Weddingbell Falls for a weenie-roast!" Hot dogs and hamburgers were cooked in the barbeque pit at the waterfall on Saturday evenings.

"I'm Daniel Boone," Eric said, "and you're Pocahontas." He was leading as we climbed on a narrow path, extending his hand to help me up the mountain. "Don't look down," he warned.

Looking down through the pine trees and mountain laurel, I saw a dense forest that made me feel as small as a squirrel. "We're too high. Let's go back! Please, Eric, please."

"Don't be such a sissy." Eric let go of my hand, and moved up the mountain. When I caught up to Eric, he was peering over the edge of a lake, watching the water tumble down the mountain.

"I found the source," Eric yelled over the sound of rushing water. "I found it!"

The lake was clear enough to reveal the rocks of its bottom. Trout swam near the surface with the tadpoles. I wished I would experience this time of discovery, this time with Eric, every day. We hiked down the mountain at an angle, so as not to slide on the slick carpet of pine needles. We stopped once to pick up an Indian arrowhead that glinted in the afternoon sun. We stopped again because Eric had to pee.

"Don't look," he ordered.

I was not planning on looking.

"And don't tell."

I was not planning on telling, either. What was the big deal? Why couldn't we just be friends without the stress of secrets? I guess the mix of blood relations and mind games was familiar to us.

I could be terribly lonesome without him. When Eric had been in bed for days with rheumatic fever, I was dying to see him. "Mommy, can I play doctor and nurse with Eric?"

"Your brother is very sick and needs to rest."

I hung out in Eric's doorway, watching him sleep in his baseball pajamas. "Mommy, is Eric going to die?"

After watching my favorite cartoon, *Casper the Friendly Ghost*, I wished for my own invisible friend who could perform kind deeds. "Please make my brother better," I whispered to the television.

Mom fed Eric chicken soup that must have been the miracle cure. There he was, skinny and pale, standing in his doorway, taunting me:

"You little pest, one of these days I'm going to squash you like a bug."

"Stay away from me. You have germs."

Yet, there was no cure for my worried mind, which produced frequent headaches. Sometimes I would lay on my mother's bed with a splitting headache.

"Mommy," I would say, "I think I'm going to throw up."

"It's all right, sweetheart," she would say. She'd put a bucket on the floor by the bed. She would place a damp, cold washcloth on my forehead. She'd empty the bucket when it got full of my worries.

I worried about my mother, who had to manage other messes. Although she brought Sandy the dog to Tanglewood Falls, I could not play with him because my grandmother said, "A honeymoon resort is no place for family pets."

"Why not Grandma?"

"He might scare away the guests. We don't have a good business if we don't have guests, and we need the business."

Sandy was kept inside a garage until my mother could find a home for him. He was tied with a rope around his neck to the handle of the double pull-up door. Eric and I knew to use the single side door to feed Sandy. As I was walking toward the garage, I saw Harry the handyman opening the double door.

"No, not that door, the other door," I shouted. As the double door was being opened, Sandy was being lifted off the floor, causing the rope to work like a noose. Sandy's paws were doing doggie paddle in the air. Sandy was being strangled, with his fur bloody red and raw where the rope gripped his neck.

"I'm so sorry. I didn't know," Harry said. He quickly cut the rope, caught the dog, and loaded him into the back seat of my mother's car. He ran to get my mother, who ran to tell my grandmother, who was tied up with Carmello the cook.

In the storeroom of the hotel kitchen, my mother flipped through the phone book and called a vet. "I have a strangled dog. Yes, he is still alive. How do I get there? Turn right? Turn left? Then what?"

My mother raced along the roads, her mind racing with worry. "I hope we find this vet before he closes for the day."

I sat in the back seat with the dog, a piece of rope embedded in his fur. Our dog whimpered with its tongue hanging loose; gross green and white foam spilled from his muzzle. "Can they fix Sandy?"

"I hope so, honey."

Down a country road, she spotted the vet's shingle. After the vet lifted the dog from the back seat, I waited in the car. When my mother returned, she said, "I'm sorry, sweetheart, but the vet had to put Sandy to sleep."

"Will Sandy wake up by tomorrow?"

I was used to being scared, but seeing Sandy strangled was as scary as it gets. On one hand, I understood why Grandma always did what she thought was best for business. On the other hand, I wondered if it would have been less scary for the tourists to see children walking their dog at a family's resort.

My grandmother had seven siblings who often visited the resort with their families. My relatives used loud voices and wide gestures to talk about one another when the other wasn't around.

"She's a millionaire. Better kiss her ass."

"Better watch your back. Freddie the freeloader will rob you blind."

"His girlfriend doesn't lift a finger. God forbid she should get her lily-white hands dirty."

"She's so hardheaded. She's liable to stab him in the back. She carries a grudge."

"Well, he carries a gun. He's using strong-arm tactics to get back at her."

"She's headstrong. Those two deserve each other."

Using a literal translation, I tried to understand the phrases that referred to body parts. I pictured one relative kissing another relative's ass. The real meaning of the comments went over my head, but my family's disapproving tone said more than the words. My relatives yelled at one another one day and gave each other the silent treatment the next. I was becoming comfortable with my family, without my father.

Winter often comes abruptly to the mountains. Even before the last leaves of autumn have fallen, arctic fronts sometimes pass through the Poconos with a cold rain. On such a day, as I was coloring “Little Red Riding Hood” pictures on my grandmother’s couch, I listened to my family fretting over the weather.

“This weather is terrible for business,” Uncle Tony said.

“It’s raining cats and dogs,” Grandma said.

I giggled as I imagined pets falling from the sky, paws treading air in the rain.

“I hope it doesn’t turn to snow before Eric comes home from school,” my mother said.

Suddenly, some kind of commotion was occurring outside. I heard my father shouting: “It’s high time I get to see my own daughter! That woman has got a lot of nerve, trying to keep me from own flesh and blood.”

Tony stepped out. “Manny, you hot head. Why don’t you go home?”

“Not without my daughter!”

I peeked out from behind my grandmother’s curtains. My father was wearing a trench coat, and waving what appeared to be a black plastic water pistol. Except it was not a toy pistol, but a real gun. My father pushed open my grandmother’s door and picked me up.

“You want to come with your daddy, don’t you?”

“But I need my rain slicker and my galoshes.”

“I’ll buy you new.”

He plopped me in his car and skidded down the hill. I looked back to see my mother and my grandmother wringing their hands in their aprons. My father was pressing the gas pedal to the floor. “Come on, come on, you piece of shit.”

“Me, Daddy? What did I do wrong?”

“Not you, silly duck, it’s this crappy car.”

At five years old, I knew my father’s car, a tan Rambler convertible. It was a trash mobile with an ashtray filled with butts. The rumble seat was littered with yellowed newspapers and empty beer cans. The car smelled liked spiced sneakers, aftershave mixed with a mildewed odor, like Eric’s old tennis shoes. Raindrops dotted the interior of the ragtop like the droplets left on bathroom tile after a shower. My father was looking behind him, and at the pistol on his thigh. Sensing the danger, I started to cry.

"Why are you crying? Don't cry. You're Daddy's little girl." He was rambling through the cigarette that never left his lips: "I love my daughter. I love my son too, but he is a mamma's boy. There is still hope for you before your mother gets to you. She cannot keep you from me. Why did your mother leave in the first place? When is she coming home? She will be sorry she ever left me. She'll regret it until the day she dies."

I was scared to death that I might never see my mother again. I was being taken away, to where, I did not know. I looked back.

"Don't look back," he grumbled.

Although it was hard to see through the cloudy plastic of the rear window, I had looked behind long enough to see Tony's Cadillac. The Cadillac closed in on the convertible and sideswiped it, practically running it off the road. My heart twitched as I looked down the steep mountain slopes where the guardrail was gone.

"Let Lynnie go!" Tony yelled through the open window.

"No! She's mine! Get the hell out of my way."

"I'll get the state troopers after you. You'll rot in jail for kidnapping!"

"She's my daughter!"

As my father was shaking the gun out the window, the car swerved off the shoulder. Then, the cars bumped into each other, and my father and uncle stopped their cars in the middle of the road.

My uncle shouted, "Lynnie, get in my car."

My father shouted, "Lynnie, stay where you are."

Even with the gun in plain sight, my uncle got out of his car and scooped me out. My father skidded away. After all that, he just drove away, leaving me to wonder what I'd done wrong. He'd involved the whole family, only to abandon his own daughter. When my uncle handed me over to my mother, she would not let me go. "Did you father hurt you? Are you all right?"

I felt wounded in some way, but it didn't have a name like a cut or a bruise, so I pretended I was all right. The relatives talked about my father as if I did not understand.

"Manny is a certifiable candidate for the insane asylum."

"They ought to lock him up and throw away the key."

I knew more than they thought I knew. I knew that my daddy was a bad man. I knew that I couldn't be good enough to make him a better man. I knew that.

As I was telling Karen about my childhood, I was overwhelmed with emotion. Like a gymnast performing a succession of somersaults, I'd tumbled from one calamitous event to another without a pause. As a child, I had had no time to collect my thoughts and feel the emotions.

As an adult, the suicidal feelings still surfaced when I was stressed. Remembering my childhood opened wounds that bled me dry between my breasts and ripped my heart apart. Perhaps I could smother myself with a pillow, a slow and steady suffocation. How long could I go without breathing? In a fit of frustration, I told Karen that I did not care to continue with counseling.

"You've taken giant steps," Karen said. "Why do you want to terminate therapy?"

"I already told you, Karen. I must be crazy."

"You are not crazy. The symptoms of anxiety and depression you experience are not personality flaws but the consequence of childhood wounds. You've come so far in healing. Let's continue."

I tried to cancel appointments, but Karen intercepted. "I understand how hard this is," she said. "Please don't immobilize self in fear."

'I still have the thoughts of suicide," I confessed.

'Tell those thoughts to go away. Suicide is no longer an option, remember?"

"But the thoughts intrude at random," I complained.

"Suicide is not a psychiatric condition," Karen explained. "It is an extreme reaction to extremely harsh human conditions. You endured abuse. You were conditioned to fear and your body responds in a fight or flight fashion."

"Do you think it's better to run or to fight?"

"What do you think?" Karen asked.

I recited a poem I'd written in high school:

If I could die it would be so easy,
Just to leave it all behind.

To fall into a silent peace,
And ease the pain of my troubled mind.

"The intention was to swiftly end the pain that plagued my psyche," I told Karen. "I thought running from pain by committing suicide was easier than fighting for my life."

"What do you think now?"

"I think I'd rather fight."

"Yes! You have the courage to continue with counseling. There's so much more for us to talk about."

"Like what?"

"We were talking about trust."

"Well, if I can't trust my own father, who can I trust? The people who were in positions to protect me were the harbingers of harm. How do I know who I can trust?"

"As you develop self-awareness, you will attract appropriate, trustworthy people into your life. Self-awareness allows you to be conscious of your feelings. The better able you are to determine your own emotions, the better able you will be to discern the motives of others."

"I can't discern excitement from anxiety because emotions are all the same to me. If a real feeling rears its head, it's ugly and scary. I don't even remember what a normal emotion *feels* like."

"Your normal self was altered by abuse."

"Yeah, like having an out-of-body experience. Afterward, I felt normal only when my consciousness was altered. So, what is normal?"

"Normal is having the skills to identify, express, and manage your emotions. I'll help you learn those skills. Keep your commitment to changing your life!"

I'd once thought that reincarnation was required to change my life. Karen was inviting me to embark on a journey in the here and now. I could use my inner resources to reestablish normalcy or invent a new normal in this life. I could call upon my courage reserves to navigate the hurdles and overcome an obstacle course of adverse circumstances. It would take courage to tune in to feelings rather than numbing out. It would take courage to clear the past to find clarity for the future. With Karen as a trusty guide, I could trek through the wasteland that was my life toward more fertile ground. At least, I decided to try again.

Resonate and Reunite

Courage is fear that has said its prayers.

Dorothy Bernard

I pulled up to the center for the next appointment and saw Karen sitting at a table. The hazy daylight caused shadows to fall across the room, so she appeared to be in silhouette. Although she was smiling, she seemed more businesslike than usual. I settled on the edge of the couch, plopping my purse on a cushion and placing a pillow at my stomach.

"Are you comfortable?" she asked.

"Well, yeah, why?"

"Could I see the homework assignment on God?"

She had been serious! From the bottom of my purse, I dug up the paper.

Karen was reading, "God hates me, therefore God punishes me." She was silent for a few minutes, and then went to the vending machine for a soda. When she returned, it looked like there were tears in her eyes.

Karen used her down-to-earth tone: "Obviously, the connection to God was severed in the pain of the past. Although your words were written with fear, they indicate some belief in the existence of a higher power. You recited the Lord's Prayer when you attempted suicide. What were you praying for?"

"Assuming there was a soul and presuming that God heard prayer, I prayed for the possible redemption of my soul."

Karen explained, "That prayer was a seed of faith in the healing power of God. You do not have to beg or plead or bargain with God. All you have to do is ask and listen."

"But I want the writing on the wall that guarantees that God hears prayer." Even as I spoke, I was learning that an answer to prayer is not always in the form of a physical manifestation or a problem solved. Answered prayer can come in the form of an insight, or an understanding between people, or a timely coincidence, or a moment of peace, or an experience with nature.

Karen asked, "How did you develop a vision of God as a source of condemnation?"

It started with the dire warnings from my relatives. Before first grade, my mother gave me choices for church. If I wanted to go with Ruthie and Annie, I could. However, if I missed Mass, my aunt would say, "God will punish you for that!" Since she was my godmother, I assumed she received exclusive information directly from God.

Grammar school vocabulary swelled with words such as hypocrite and contradict and excommunication, and the language of the Catholic congregation: catechism, confession, contrition, communion, confirmation, and the rituals of the Catholic church: The stations of the Cross, the Cross on the Rosary, and the Sign of the Cross: *"In the name of the Father, and of the Son, and of the Holy Ghost."* That included all the important people, but what category did little girls fall into?

Parochial school even implanted discrimination before school children learned how to print the alphabet. According to the clergy, the Catholic Church was the one true church, and Protestants were sinners. "If you encounter a Protestant, it is your duty to preach conversion." Otherwise, it was best not to play together.

On Holy Days of Obligation, Mass was mandatory, so the entire school marched single file to the church, like penguins in habits and uniforms. As we entered the vestibule, the nuns' faces took on a holy glow, and their hands skimmed across their rosary beads. While we were in God's house, they disciplined with hushed voices. The simple acts of sitting, standing, and kneeling were timed to silent cues from the priest at the altar. The nuns glared at a child who accidentally knelt in the pew when standing was expected, and sometimes yanked a naughty boy out by his ear.

Mass was a mystery since it was conducted in Latin, except for the sermon, which I never understood, even in English. Sometimes I could not tell when the priest switched from Latin to English because his words were gibberish, something about "man's inhumanity to man."

In Sunday school, I imagined God as a male figure on a throne in the clouds who shook his finger at unruly children. It was difficult to grasp the concepts of omnipotent and omnipresent, but I dared not question the doctrine. I dared not answer a question, even if I knew the right answer. Nuns often whacked kids across the knuckles for not knowing the difference between a cardinal and a mortal sin. Other children seemed to accept whatever was taught, so I pretended to believe, too.

Sister Mary Austin prepared the children for First Holy Communion. "Jesus Christ died for you. He died for your sins. All souls are pure until they are born, and then they are born with Original Sin."

Prior to the First Confession, we were instructed to examine our conscience for sins. "What is a sin, class?"

"Anything that is not pure in thought, word, and deed, Sister."

Often I did not sin at all, but since Confession was mandatory, I invented sins, such as fibbing. To perform the rites of a good Catholic, I lied to the priest about how I had fibbed to my mother.

The First Holy Communion was a confusing rite of passage. We were coached into accepting a wafer as the body of Christ and drinking the juice as if it were His blood. The symbolism escaped me, and skepticism was a sin I dared not confess.

Sister Mary Frances instructed us to contemplate what became of our souls after death. "Saint Peter will meet you on your Personal Judgment Day to determine your after-life fate. You have to redeem your soul to get in Heaven. If you commit a grave sin, your soul will burn in hell with the fallen angel Lucifer."

As an altar boy at only eleven years old, Eric was on a sure path to Heaven, even learning the incomprehensible Latin. Our aunt watched him at the altar with the Monsignor. "Look at your brother. He is such a saint."

Annie giggled, whispering in my ear, "Just call him Saint Eric."

After church, our aunt encouraged Eric, "You look so pious and pure, you could be a priest, but you'll have to be a virgin. You're what, ten? Eleven? Of course you're a virgin. Do you have a girlfriend?"

"No," Eric stammered in embarrassment. His face turned as red as the robe required when assisting with sacraments. The church considered sexual inhibition to be a positive attribute of the most sanctified, indicated by celibacy. Although Eric was barely in puberty, he decided that he would have his own normal family, which was not possible for a priest.

I was in search of a sure path to Heaven. When Mother Superior asked girls to clean the convent, I volunteered to dust the home of the devout sisters of a holy order. Sister Mary Agnes led me past the rectory to the convent. As I stepped into the habitat of this secret society, I smelled a sweet mixture of incense, candle fragrance, and furniture polish. "Don't break anything," Sister said.

The statue of Saint Francis was larger than life, and as I dusted his feet, it seemed like the eyes of Jesus were watching. My heart flopped like a fish out of water. I prayed that I was not doing anything wrong.

On Vocation Day, Sister Mary Therese told us, "Search your soul for your calling. If you have the calling, your heart will speak to you."

The convent activity caused me to consider a vocation as a nun. Could I devote an entire lifetime to God? Well, how long would I live? Could I live with all the other sisters? What, and never talk during dinner? Could I wear that habit? Not in this heat and humidity. This particular path to Heaven was a little too difficult. Obviously, I did not have the calling.

Perhaps I could be virtuous, like the Virgin Mary. I contemplated faith, hope, and charity: Have faith in whom? Have hope for what? Who needs my charity? I waited for rapture, but after growing up Catholic, all I got was guilt.

Karen responded to my religious inheritance: "Guilt is productive as a measure of moral conscience to keep us from veering too far from our values. But nonproductive guilt, that pervasive guilt for no good reason, is counterproductive. You were not guilty of any wrongdoing."

"Whenever I was in church, I never felt right or good. I don't think a religious institution is for me."

"It's okay if traditional religion has no significance for you. Some people feel stifled by it and some use church just to gain status. Religion can be a source of strength to others. A basic premise of religion is the belief in a Higher Power. The principles of religion, such as The Golden Rule or The Ten Commandments serve to instill peace and love. There is a difference between religion and spirituality. With spirituality, humans attain an awareness that acknowledges the soul because we are intrinsically spiritual beings in human form."

"I thought the soul hovered above or around the body, but not quite in it."

"The body is a vessel for the soul to inhabit, and the soul is the essence of love as it manifests in the world. God's love is alive and present in the soul. Our spiritual connection is our unity with God, and the love of God in the universe. Every soul finds redemption as a child in God's family because love is perfect and pure within all of us. How do you feel about what I've said so far?"

"Well, it's a relief to hear that I'm not a heretic without hope of redemption. Spirituality takes on a new meaning, not as a means to get to Heaven, but as a way to get through each day on earth."

"You've dealt with more than your share of human suffering," Karen said. "But you also have your share of human rights and the ability to choose. You can choose love over fear."

"But what if I no longer have the capacity to feel love?"

"Remember when your mother placed a cold washcloth on your aching head? The feelings from her that nurtured and soothed you and your feelings of appreciation for her were the exchange of love. That is love in action! Why not pray to experience the love of God?"

"How?"

Karen offered passages to ponder: "I give love and receive love freely and unconditionally. I am the love of God in expression."

"What about faith?"

"Faith is the belief in that which is unseen. By practicing faith one day at a time, trust in God expands as a source of good. As you allow faith to replace doubt, a more balanced belief system forms that is based on love rather than biased by fear."

Hungry to feed my undernourished soul, I absorbed the new information and allowed the truth of the words to resonate. I was ready to make the connection and reunite with God. I expected thunder and lightning to proclaim my acknowledgement of God, and stars to fall from the sky to provide proof of a higher power.

However, it sounded too good to be true when there were still problems to solve.

Curses and Que Sera

You need to claim the events of your life to make yourself yours. When you truly possess all you have been and done, which may take some time, you are fierce with reality.

Florida Scott Maxwell

Sitting on the couch in the counseling center, Karen and I shared a pack of red licorice. Newly aware of the threads of my troubles, I wanted to unravel the knots of secrets. However, I was still tightly bound with shame.

Karen passed the sticky package back to me. “Don’t you realize that the bondage is in hiding? There is freedom in revealing your true nature.”

I was afraid to reveal my true self because I was unsure of who I really was under the muck and mire of memories. “I feel like a fake.”

“That’s because you did not allow real feelings to surface for so long.”

“That’s true.”

“How did you feel when your mother married your stepfather?”

“I don’t know where to begin.”

“Start by telling how he came into your life.”

My mother met Frank while we were still living in New Jersey with my father. Frank kept in touch with my mother after she moved us to Pennsylvania. My mother, brother, and I had been living at Tanglewood Falls for about a year when I met my mother’s friend Frank.

He came to Tanglewood Falls one autumn afternoon to see my mother, and they took me for a ride in his black Ford Fairlane. Frank drove with his left hand on the steering wheel and his right arm over my mother’s shoulder, grinning and joking. He spoke with an accent because he was from England, and he called my mother “lovey.” My mother was sitting closer to Frank than she ever had to my father, and she was laughing, a sound I had hardly heard since I was little. Sitting like a good girl in the back seat, I wanted to know what was making my mother smile. "Mommy, what's so funny?"

"We are just happy."

Oh! That's how grownups act when they are happy! Because my mother was happy, I was happy, too, as we went on our way to get a marriage license.

The next day, I was rocking on my bed, memorizing the music that was playing over the public address system. Doris Day was singing, *"Will I be pretty, will I get married? Que Sera Sera, Whatever will be, will be. The future is not ours to see. Que Sera, Sera."* My whole future was ahead of me, but it was not mine to see. "Phooey!" I thought.

My mother was standing in the doorway to my room, looking like a movie star. She was wearing a green brocade dress with gold trim and a matching hat with a veil over her hazel eyes. The colors made her olive complexion glow.

"Mommy, you look so pretty."

"Frank and I are going to be married."

"Why?"

"We want to be together."

"Why?"

"Because we make each other happy."

"Will you be in a wedding? Can I come?"

"No, sweetheart. I will be away this afternoon and tonight, but I will be back tomorrow. Grandma will take care of you. Be a good girl, okay?"

Shortly after the wedding day, my mother had some explaining to do. "We are going to start over as a family."

"With Frank? Here, at Tanglewood Falls?"

"No, dear, I want to have a normal family. We are moving to New Jersey."

"With my father?"

"No, we are moving to Levittown, New Jersey. You will enjoy going to a new school and making new friends."

"But, I don't want to. What about Annie?"

"You'll get to see her on holidays."

I was almost seven years old. Already, I had been to two kindergartens in two states in one year and a Catholic school for two years. I did not want to be torn away from Annie and everything I knew just to be what my mother called "normal."

Annie and I had a day to say goodbye. Since it was raining, we got permission to amuse ourselves in the resort game room, if no guests came. Annie and I sprawled out on the large, leather sofas, playing checkers, chess, Parcheesi, and Go Fish. We sat side by side on the piano bench playing "Heart and Soul," until a honeymoon couple started shuffling cards.

"We're supposed to go home," I said.

"I want to stay here," Annie said.

This was going to require some convincing. "Let's go to your house and get a Popsicle," I suggested.

Ruthie was playing Andy William's "Moon River" as she danced with the vacuum. Fortunately, she was in a good mood. When she was in a bad mood, she would tell us, "Go play in the traffic," and I would imagine dodging a caravan of Sunday drivers on Route 611.

Annie and I lay on her bed, watching the rain. "Let's have a contest," Annie said,

"Like what?"

"A cursing contest. Let's say all the bad words we can think of."

"What bad words?"

"You know, the ones you're not *supposed* to say."

"Oh, I get it," I said. "Words like ca-ca, only worse."

Annie giggled. "Right! Say each one over and over. Whoever swears the fastest is the winner."

"Okay, Annie, you first."

"Go piss up a robe. Gopisuparobe. Gopisupparobe." Annie said it very fast.

"That's ROPE, you dipshit," I reminded her.

"You shit head. Shit for brains."

"Go jump in a lake. Gojuminalake. Gojunalake."

"Faster, Lynnie, like this: shit shit shit dam dam dam. Shishishidamamdam."

Annie repeated swear words while I doubled over in laughter with my sides aching. Uh Oh. The music was off, the vacuum was quiet, and Ruthie was shrieking. "You brazen brats. God will get you for this. You two will go straight to hell." She yanked Annie by the hair and pushed her into the bathroom. "Lynn, you better come in here and see what happens to bad little girls. I have a good mind to tell your mother how bad you can be. Ann, clean your mouth of those dirty words this minute. Clean it!" Ruth was shoving a bar of soap into her daughter's mouth and Annie was gagging, rolling her eyes up, trying not to cry. "Shame on you children. Shame, shame, shame. God have mercy on your poor pitiful souls." When she got away from her mother, Annie whispered, "Bitch, bitch, bitch." Maybe I'd be in trouble less often if I saw Annie only on holidays.

I was already in trouble with Frank. After school, the bus dropped me off under the heart-shaped sign that said "Tanglewood Falls." Beneath the sign was the wishing well, where pennies glinted with the gold fish. The sign also happened to be outside the cocktail lounge. Walking through the bar, I was enchanted by the various shapes and sizes of the bottles reflecting their colored glass in the mirrors. Over the bitter smell of stale cigars, I could almost taste the sweet liquor.

Steve the bartender was always friendly, and we invented an afternoon game. He would ask how my day was and I would answer, "Not so good," with a pretend pout.

"How about I fix you a tall one," he would ask. Steve would fix the usual, which was a fizzing cola over miniature ice cubes, with cherry syrup and four maraschino cherries and an umbrella straw. He would say, "Cheers, young lady," and we would clink our glasses together. The delicious taste of the cherry coke brought an instant grin to my face. "Feeling better, Miss?"

"Much better. Thanks, bar-keep."

"My pleasure, Miss."

The show was over one afternoon when Frank walked through the bar, just as I was saying the "not so good" line. Frank was furious. "Whenever someone asks you how you are doing, you say, 'Fine, thank you,' no matter what."

"But!"

"Speak only when you are spoken to."

"But!"

"No ifs, ands, or buts about it."

"But! Steve said."

"Steve? You address your elders as Mr. or Mrs. And I don't want to hear another word from you."

The mirror over the bar showed my cheeks blushing as red as the cherry syrup.

When Steve started to explain, Frank interrupted him. "Children don't belong in a bar at any time. You should know better." Then Frank turned to me: "From now on, you are to walk outside, around the bar. Don't be bothering the help."

Was I a bother? Steve never said I was a bother; maybe he was friendly to me because it was his job, or because my grandmother was his boss. As for Frank, he was not my father. He was not even friendly, but we were moving to Levittown to live with him.

Lynn C. Tolson

Rejection and Responsibility

The willingness to accept responsibility for one's own life is the source from which self-respect springs.

Joan Didion

"What was Levittown like?" Karen asked.

"It was not at all like the Poconos."

I recalled how no distinguishing landmarks pointed the way to Levittown. There were no spruce or pine trees to set our house apart from the rows of other newly built homes. Maple sprouts as spindly as the legs of newborn colts lined the sidewalk, and cornfields grew beyond the back yard to the flat horizon.

The public school was a whole new world of teachers in street clothes and children in tight cliques. After practicing cursive penmanship, I tried to write a letter to my cousin Annie. Words would not form sentences in the simple language she and I had once shared. How could I tell her that not only were there ordinary fire drills, but also duck-and-cover practice? When the sirens sounded, the kids had to hide under a desk. During the Cuban Missile Crisis, doomsday was looming, indicated by the orange signs that pointed to community bomb shelters. How could I say how dangerous ordinary mosquitoes were? Every other week, every other neighborhood block was sprayed with bug killer to prevent a plague. On those evenings, we were warned by foghorns on police cars to stay inside and to close the windows. The cars had to be covered so the paint would not be eaten away by the pesticides. How could I explain that Levittown was the end of the world?

The houses were considered middle-class cookie-cutter styles. My mother infused the house with her first-class taste, using her talent for domestic arts to manufacture a home. She scanned the newspapers for sales, able to find a unique gem in an ordinary store. A lighted étagère with glass shelves displayed a tall vase the color of sapphires, and a square candy dish sparkled like rubies. She puttered around the house with a plan to make the house a home.

My mother had a knack for first-class cooking, too, using common recipes clipped from the newspaper to make gourmet meals. She would have me set the table with placemats indicating who would sit where. As we ate salad tossed with homemade vinaigrette and lasagna layered with ricotta cheese, we agreed that she was the best cook. The family functioned around food and mealtime made us "normal."

Our new stepfather took charge of Eric and me as though we were soldiers in a boot camp. Perhaps that's because he had been in a war for the British Army. Hail to the King! Then he had been a tank mechanic for the US Army. Hail to the Chief! Now he was a mechanic fixing "kaput" Mercedes cars. After a ten-hour day at the body shop, Frank came home smelling of cigarettes and motor oil. He showered, watched the evening newscast, and drank scotch-on-the-rocks. Sometimes he grumbled about his belly being on fire, and my mother would warn us not to rile him. I imagined the flames from hell inside his stomach, and a devil's fork poking his sides, riling him from the inside out.

Eric acted like the world was coming to an end. He was mad. He was bad. He hated Frank. "My mother and father got *divorced.* Divorce is a sin subject to excommunication," Eric would lament. He would point to Frank: "It's all your fault! It's a sin! We're all going to hell! You're to blame!"

Frank would tell Eric, "You've been swayed by overzealous clergy. Who gives a damn about excommunication?"

Every now and then my mother would speculate about Eric's attitude. "Perhaps Eric rejects Frank because he thinks that a stepfather will take his mother's love away from him." "Perhaps Eric thinks that Frank takes away his position as man of the family." That stuff messed with my head.

"Mom, what am I supposed to call Frank?" I asked.

"The kids can call me sir," Frank answered. "And they should call you ma'm."

My mother was Mommy and nothing else felt natural. Eric raised an eyebrow.

"My children are not soldiers or subjects of a king and queen," Mom declared.

I imagined myself as a pretty princess, wearing a tiara, carrying a wand around a castle, and willing my wishes into reality. My mother was bursting my bubble. "Kids, how about if you call Frank 'Dad'? Okay, Eric?"

Eric rolled his eyes. I agreed to call Frank "Dad," but Eric refused to call him anything. Eric demonstrated his contempt by throwing darts at the dartboard outside. Oops! A dart landed in the air-conditioning compressor. Eric sheepishly showed our mother the errant tip in the grill with the stiff feathers of its tail sticking out of the metal.

"Wait until Dad gets home. He'll have a conniption fit."

We waited in suspense for our stepfather to inspect the damage. When he did, commotion ensued equal to that caused by my real father. Frank, Dad, was shouting, "That's a new compressor. Who is going to pay to fix it? I will have to take the costs out of his allowance. He is grounded."

With Frank's belly full of fire, I was afraid Frank would forever fan the flames of anger on Eric.

"It was an accident," Eric said.

"My son would never do anything bad on purpose. Try not to be so intolerant of my children."

"Children should be seen and not heard," Frank replied.

I imagined Eric and I as sketched cartoon characters, like in the Sunday funny papers. Our faces had no expressions and no phrases were printed in the word balloons.

"If we are to function as a family, we could do with some rules. What these kids need is responsibility," Frank concluded.

Responsibility came in the form of chores, which we would check off from the to-do list on the refrigerator. I made my bed as usual before school, but Frank made it harder by insisting on military corners. After I finished a long list of tasks, my mother said, "I am so proud of how you handle responsibility." How I loved to make Mom proud!

"Dad would love it if you have his slippers and the newspaper by his chair when he comes home. He would love it if you polished his shoes, too."

"But I don't know how to polish shoes."

"Dad will show you."

As I sat on the floor with his loafers around me, Frank suggested, "Use more elbow grease. You should be able to see your face in the leather."

Perhaps the better I did chores, the more love I would receive. Eric did chores too, but we didn't talk about it. Conversation with Eric was impossible since he was like the robot on *Lost in Space* with his mechanical responses: "Yes please, no thank you." There was no laughter or tears, only a resolute expression in his steel-blue eyes. Wasn't there a key I could turn to restart his engine?

On Sundays, my mother would prepare Frank's favorite foods from England. We ate roast beef with Yorkshire pudding, and trifle, a dessert made with layers of ladyfingers, custard, fruits, and whipped cream. I did the dishes as best I could.

Since Mom wanted our first Thanksgiving as a new family to be normal, we were not going to Tanglewood Falls.

"What? No Grandma? No Annie?"

"You can see them another time."

Mom sang Sinatra songs as she dressed the turkey, mashed potatoes, baked yams, stirred gravy, and baked pumpkin pies.

At the table, Eric said grace in honor of the pilgrims: *"Thank you Lord for these thy gifts which we are about to receive."*

While our stepfather carved the turkey, he announced that he was grateful for finally being beyond the army's draft age. That spurred a series of questions only I dared to ask:

"What did you do in the army?"

"I learned survival tactics."

"What does that mean?"

"I ate maggots for protein."

My mind flashed to maggots squirming on the garbage. "Gross!"

"What else did you do in the army?"

"During the Korean War, I was a sniper, climbing trees in the jungle to sight the enemy with a rifle. The troops called me Eagle Eye."

Eric butted in: "Did you ever kill anyone?"

"Do you mind?" Mom asked. "War stories are unfit for dinner conversation."

As we were finishing our meal, I was imagining Frank wearing a helmet in a foxhole, just like on the television war movies. Maybe the bullets ricocheting off his helmet was what had made him mean.

Shortly after Thanksgiving, my mother was sick for several weeks with phlebitis, an inflammation of the veins in her legs. Blood clots could form if she stood for too long, so the doctor prescribed pills and bed rest. After school, after chores, I read Nancy Drew mysteries, two or three in a row. When I finished with those, I borrowed Eric's Hardy Boys adventures. No amount of reading could quench the thirst I had for my mother's company. Only she could fashion a tea party from a card table; she'd invite the stuffed animals from "high-society," dress them in costume jewelry, and serve the guests almond biscotti.

After creating a greeting card like a valentine, I got to visit my mother in her sick bed. Her cheeks were soft like a rose petal, and fragrant with face lotion. "I miss you, Mommy."

"I miss you too, sweetheart."

"What's this?" I handled one of the bigger bottles by the bed.

"Vitamins."

"Like the cod liver oil you used to make me take?"

"Something like that. You hated that tonic, didn't you? I'm sorry I made you kids swallow it, but the doctor said it was good for you."

"Can I look in the jewelry box?"

"Sure, put it on the bed."

Sifting through her treasure chest, we played show and tell.

"Grandma gave me that," she said about an emerald pin. "That bracelet was a wedding present from Dad." When I put a pearl ring on my finger, it slipped to the underside. "Your father gave me that, before we were married. He probably stole it." I put the tainted ring back in the box.

Eric and I watched TV with Frank in the evenings, absorbing his condescending assessment of society. While Frank was watching a boxing match with Muhammad Ali against Sonny Liston, he voiced his opinion, "Cassius Clay, Ali Shamali, he should pick a name and stick with it."

I wondered what was wrong with changing names. After all, even places changed names. There had been many cities named Levit town: Levittown, New York; Levittown, Connecticut; Levittown, New Jersey. The mayor changed the name of our Levittown to Willingboro.

Eric and I started imitating the boxers, dancing around "the ring" in the living room.

"Remember the basic rule," Eric said. "No hitting below the belt."

"I'm not wearing a belt," I said.

We circled each other in a round, clenching our fists. "Jab right, jab left."

Ouch! A karate kick landed on my private parts, a blow by Eric's heavy black shoe. Stunned not only by the pain, but also by the intentional violation of the rules, I doubled over, holding myself. "I have to see my mother," I wailed.

"Don't disturb your mother," Frank said. "She's had a bad day and she needs to rest."

Running up the stairs, tears stinging my eyes, pain surged where I peed. I knocked at my mother's door, whispering, "Mommy, Mommy!"

"Come in." In the soft light of her room, I saw that her shoulders were propped on pillows, and her legs were under the covers. "Sweetheart, what's wrong?"

"Eric kicked me down there."

"May I see if you're hurt?" Mom gently lifted my blouse and lowered my panties to check out the sore spot. She got out of bed, wearing a cotton nightgown, and she wet a washcloth. As she pressed the lukewarm washcloth to me, she asked, "Do you mind if Dad looks to see if there has been any damage?"

Frank had been standing in the doorway, and then sat on the bed. Facing him, I lowered my panties and looked down to see a black-and-blue welt, tinged with yellow, forming below my belly button.

My mother whispered to Frank, "Her hymen could be broken. Maybe I should call the pediatrician."

I did not know what could be broken but was glad when they decided I did not need a doctor; I could not stand the humiliation of exposing myself again.

"Your mother needs to rest now," Frank said. "You, too, Lynnie. Put on your pajamas and go to bed."

I got the impression that, no matter what I had been exposed to, it was insignificant compared to my mother's experiences.

"Frank, please tell my son I want to see him."

In my room across the hall from our mother's room, I could hear her explaining to Eric. "You must miss me. If you are angry, don't take it out on your sister."

"It was an accident," Eric claimed.

Panties hurt, peeing hurt, and dabbing my swollen, bruised private parts with toilet paper hurt. Accident, my foot!

Soon, Santa Claus was coming to town. Frank warned us that if we were bad, Santa would leave us a lump of coal in our stockings. However, if we were good, Santa would leave us an orange. That's what kids got from Kris Kringle in England, since citrus fruit was a delicacy in the foggy British Isles.

What I wanted for Christmas was the Chatty Cathy doll. Pull her string and she talks: "I'm hungry, I'm thirsty." Perhaps I could get the doll to speak for me: "Lynnie feels scared of her stepfather. Lynnie thinks her real father doesn't love her. Lynnie's brother hurt her on purpose."

"Santa already picked out your presents," my mother said. "If you want the doll, you will have to ask your father."

"When do you think he will call?"

"Your father will call when he's good and ready."

Calling my father was impossible because he moved around too much. First, he was evicted, then he was staying with one of his six siblings, or he was staying in a hunting cabin or a fishing camp. Did he really exist? Did he even know that I existed?

Our mother left her bed to decorate, singing carols along with Johnny Mathis records. Sitting on the couch, Eric and I watched as Frank hung red felt stockings with our names embroidered on the fluffy white trim: Mom, Dad, Eric, and Lynn. My mother was putting ornaments in their places. "Smaller balls on top, large balls on the bottom. This blue ball looks good here, hang the icicles over here, and the starbursts should go here. Come on, Lynnie, throw some tinsel on the tree."

"No, thank you. I'll just watch."

A spell had been cast over the family that made us look like normal. What if I put a decoration in the wrong place? I could shatter "normal" into pieces like a glass ornament that slipped off a branch and fell to the floor.

A picture of me sitting on Santa's lap from the year before reminded me of what I really wanted. More than a Chatty Cathy, more than a normal family, what I needed was a daddy's love.

When I was about five years old, I was sitting on my father's lap when he said, "You're Daddy's little girl, aren't you?"

"Yes, Daddy. I love you."

My father jerked his hand away and interrogated me as if I had committed a crime of passion. "How do you know what love is? How do you know what love feels like? How could you say things when you don't know what you are talking about?"

Maybe that is why he never said he loved me, because he di know what love meant. That did not stop him from saying things he did not mean. Perhaps he needed a storybook, with w that spelled L-O-V-E and pictures of fathers and daughters smiling at each other. Whatever, his rejection cut to the core of my being. Never again would I speak those words, never again would I reach out to hold hands. I would harden my heart and guard it behind iron bars and barbed wire, and no man would ever break into it again.

Sometime after Christmas, my father called. After the usual quiz about my mother, I told him about Chatty Cathy.

"You want a doll? I'll get you a doll."

"Promise, Daddy, promise?"

"I promise. Anything for Daddy's little girl."

"When will you come see me?"

"Ask your mother what day would suit her."

"Mom," I hollered, "what day can my father visit?"

I was holding the phone at arm's length so my father could hear my mother. He heard: "Just tell your father to pick a day and stick with it. I'm sure it will be a day that's convenient for him, if not for me."

"Tell your mother to get off her high horse," my father responded.

On the designated day, I waited inside with my hat and coat on, watching for him through the clear glass of the storm door. What if my father did not see me? He might drive past our home, since the houses looked alike.

"Don't expect anything," Eric advised. "That way you won't be disappointed." He rode around the block on his bicycle, looking for our father. He didn't arrive that day.

Long after the New Year, after the class exchanged cards for Valentine's Day, our father finally visited. "How's Daddy's little girl? You missed me, didn't you? Have you been a good girl?" He lifted me and squeezed me hard, emptying the breath from my lungs as if I were an accordion. Eric was circling us with his bicycle.

Although I was happy with what Santa had left, I still hoped for the Chatty Cathy doll my father had promised. While he talked with Eric, I peeked in the back seat of his car. No doll. When he opened the trunk, I glanced in. No doll. I could not stand the suspense any longer. "Daddy, what about the Chatty Cathy doll?"

"Aren't you too old to play with dolls?"

It was only one doll, the only doll I ever asked for, and I was not too old when I first asked for it. Now who was going to speak for me?

Our father pulled a long pole with handles at the top and bottom out of the trunk of his car.

"It's a pogo-stick," he said. "You two kids can share it."

The next-to-last thing I needed was a plaything to bicker over with my brother. The very last thing I wanted was something else to jump-start my rattled nerves.

The disillusionment with my father became greater than the desire for anything. Why couldn't my father be like a real daddy, full of hugs and kisses and presents wrapped in pretty packages that got delivered at the right time and in the right way? Whatever it was, I was not good enough to receive it.

Meanwhile, Frank wanted to legally adopt Eric and me.

"What will be my last name?" I asked.

"You can choose between your father's name and your stepfather's name."

"I'm fed up with my father."

My first name was my mother's middle name, and my middle name was her first name. I decided I would change my name to my mother's new last name but after practicing my signature, it did not look right, so I changed my mind back to the name I already had.

"Eric, what name will you have when we are adopted?"

"I don't want to be adopted. I don't even want to be Eric."

My brother said he wanted to be called "Matthew," which was his middle name.

"This is becoming an identity crisis," our mother said. "Let's just drop the subject."

Our father went berserk over the proposed adoption, demonstrating at our house, banging on the door, brandishing a gun. He was hollering to the door: "Who do you think you are, you grease monkey? You took my wife and now you want my kids? No one is going to adopt my kids as long as I live. I want my daughter. Give me my daughter."

Maybe my father loved me, after all.

I whispered to Eric, "Why is it always me?"

"Because you are little. It's easy to pick on you."

"What if he breaks into the house and steals me again?"

"He can have you, if he wants."

Frank yelled, "Eric, take your sister upstairs now," then he went outside.

"I better do something," our mother muttered, "or else they will kill each other."

Eric and I watched through a bedroom window as our real father and stepfather stood face to face in the street. Their fists were rising and falling in the air and their mouths were showering spit and swear words. Why couldn't our father just pick his kids up like any divorced daddy? Why did he have to pick a fight?

Our father was raising the gun. "Let a limey foreigner adopt my kids? Over my dead body!"

Frank yelled, "Put the gun down, you trigger-happy wop."

I had seen my father shoot at beer cans lined up on fence posts. The chances of him hitting a target were about fifty/fifty. Frank had been a sharpshooter in the military. How could they even the score?

Our mother shouted from the front door, "Stop, please stop, you'll scare the kids."

Neighbors stepped out. "Call the police! They are disturbing the peace!"

The police apprehended my father, using all the drama of *Dragnet*. Frank had the body shop tow his car. The court granted a restraining order. However, my father was driven by an unrepressed impulse to make others miserable. He would call our house ten or twelve times a day, day in and day out, letting the phone ring twenty or thirty times. We kept count.

"Don't answer that," Mom would say. "It's your father."

"Mom, talk to him, make him stop."

"What makes you think I want to talk to him? You talk to him," Mom replied.

"Eric, it's your turn. You talk to him," I said.

"I don't want to talk to him, you talk to him."

"I had to talk to him last time," I objected.

Mom had an idea: "Pick up the phone and put it back down. Maybe then your father will get the message."

I hated to do that, I really did, but my ears were ringing. I lifted the receiver, slammed it down, and it got quiet for a minute. Ring, lift, slam, and quiet. Ring. I had a better idea: "Mom, can't we just keep the phone off the hook?" Off its cradle, the receiver delivered the fast-busy sound: beep, beep, beep. So much commotion centered on the telephone, an instrument designed for communication. When we were blessed with peace and quiet for a few days, we were suspicious.

"What do you think your father is up to now?" Mom asked.

One afternoon, there he was, in his car, at the corner. "Mom, Mom! He's here!"

"Give me the phone so I can call the police."

The Willingboro police cruised past our house to the corner, slow enough so as not to alert the alleged villain. I read the side of the car, *"To Serve and To Protect."* My father had defied the restraining order, and was put behind bars.

"Out of sight, out of mind," my mother said. Although I couldn't see my father, I could picture him with my mind's eye or in a dream. He appeared to me as the eye of the storm, and he hit my heart like a hurricane, destroying everything in his path.

In the counseling session, I told Karen, "I hate to bore you with dreams. But I've had a recurring dream since I was seven years old, and it still haunts me."

"Do you want to tell me about it?"

"Do you want to hear about it?"

"Go ahead, Lynn, you can tell me."

I am walking home from school when the weather changes from warm and sunny to cold. Wearing only a blouse, skirt, and sandals, I am shivering. The sky darkens with whirling clouds and a wild mixture of rain and snow starts to fall. It is difficult to see the way home. Houses I pass are shut tight. I am alone on the sidewalk until a black car slowly follows me. It is driving on the wrong side of the road, slightly behind my right shoulder. There is a dark figure in the car that does not reveal itself. My heart is thumping with fear as I try to walk faster and faster, struggling against the wind. Who is following me? Why is it taking so long to get home? Where is home? Am I lost? I turn a corner and see the darkened neighborhood brightened by the outside lights of my home. I am running to safety when the black car turns the corner after me. As I approach my house, the lights go off and I am unable to find a way to the front door. The black car parks in front of the house; only a dark shadow appears behind the wheel. The house ahead no longer looks like a safe place and I am not safe with the black car in the driveway. Scared to death, I stand still.

Karen asked, "Did you tell your mother about the dream?"

"When I told my mother how disturbing and frequent this dream was, she consulted the pediatrician. The doctor said it was common for children to have recurrent dreams. That report meant nothing to me. I wanted to know who the dark shadow was and what the dream meant."

"What do you think the dream meant?"

"My real father was just a shadow and real safety was merely a mirage."

"Your dream has a universal theme. It shows a threatening aspect of the family culture. What else do you remember about living in Levittown, I mean, Willingboro?"

"Well, what I recall may seem trivial."

"So far, nothing you have told me has been trivial."

"When Beatlemania swept the country, the girls at school swooned over John, Paul, George, and Ringo. We traded Beatles' cards the way boys traded baseball cards. I waited with anticipation to see The Fab Four on *The Ed Sullivan Show*. However, Frank forbade me to watch the show: 'The whole world has gone bloody hysterical over a bunch of mop-haired, no-talent freaks. Those hooligans are out to ruin American youth and embarrass Great Britain. You call that music? I call it crap!'"

"What did this event mean to you?" Karen asked.

"It caused me to question the validity of anything that interested me, as if I did not already have enough self-doubt."

"Yes, your own inner messages were stifled by the opinions of others," Karen suggested.

"I think my interests and opinions do indeed matter. At least, they matter to me. And I have a responsibility to acknowledge them."

Competitions and Homecoming

Love doesn't just sit there like a stone; it has to be made, like bread, remade all the time, made new.

Ursula K. LeGuin

"What else happened in Willingboro?" Karen asked.

I recalled that as the winter ended, my attention was turned to the arrival of a baby. While my mother was expecting, she rested in bed. Before school, Eric fixed hot chocolate and toast and Cream-of-Wheat cereal. Although he was just eleven years old, he appeared so grownup when he made breakfast. Still, he was distant, as if he was not quite with it or a part of whatever he was doing.

On my way home from school one afternoon, I saw an ambulance in front of our house. A body lay on a stretcher on the sidewalk. Was that my mother? It was!

"What's wrong with my mother?

"She is going to hospital to have a baby," answered Nanna, my stepfather's mother.

"When will she be back?"

"Soon, Lassie, soon." Nanna was petite and plump, and sat with her legs crossed at the ankles and her hands folded in her lap. Like my mother's mother, she was born to boss, utilizing a tongue as sharp as her knitting needles. "Turn off the telley! Do not waste electricity! Stay where I can keep an eye on you!"

To solve these problems, I draped a long rectangular tablecloth over a square card table, and fashioned a tent to read in with the flashlight. The tent was across the couch, in front of her face.

"Come out from under there! That is no place for a proper lady! I know you miss your mum, but keep a stiff upper lip! Obey your elders!"

At my age, everyone was an elder.

"Come, Lassie, let's knit for a bit."

Knit one, pearl two, click clack, click clack,
When is my mother coming back?

My baby brother Rusty was born two weeks before my eighth birthday, so I considered him a birthday present. All normal families got new members every now and then. My mother tried to include me in the daily routine. "Here, you can pat his bottom with baby lotion. Be careful with the top of his skull. See this indentation? It's very delicate."

The fragility frightened me. What if I did something wrong? I changed diapers so my mother could sleep late. What if I accidentally stuck the baby with a pin? The baby peed up in the air during a diaper change. What did I do wrong? As I fed him, he gurgled, clapped, and rubbed food on his high chair. What was he so happy about?

Often, I would sit in the rocking chair in his nursery to watch him sleep. Walking toward his room one afternoon, I saw my mother holding the baby as if he was a prized possession. A jealous twinge twisted in my chest. When Rusty said goo-goo or da-da or crawled or sucked on a straw or took his first step, Mom and Dad marveled as if watching a magician bring a round dove out of a top hat. How could I compete with his magic tricks?

The more attention the baby received, the less important I felt, until I reduced my place in the family by calculating relationships like an arithmetic formula. Since my mother was my biological mother, I belonged with her. Since my mother was Rusty's biological mother, he belonged with her too. My stepfather was Rusty's biological father, so little Rusty belonged to Frank. Rusty was my half-brother and Eric was my whole brother; did that make Eric more of a brother than Rusty? Eric divided himself from everybody. The family meant my mother, my stepfather, and their baby. How did I fit into this equation? Sensing my insecurity, my mother reassured me: "Sweetheart, I love you. And Dad loves you too."

While I was telling Karen about those years in Willingboro, I was thinking about my real father. "Love was a one-way vacuum with him," I told Karen.

"What do you mean?"

"Well, he sucked the love right out of me and he never blew it back. There was never enough attention or affection."

"How did you feel about that?"

"I felt a void so enormous it seemed impossible to fill. I traded my fixation for my father's love, or lack of, for other equally intangible entities. The obsessions ate me up alive, wasted me, spit me out."

"That's excellent insight," Karen said. "Constantly craving more is a set-up for an addictive personality. There are healthier ways to fill the void."

"Like what?"

"Know that there is enough of God's love for every one. There is no need to compete for God's love. Each of us is equally important to God and worthy of love as we are."

"It may take me a while to fully understand that I am valuable just being."

"It's a whole new way of thinking, isn't it?" Karen responded. "What else from your childhood do you want to talk about?"

"I don't want to talk about any of it. I just want it to go away."

"You've done a great job so far. You know that it's necessary to access the truth to continue the healing process. Please, go on."

"As the confusions of my childhood continued to mount, I could not decide whether to ask for a cheeseburger or a hamburger at a fast food restaurant. If I eat this, then I cannot have that. It is one thing or another, or nothing at all. If I could not make up my mind, I would say, 'No, thank you' no matter how hungry or thirsty I was. Even after I said I was sure, I was not sure at all."

"Why do you think it was so hard to make decisions?" Karen asked.

"Maybe I was afraid of making the wrong choice," I said.

"What did you think would happen if you didn't make the right decision?"

I was thinking out loud. "A bad decision might have led to a total lack of love."

"Eventually, you couldn't decide on anything for yourself."

"Yeah, that's right," I responded, and I told Karen about times when it seemed like I could not do anything right. When my mother could not stand for long periods, one of my dinnertime chores was to peel the potatoes. As I stood on a stool over the sink, my mother showed me how to use the potato peeler.

"Dig out the eyes," Mom instructed. "Never eat the eyes because they are poisonous."

Carefully, I was digging the eyes out, when Frank started shouting over my shoulder. "What kind of half-assed way is that to peel a potato? What is the matter with you, wasting a whole potato?"

Mom came to my defense. "Lynnie is a little girl. We are not in war-torn England. You are not being rationed in the army. There are plenty of potatoes."

"Your daughter should be more careful. If she can't do it right, she should not do it at all."

Not only did my stepfather hurt my feelings, but also, he never said he was sorry, as if my feelings did not matter. Plus, he always had to have the last word. My mother seemed frustrated with Frank, saying, "The gasoline fumes must be getting to him."

I was fuming myself, over my real father. When the restraining order was lifted, he called with a promise to see me on my ninth birthday. My birthday came and went. Another year came and went, but he never showed.

"He's so full of baloney," Eric said. "Don't bother waiting."

In the afternoons of late spring, Eric and I would catch caterpillars from the cornfields. In the evenings, we would catch lightning bugs. We would put our prey in jars to see who could collect the most. But after school one day, I cancelled plans to stalk innocent insects because my head hurt.

"I have to take a nap," I told Eric.

"Only babies take naps. What are you, some kind of baby?"

I was going on ten years old, and hadn't napped since I was little, but all I wanted to do that afternoon was sleep. I was lying on my bed, squirming like a section of severed worm on the sidewalk.

"Mommy, help! My head hurts more than normal."

"What does it feel like?"

"It feels like a soldier is stabbing my temple with a sword. It's making me sick to my stomach." First, I was freezing cold and sweating, and then I was burning hot and shivering. I barfed a baloney sandwich onto the bed. That's what my father was, full of baloney.

The pediatrician made a house call and diagnosed a migraine headache. The treatment was bed rest and a couple of aspirin.

Another day after school, I followed my brother into the house as usual only to notice that nothing felt normal.

"Mom? Mom? Eric, where's Mom?"

"How should I know?"

My mother was in her bedroom, packing a suitcase with Frank's boxer shorts and undershirts.

"Where is Dad?"

"He is in the Veterans Hospital because his ulcers ruptured."

"Is he dying?"

"No."

"Can we see him?"

"You go see him," Eric said. "I don't want to see him."

"We are all going to see him," our mother said. "Children are not allowed inside."

"Then how can we see him?"

Mom, Eric, and I stood in the parking lot and looked up at the white brick building with stories of small windows. "Wave to that window," Mom said, holding baby Rusty and flapping his pudgy arm. "Wave to Da-Da."

"Mom, which window?"

"That window," she pointed toward the roof.

Although I could not seem to get which window, I waved.

"Wave, kids, wave. It's important for him to see us."

Eric stood there like a tin soldier, giving me the notion to hand my brother a white handkerchief to wave in surrender of the enemy.

I was acutely aware of the possibility of being without a stepfather. The fear was as palpable as standing on the high-dive of the swimming pool, about to leap into thin air. I had a real father who was out of his mind, a thirteen-year-old brother who was in a world of his own, and now my stepfather was about to disappear off the face of the earth.

Frank came out alive, and as he recuperated, he seemed subdued. He was trying to reduce the stress left over from years in a war and the everyday battle of earning a living. Instead of the national evening news, he listened to bagpipes. Instead of scotch whiskey, he drank milk in the highball glasses, and he quit smoking. When he quit his job, my grandmother offered him a job as the kitchen manager at Tanglewood Falls.

Mom and Dad were selling the house in Willingboro. We were returning to the resort. There was one thing Eric and I could agree on: We both felt like we were going home.

Clichés and Confucius

Half the misery of the world comes of want of courage to speak and to hear the truth plainly, and in a spirit of love.

Harriet Beecher Stowe

"You were happy about returning to Tanglewood Falls," Karen asked and answered.

"Yes, but things were not the same as when we'd lived there two years earlier."

"What do you mean?"

I explained that I'd noticed different family dynamics with my stepfather on the scene. Evidently, the family stuck together during a crisis but was barely civil to each other on a day-to-day basis. While Frank worked for my grandmother, they disagreed on everything, from how many turkeys to order to how to cook a turkey. Some days they worked in the kitchen together and barely spoke to each other.

On Thursday nights, the family ate at Grandma's apartment. The adults talked about the weather, the business, and each other. Sometimes I was attentive to their conversation; other times I tired of trying to translate adult double-talk. When their chatter was like the annoying static on a transistor radio, I sat outside after dinner, in the webbed rocking chair on my grandmother's patio.

I tuned out that station and moved my mental dial and, quite by coincidence, tuned into good vibrations. As I rocked, my mind wandered to the wonders of Mother Nature. Chipmunks scurried across the rocks, and ducks skimmed across the lake. Wind rustled through the trees and stirred the scent of Pocono pine. Oh, this was the life. In that moment, I was content to rock in absentminded bliss.

On the way home, my mother and stepfather discussed the dinner conversation with each other. She would say, "I'm sick and tired of the way my mother plays favorites with her own children. She plays one of us against the other. And after all I've done for her!"

It was true that Maria adored her son, who devoted his life to the family enterprise. In contrast, Maria often criticized my mother. My mother tried to please her mother by taking reservations or by cleaning the cottages, but nothing Sophia did was good enough. In their company, I cringed at all the criticisms.

After every visit, my mother would say, "The tension was so thick you could cut it with a knife."

Frank would respond, "What did Tony mean by that snide remark? What is he trying to pull?"

She would say, "I swear, he's out to get me."

She would say, "What do you suppose Ruthie has up her sleeve? Does she think I can't see through those back-handed compliments?"

He would respond, "After the stunt she pulled, you would think she would know to put her best face forward."

Karen was leaning forward, shifting in her chair. "What did you learn about your family's communication patterns?"

"I learned that what my relatives said could not be taken at face value. Latent evil messages lurked beneath even idle chitchat. I learned that they spoke in clichés to evade honest communication."

"That's sounds like an accurate assessment. What did your family do for fun?"

"That was their fun, bashing everybody. I don't remember having fun with my family. Maybe we had fun, but the bad times were more important than the good."

"Okay. What did you do for fun?"

A love of horses made me eager to take riding lessons at the stables. As my mother approached the stables to inquire about the lessons, she was saying, "I don't know if I can put up with the stench of manure every week."

My heart was leaping to the smell of horse and leather. "Mom, I don't smell anything, except horses."

"Then you go in to the office and ask the stable manager how much for how long."

I looked at pictures of equestrian events as the manager gave me the rider's regulations· "You will need boots with heels." The stable manager informed me, then I informed my mother, then Mom informed me that I had to ask my father.

My heart was sinking at the dreadful task of asking my father. "But, Mom, you know that I don't even know where he is and that I haven't seen him in years."

"It will be some rigmarole trying to find him, but I'll help you, if you want." She called my father's brother who called my father to tell him to call my mother. When my father finally called, my mother called me to the phone. "Your father's on the phone. He's in such rare form, it's hard to get a word in edgewise."

"Hi, Daddy."

"How's Daddy's little girl?"

"Fine, thank you."

"What kind of answer is that? Why is your mother in such a huff? What did you tell her?"

"Nothing. Can I ask you something?"

"You must have told your mother something. She did not let me see you for two years. She's driving a wedge between us. Now that you want something, she's doing an about-face."

"May I please have riding boots?"

"So Daddy's little girl wants to be a cowgirl. Sure, I'll get you boots."

It was just another battle, with words as ammunition, with me on the front line, trying not to take sides, all over a pair of boots.

"Mom! He said he'd send the boots!"

"Good. I hope for your sake he keeps his word. Did you tell him what size? Did you tell him the address?"

"Was I supposed to?"

"Lynn, I cannot think of everything. If you want your father to send you boots, you have to give him the address."

Karen was trying to steer me back on track again. "Were the lessons fun for you?"

"I loved the lessons, the trail rides, and the arena practice. Heels down, toes up. After entering a competition, I skillfully maneuvered a Palomino through an obstacle course and won a red ribbon. But."

"But what?"

"Whatever I was doing, I was driven by the desire to please my parents. But my father never came to see me ride, so I quit. Unable to articulate that I was feeling abandoned by him and unworthy of his attention, I abandoned the very thing I loved the most before it too could desert me."

"What else did you do for fun?"

I recalled how Tony had an enormous house built for his family at Tanglewood Falls. There was a room for every purpose, a maid to clean each room, and quarters for the maid, with its own bath and entrance. Ruthie spared no expense in decorating the house with Spanish tile, Italian murals, and Swedish crystal. The house was the talk of the town, and its grandeur was displayed in *House and Garden* magazine.

The hours I spent there with Annie were fun. On rainy days, we played Monopoly on the screened-in porch, or Ping-Pong in the recreation room. On sunny days, we played croquette on the manicured lawn. Saturdays were for sleepovers, and some Sundays I ate ziti and sauce with my cousin. Fierce quarrels were a mainstay of their meals, like a loaf of crusty bread or a plate of spiced sausage.

Some Sundays, Tony asked Ruthie, "Why doesn't she eat with her own family?"

"She is family, she's your sister's daughter. She's your niece. Apologize to her."

Maybe he was mad because I knew about the holes in the wardrobe doors. Tony had used his fist to express frustration over Ruthie's spending. I had inadvertently eavesdropped on that fight, which was not difficult because they were so indiscreet. He had shouted words that I later looked up: pretentious, ostentatious, and gaudy, which described Ruthie and her taste.

Tony also built an ice skating rink at Tanglewood Falls. Eric was in charge of the sound system, like a disc jockey, and sometimes he canned the corny "Blue Danube Waltz" to play rock-and-roll records. I learned to skate backwards by moving my hips to the beat of Chubby Checker's *"Let's do the twist."* Nothing was more exhilarating than the swish of the blades and the chip of the ice from the toe-pick.

Annie and I were taking skating lessons together, jumping and spinning, both able to perform cartwheels on figure skates. Almost every afternoon, we sat side by side on the bench in the rink, heads bowed as we laced our skates. One Monday after school, I noticed bruises under Annie's sheer tights.

"What happened to you?"

"I fell on the ice," Annie lied.

"I don't remember any fall."

"Remember last Saturday when my mother pulled me off the ice to go to Confession?"

I remembered Ruthie having a fit because she was late. Annie had a fit in response because she wanted to skate.

"I had to wear my skating outfit to church," Annie explained. "When we got home, my mother hit me with the wooden spoon. It's my fault for telling her I didn't want to go to Confession."

"Annie, my mother never hit me like that. We should tell my mom."

"No, don't tell your mother."

"But my mom is your godmother. She can help."

"No, Lynnie, please don't tell. Promise. Hope to die."

"I promise. Cross my heart and hope to die."

Annie and I floated onto the ice, faced each other, crossed our arms at the wrists, held hands, and spun around in a spread eagle. Like the bird, we spread our wings wide, flying free on the ice.

Early one morning, Annie and I watched Eric as he resurfaced the ice. He drove the machine over slush, fresh water spilling from a chamber to make a new, solid surface.

"He ain't no fucking saint," Annie whispered as she scowled at my brother.

"What do you mean by that?"

"Nothing."

"You've been pissy with him since last week, when I saw you two coming out of the boiler room, mad at each other. He was in there, sharpening your blades, right?"

"Something like that. The trouble with him is that he needs to get laid."

"What do you mean?"

"Oh, Lynnie, you are so *intense*. Never mind. Just forget I said anything."

Occasionally, my mother came to the rink. "Lynnie, you are a butterfly on ice."

I thought her praise was due to pity and parental obligation, and I reduced any ability to that of a lowly caterpillar. "How come you won't let my father come to see me skate?"

"I have my reasons," my mother explained.

Karen interrupted my recall. "Although you wanted desperately to please your parents, you disregarded your mother's praise. It's okay to take compliments as support of your unique God-given talents and abilities."

"I never thought of talents as gifts."

"Everyone has gifts. You are gifted too."

"Yeah, but, my father never saw me skate."

"What kept him from seeing you?"

"Well, the restraining order had been lifted because the lawyers said there was no due cause to curtail visiting rights. I think the reason had something to do with a time he had visited me, before we returned to Tanglewood Falls."

"What was that visit about?" Karen asked.

I was about eight years old when my father called the house in Willingboro. He wanted to pick me up on a Saturday. I think Eric had a weekend Cub Scout meeting planned for the weekend. My mother bought me a burgundy jumper with a white blouse, ankle socks to match, and new Mary Jane shoes.

I wondered what was wrong because my father was on his best behavior. "You want to take a tour with Daddy, don't you?" he asked when he picked me up. "We'll see the Queen Mary, okay?"

We drove through the Lincoln Tunnel under the Hudson River, and past the row houses with iron gates. "We're near Greenwich Village," my father said. "Better lock your door. There are dope-fiends and hippies and all kinds of weirdoes." At the pier, my father held my hand as we watched tourists go through a turnstile and walk on a plank.

"See? That's the Queen Mary."

"Where is she?'

"The ship is the Queen Mary."

"Oh. Are we going on the ship?"

"No, not today, they are sold out of tickets."

My father was quite capable of purchasing tickets for boxing matches and applying for hunting licenses in advance. However, he could not get his daughter on board a boat, as promised. After eating hot dogs and pretzels sold by street vendors, we drove over the Brooklyn Bridge to a room he was renting.

He lived in one room of somebody else's house. In the bedroom, I recognized the Zenith television with the foiled antenna from our first home in Passaic Heights. Not much else was in the room except his dresser, nightstands, and a bed. There was no place to sit but on the floor or the bed. When he left the room for a while, I sat on the floor with the funny papers, pressing and peeling Silly Putty.

When he returned, he took off his shoes, pants, and shirt, and flung them across the bed. He was wearing a tank T-shirt, boxer shorts, and socks. When he took his shoes off, he had the smelliest feet.

"You're tired, aren't you? You need a nap, don't you?"

"I don't take naps anymore."

"Is that so? It has been a long day. You are getting sleepy. Be a good girl. Come here on the bed with your daddy."

I am being a good girl. I am sitting on the edge of the bed and watching my father prop himself on three pillows, leaving me with only one. He is not sharing fair. Coins spill out of his pockets. He is rolling onto the coins. He is pulling me closer. He puts his left arm around me. I thought he did not like left handed. My head does not reach into his hairy armpit. "You're Daddy's little girl, aren't you?" He rubs my face with his finger. His finger feels rough. "Your skin is as soft as your mother's."

He has to bring up my mother because he loves her. I must be special to be like his queen. I wish I were a princess. He tickles my belly. He raises my blouse. This is scary. "You're squeamish like your mother, aren't you? Let's play a game. Give Daddy a kiss." I peck his cheek. It feels stubbly. "Give Daddy a kiss on the lips, like your mother used to." I kiss his lips. They feel greasy.

"Come closer, closer, closer. Don't be afraid, Daddy is not going to hurt his little girl." He pulls down his underpants. I try not to look. My eyes move. He has hair down there. He puts my hand between his

own, and pushes and presses our hands down there. He says, "After you take a nap, you won't remember anything. If you do, do not tell your mother, it could make her go crazy. Or it could kill her. Let's keep our afternoon a secret, just between us, something special. Don't breathe a word of this." I take in a breath. I hear nickels, dimes, quarters, and keys clinking together. My nerves are jingle-jangle. He asks, "Do you want the change? Give Daddy the quarters, for the toll booth."

Can I breathe? What happened? If I could put words to what happened, it would make my mother crazy. Or she could die. Either way, I would be stuck with my father. What did I do to deserve that?

When I got back home, our mother was sprinkling Rusty's butt with baby powder before bed.

"Hi Lynnie, how was your day?"

"Fine thanks, Mom."

"Did you see the Queen Mary?"

"Sort of."

"You were supposed to be back by 7 and it's 9. What's his excuse this time?"

"He made me take a nap this afternoon."

"You don't take naps anymore. Were you tired?"

"Not really."

"Where did you take a nap?"

"On his bed."

"What was he doing while you were napping?"

"Napping."

"He was napping on the bed while you were napping? What else happened?"

"He gave me change from his pockets, but not the quarters. Can I take a bubble bath?"

"It sounds like he was making seductive overtures," Mom said. "Your father used to take his buddies and your brother on fishing trips. I didn't like the sound of *that*, either. Who knew what went on? Next time I talk to him, I'll see what he has to say for himself."

I had to see what the dictionary said about the word "seductive."

My mother said I was not the same after that Saturday with my father. I did not feel the same, but I did not know in what way I was different.

Karen asked, "When did you see your father again?"

"That's another story within a story."

"I'm listening," Karen said.

One summer evening, my aunt and uncle took Eric, Annie, and I to a drive-in movie, which Tony had purchased. It's not that he purchased tickets for the movie; he had purchased the entire drive-in theater. During intermission, I could not decide on a snack. With no parent of mine to tell me what I wanted, I chose everything: buttered popcorn and orange soda and a hot dog with mustard and a hot fudge sundae. By the time my uncle dropped me off at home, my stomach was rumbling. I lay awake all night, and listened to my stomach gurgle and churn until the next morning when I finally told my mother.

"Why did you wait all night to tell me you're sick?"

"I don't know." I had suffered in silence because I thought I deserved punishment for eating an assortment of snack foods in one sitting. Besides, I did not want to wake my parents up in the middle of the night and bother them.

"Do you mind if I feel your belly?" Mom lifted my pajama top. "It feels lumpy. Do you mind if I ask Dad what he thinks?"

Frank leaned over my bed and pressed my tummy. "Could be appendicitis."

Mom hurried to the hospital. As I walked into the emergency room with my arms folded across my stomach, a nurse asked, "Are you all right?"

"Fine, thank you!"

"Do you want a wheelchair?"

"No, thank you!"

In the operating room, I was told to breathe into a mask while counting backwards from one hundred. That gave me just enough time to wonder if that was what it felt like to be dying.

As I recuperated, I occupied myself with coloring books and crossword puzzles. Only the sound of hushed voices passed from adjacent rooms. I was enjoying the peace and quiet of the hospital. Mom visited every evening for three days.

"Eric is watching Rusty so I can see you, sweetheart. How are you?"

"Fine, thank you, Mommy." Referring to my stepfather, I asked, "How come Dad doesn't visit?"

"Your grandmother won't give him the time off."

On the fourth day, Mom brought me the latest family news. Like a bold headline in *The Pocono Record*, she announced: "You have a new stepmother."

"What?"

"Your father got married. He has a new wife. And they're here to visit."

"Now?"

"Yes, now. Your father didn't give me much advance notice of his arrival."

My stepmother walked into the room with my father, who appeared as large and looming as ever. Without asking, he lifted my gown to feel my belly. "How's my little girl?"

"Fine, thank you."

"Is that all you have to say? This is Holly, your stepmother. Can you say hello?"

Holly had a whole different look than my mother. My stepmother had pale skin, cornflower-blue eyes, and jet-black hair. She was wearing a mini-skirt with an orange and red flower print, sling-back sandals, and huge plastic hoop earrings. Holly's freckled breasts showed when she leaned over to say, "How are you doing, honey?"

"Fine, thank you."

"I have a bone to pick with your mother," my father said. He went out to the hall and left Holly in the room with me.

While my mother and father talked outside the door, Holly asked, "Do you like my hair? It's usually plain brown, like yours, but I dyed it for fun."

"Holly, I like your perfume!"

"Thanks, honey, it's called 'Jean Nate', and I'll get you some."

"Really? I can wear perfume, too?" My mother never let me wear a fragrance more mature than baby oil.

My father was raising his voice, "You could have let me know sooner that she was in the hospital. She's my daughter, too, or have you forgotten that?"

"It's not easy to find you, with all your gallivanting. Besides, I did not like the tone of your last visit with her."

"What tone are you talking about?"

"She said you took a nap."

"What's wrong with that?"

"I didn't care for the sound of it at all!"

Their shrill voices amplified my embarrassment. A nurse asked them to be quiet.

In a voice as obnoxious as before, my father said, "I'll have you know I'm a changed man, with a new wife, and a house in East Paterson."

"You can't pay your children's dental bills and you bought a house?" My mother was not asking, she was telling.

"Don't throw that bullshit in my face! I have every right to see my kids."

Holly was pretending not to hear the argument. "You could visit us in New Jersey," she said. "Your father just wants to have a normal family."

My father stood in the doorway. "Holly, it's time to go. Say goodbye, Lynnie."

After he left, my mother said, "I am furious! Your father drove all that way just to pick a fight. The louse claims he can't pay child support. His wages were garnished for that head-on collision. You know, he was driving drunk on the wrong side of the road. Drunken driving! He can't have a driver's license, yet he bought a house for that hussy. He has no scruples. What a flimflam man! All his wheeling and dealing must have paid off. God forbid he should dole out a few bucks for the hospital bills."

My mother never had a good word for my father. The bad words made me feel ashamed. I was a part of him; when he did something wrong, I felt as though I'd done something wrong.

On the fifth day after the operation, I was ready for discharge. Mom was packing the get-well cards when the nurse brought a wheel chair into the room.

"Congratulations! You're going home," the nurse said. "Have a seat, dear."

"No, thank you."

"It's hospital regulations. Most kids like a ride in the wheelchair."

I'd just settled into the wheelchair, ready to ride, when the hospital lobby came into view. Through the double doors I could see Mom's car, a big, beautiful black Buick, waiting to take me home.

"It's so good to have you home," Mom said. "Do you need anything? Can you watch Rusty while I make dinner?"

"What are we having?"

"Pork chops, applesauce, and lima beans. By the way, your father wants you to visit in a couple of weeks. You can get a feel for your stepmother. From the looks of her, she's young enough to be your father's daughter."

Holly was like a character in a Nancy Drew novel, full of intrigue. Her story was a mystery that begged to be solved.

One spring Saturday, my father and stepmother picked me up. Instead of the two-seater sports car, he was driving a station wagon with wood panels on the sides.

"Hi honey," Holly said. "Too bad Eric couldn't join us. He sounds like such a sweet boy."

"He's working at his grandmother's resort," my father said. "He's what, fourteen? It's good for him to spend his spare time earning his keep." My father was holding a lighter for Holly. "Just as well your brother is not here," he said. "Who knows what Sophia told my son about my new wife. Lynnie, what did your mother have to say about Holly?"

"Nothing."

"Nothing? She said nothing? I can't believe your mother had nothing to say. Tell me what she said."

"Well, she said Holly was old enough to be your daughter."

"That's what she said, huh?" My father grinned, as if he was proud that Holly was young.

Holly turned around to look at me. "You're eleven. Right, honey? Then technically, I'm old enough to be your mother, if I had been pregnant when I was eighteen."

Holly didn't look like she could be anyone's mother. Her hair was colored a lighter shade and it was swept up in a ponytail. She looked like a go-go dancer in her fishnet stockings, mini-dress, and dangling earrings.

"Holly. I like your hair. I like your earrings, too."

"Thanks, honey. I colored my hair strawberry-blonde. Are your ears pierced? No? If they were, I'd let you borrow my earrings."

We turned down a street that had branches of elm and maple trees crossing above it. As we drove under the trees, I thought of the pictures of military weddings I had seen. The car was like the bride and groom that marched down the aisle; the trees were like the swords meeting point to point, arched over the couple. My father parked the car in front of the detached garage. The two-story house stood on a small lot, and an extension ladder was propped against a second-story window. Chain-link fences separated the yard from the close neighbors. A side door led to the kitchen, where a white miniature poodle was wagging its tiny tail.

"This is Irma La Deuce," Holly said. "I had her before we got married." Holly hugged her pet and rubbed its clipped fur on her cheek. "I took her to the grooming shop so she'd look good for you."

"She's wearing a bow!" I exclaimed. "How cute! Can I take her out?"

"Too late for that," my father said. "The mangy mutt crapped."

"We were gone for hours," Holly explained.

The puppy had peed and pooped inches from the edge of the newspaper Holly had placed on the floor for accidents. Manny grabbed the dog by the fur at the back of its neck and it peed in the air, yelping for mercy.

"Manny, don't hurt my dog!" Holly pleaded.

"There's only one way to train a dog," my father said. Then he rubbed the puppy's nose in the puddles and piles. "See? See what you did?" he yelled as he used rolled-up newspaper to spank the puppy. He hit the helpless animal until it lay quiet and still, playing dead for protection. "Now that's the way to teach an old dog new tricks. Beat it into submission," he said.

"Manny, I wish you wouldn't treat my dog like that," Holly said submissively.

Actually, the puppy was smarter than it appeared because it would not put its paws on the newspaper that could beat it.

While Holly was drinking a Tom Collins, she broiled steaks, baked potatoes, and tossed a salad. She also tossed me some food for thought. "Honey, I haven't had a chance to read the horoscopes. Do you want to read them to me while I cook? Get the newspaper. It's probably in the den."

My father was sitting in the den, drinking from a jug of wine, and smoking a pipe. "Watch this!" he said. He inhaled from the pipe and then exhaled rings of smoke that drifted and vanished. The rich aroma of the tobacco thrilled my nostrils.

"Can I try?"

"I won't allow my little girl smoke. Smell this." He put a pouch of tobacco leaves under my nose.

"Smells so good," I said. I wished he'd show that side of his personality more often. He grabbed me and pulled me onto his lap and tickled my ribs. *This* was the side of him that I could do without.

"Honey, did you find the newspaper?" Holly called from the kitchen.

My father let me go. At the kitchen table, Holly taught me the signs of the zodiac. "You are an Aries, which rules the head. Aries are smart, spontaneous, and interested in everything. Good jobs for Aries are acting, writing, or sales. Manny is an Aries, too. That's why he is such a good salesman; he could finagle the Pope into buying swampland in Florida."

I was thinking that my father was impulsive, interested in nothing but himself, and a cunning liar.

My father yelled, "Hitler had the same birthday as me. And he killed himself."

"What?"

Holly put folk music on the stereo. "Listen, it's my favorite," she said. "It's Peter, Paul, and Mary." Holly was strumming her guitar and singing along, *"Leaving on a jet plane."*

She put her pick down. "Have you ever heard of deja vu?" she asked. "It's that feeling of familiarity, as if you've been in the same place before, or you knew the same person before, even though this time is the first time."

Later, while my father was sitting with a fixed stare, as if we were not there, Holly lit candles. She turned off the lights, and placed a board game on the kitchen table. "Let's use the Ouija board and see what the future holds for you."

"Will I get married?" The wand spelled "Y-E-S."

"Will I have children?" The wand spelled "N-O."

Then, Holly peered at my palm, "Oh, look at your life line."

"What?"

"Have you heard about the witches of Salem? Let me show you some potions and spells. You know, I can zap somebody. Remember that driver who cut us off on the parkway? I zapped him. I hope he gets four flats. It would serve him right."

Holly warned me with superstitions: "Never let a black cat cross the path or you'll be jinxed for life. If you break a mirror, it's seven years bad luck. Don't even bother to get out of bed on Friday the 13th because nothing good can come of that day."

My father came out of his stupor with some suspicions of his own, rambling, "What are yous? Some kind of Communists? The Russians are coming. Big brother is watching you. This town is crawling with spies and they're all out to get me. Remember what Confucius says!"

"What?"

"Confucius says," he said, then trailed off with mumbo-jumbo.

Was this my new normal family? We were all play-acting in some super-natural family show, like *The Addam's Family*, with my father cast as Lurch and my stepmother as Morticia.

While my father and stepmother were driving me back to the Poconos, I thought about how Holly called me "honey" as if she was fond of me. She endeared herself by sharing the mystery of the universe and by bewitching me with her hip attitude. I wanted to be cool like her.

When we arrived, my father walked to the door with me while Holly waited in the car. Since we were late, Frank was standing by the door, with my mother standing behind him. "You better have a good excuse for being late again," my mother said to my father.

"Mom, may I get my ears pierced like Holly?"

"No you may not. You can wear clip-on."

"Why? Why can't I get my ears pierced?"

"Let me tell you why!" Frank said. "In England it's a sign of solicitation in the red light district. Only tramps have pierced ears."

"Are you calling my wife a tramp?" my father shouted.

I was afraid they'd have a fistfight. My mother stepped into the foyer, saying, "Frank, don't! Manny, don't! Lynn, get in here!"

"Get in the house!" My stepfather pulled me inside with him and shut the door in my father's face. I parted the sheer curtains at the front window to see if my father was leaving. "Get away from the window!" my stepfather ordered.

For the next few weeks, Mom and Dad and I fought about whether or not I could get my ears pierced. When I next visited my father and stepmother, I convinced Holly that I had gotten permission to get my ears pierced, even though I hadn't. She took me to the piercing pagoda, where I picked out gold studs and silver hoops. The piercing gun caused a second of pain, but the pleasure of being hip like Holly was worth it. Back home in Pennsylvania, a crusty infection revealed my newly pierced ears.

"You have holes in your ears! Didn't you hear what I said? How dare you defy my direct orders! I am your mother. You are my daughter. I know what is best for you. I have a good mind to never let you see that floozy again."

That only made me want to see my stepmother more. When I saw Holly again, she was wearing hip-hugger bell-bottoms and halter-tops, with her blonder than strawberry-blonde hair loose on her shoulders.

"Where's your poodle?" I asked.

"Manny couldn't handle the barking anymore. He made me get rid of Irma. I took her to the pound. I miss my pet, but she was driving your father crazy."

I watched as Holly put on makeup. She was moving her hands from cigarette to mascara, puffing and powdering with her fingers shaking. As if I were her new best friend, she began confiding.

"I'm afraid of Manny's temper. He gets out of control. I told him we should see a marriage counselor. He thinks that head shrinks are for crazy people. But he wants the marriage to work, so he agreed to see a psychiatrist. He went to an appointment and was evaluated with inkblot tests. He went once again with me, but in the middle of the session, he stormed out of the office. I had a private talk with the psychiatrist. He told me that Manny is paranoid schizophrenic with suicidal and sadistic tendencies."

"What?"

"In other words, he is a psychopath. Without psychotherapy and medications, he is considered a danger to himself and others. Since the office visits cost seventy-five dollars an hour, the psychiatrist offered to reduce the fee. He says it is urgent that Manny has therapy. Your father refused, saying that even if it was free, he wanted nothing to do with that hocus-pocus."

Then Holly flipped tarot cards to predict my future: "Honey, I'm telling you this for your own good. You should keep in mind that mental illness is often inherited. Sometimes it skips a generation, but sometimes not."

Which generation did I belong to? The sometime hit, or the sometimes missed?

"Whatever happens, I would never leave him. He has been good to me. This house! If it were not for him, I would still be on the streets. That's how I met him, you know."

"You lived on the streets?"

"You could put it that way. I never finished high school. I got C's and D's, and got kicked off the cheerleading squad, so I figured, what's the use?" Holly pursed her lips, and glided raspberry flavored gloss across my lip with her shaky finger.

I was thinking about our private talk as we were driving back to Pennsylvania. My father was getting annoyed at the tourists parading to the Poconos. "Damned Sunday drivers." Then, he noticed me, "Why are you so quiet? What's the matter with you?"

What was I supposed to say? I know you are crazy as a rabid dog cut loose on a litter of defenseless kittens?

Karen said, "Your parents expected too much of you. It is especially irresponsible for an adult to share information that is beyond a child's capacity to comprehend. How did you deal with this information?"

"I looked it up in the dictionary: To be paranoid is to show unreasonable distrust, suspicion, or an exaggerated sense of one's own importance. Schizophrenics have psychotic reactions characterized by withdrawal from reality, with variable accompanying affective, behavioral, and intellectual disturbances. Sadistic means being deliberately cruel. Suicidal is to be a danger to oneself. A psychopath is a person with a personality disorder, especially one displaying aggressive antisocial behavior. That was my father, all right!"

"Do you understand that a diagnosis may offer some explanation for bizarre behavior, but it does not relieve him of responsibility for that behavior?" Karen asked.

"Yes. But those clinical, multi-syllabic diagnostic labels didn't help me verbalize the scourge of a schizophrenic father."

"What did you tell your mother?" Karen asked.

"She must have known he was violent because she told me about his boxing buddies. She said that when we lived in Passaic Heights, before she left him when I was five years old, he'd go to the gym to box. One of my father's friends told my mother that the guys refused to get in the ring with my father because his temper got out of hand. They wouldn't spar with him anymore. A man must be very violent to scare his boxing opponents! She also told me that she had once asked him to go to therapy, but he had been an ass about it. So she left him and *she* went for therapy."

In my counseling session, I revisited how often my mother had bad-mouthed my father. When she talked bad about my father, my mother could be seen as the good parent. She also always referred to my father as "your father." It was as if *I* owned him. She never referred to him by his first name, which would indicate a relationship. She never referred to him as her ex-husband; that way, my mother could be relieved of the responsibility of having married him. Perhaps on a subliminal level I realized that she had abdicated all responsibility as a parent, and that's why I didn't tell her everything.

Ripples and Tidal Waves

Destiny is not a matter of chance, it is a matter of choice. It is not a thing to be waited for, it is a thing to be achieved.

William Jennings Bryan

For a change of pace, Karen moved the counseling sessions to a small office on the second floor of the center. When I arrived, she was sitting at a metal desktop that was covered with manila folders. Her family photograph was perched on a pile of papers.

"How are you today?" Karen asked.

"Fine, thanks." I sighed as I answered, tired of the sound of my own voice. "How are you?"

"I'm great. I'm having a great week. How's your week been?"

"Are you always like this?" I asked her.

"Like what?"

"So nicey nice."

"I have an even temperament," Karen responded. "Why do you ask?"

"Your life seems so perfect. You have a husband you love and trust, and those three beautiful children who love you."

"Like anyone else, my life is far from perfect," Karen responded. "I've had my share of hardships, but I count my blessings. One day you will, too."

I nodded.

"What would you like to focus on today?" Karen asked.

"I don't know."

"Why don't you tell me when you saw your father again?" she prompted.

I was remembering that my father had arranged for Eric and I to visit during summer vacation. The visit got off to a bad start from the moment we arrived in New Jersey.

My father never read anything other than the sports page. However, when I was dusting the living room I saw a copy of *The*

Rise and Fall of the Third Reich. I knew from social studies class that it was a comprehensive book on Hitler and World War II. It seemed odd, too, that he had named his German shepherd puppy "Adolf." The dog was swatting a small oval ball with grooves across the kitchen floor. The ball was green and brown, and it had a rim with a hook, like a Christmas tree ornament.

Holly stepped in, "Jesus, is that a hand-grenade?"

A hand-grenade? Like in the World War II movies?

Holly was shrieking, "Are you crazy? There are children in this house!"

My father was smirking, "Are you afraid of that? It's not even live. And how dare you call me crazy!"

In the mid 1960's, pictures of the race riots covered the front page of *The Bergen Record.* African-Americans were fighting for their civil rights. The paper showed photographs of fires in the streets and stores with smashed windows. The evening news reports showed cops beating blacks with clubs and knocking them down with fire hoses.

"Sic 'em!" My father wrestled with Adolf. "I'm trying to protect my family here. Those Negroes are rioting around the corner, in Newark." The brown and black fur on the dog's neck stood up and his paws gripped the floor with spread claws. Adolf sunk his fangs into the padded sleeve my father had wrapped around his arm. Adolf growled in aggression. Holly objected to the training and insisted on obedience school. I wasn't sure if she meant for the man or the dog.

A few days later, Adolf tore the ear off a four-year-old as she strolled up the street. From the living room, I heard frantic neighbors on the front lawn talking about the hospital, insurance, and reconstructive surgery.

"Put a muzzle on that animal."

"Take it to the pound."

"Throw a piece of steak laced with rat poison."

Police cars parked at the curb, issuing a cease and desist order to my father. "Vacate the dog from the property, or we will have to take matters into our own hands."

"My dog is the cream of the crop."

"You have two days to dispose of the dog."

"I'll take care of my animal myself."

That night, when Holly and Eric were watching television, I moved a tin of Jiffy-Pop over the burner. As the popcorn swelled in its balloon, I heard a couple of Fourth-of-July firecrackers exploding outside. Then, the kernels were cooked, and the night sounds faded. I carried a chair to the window that was over the sink. When I stood on it, I saw a streak of light bobbing in the back yard. The light beamed to a shovel that was leaning against the fence, and dirt was piled up between the lilac bushes. There was my father carrying a fur coat to a hole in the ground.

I dream that I am cold, very cold. My father comes into the room and wraps me in a fur coat. The coat has no buttons or snaps and won't close. I am still cold.

The next morning, Holly and Manny were arguing, as usual. He wanted to deep-sea fish with his buddies off the Jersey shore.

Holly said, "You're going on a fishing trip? Don't you think it's inconsiderate to desert your kids during their vacation?"

"Don't tell me how to raise my kids."

"You could at least bring your son, like you used to."

"This trip will sort the men from the boys, and he's such a mama's boy. He gets seasick."

"He's a teenager!"

"He's not man enough to go on this trip. Besides, I need to get away from it all! Fix me something to eat." While he packed fishing gear, Holly wrapped liverwurst sandwiches in wax paper. When he was gone, Holly started talking. "Kids, I hate to be the one to tell you this."

Nothing good ever followed that phrase. As Holly whipped up cream cheese and jelly sandwiches, she stirred a witch's brew of rumor and innuendo. "What you don't know is that your mother knew Frank long before she left Manny. Those two had an affair, and that's the real reason for the divorce." I imagined my stepmother standing over a cauldron with a stick, boiling poison from a bottle with an X on it.

Eric was shooting daggers at our stepmother with his eyes. "That can't be true," he muttered.

"I'm afraid it is," Holly said. "Your mother has a talent for painting a picture that puts herself in a good light, and to hell with the rest of us."

Eric raised his eyebrows, but never raised his voice. Maybe the white bread sandwich was sticking in his throat. I licked cream cheese from my finger, wondering *why* our stepmother was knocking our mother off her virtuous pedestal.

That evening, our father burst through the door, smelling of fish and beer, proudly displaying the catch of the day. "Fix some hash-brown potatoes and corn-on-the-cob. And get me a cold one. I'm hot, I got a headache, and I'm hungry." He beheaded the scaly fish on the kitchen table, and blood and guts oozed over the Formica. He'd often eat sardines straight from the can, delighting in our disgust. Filleting fresh catch in front of us was even grosser. I gagged, and Eric's eyes widened as he gulped.

Our father looked at us with blood-shot eyes. "What are yous?" he slurred. "Are yous both wimps? Your mother made yous so thin-skinned. It's a wonder yous are not both queer. It's about time you kids toughen up. You got a lot to learn and like it or not, I'm gonna teach it to you."

My heart was doing flip-flops as my father began to unbuckle his belt. Was he going to beat me first, then Eric, or vice-versa?

"If you hurt either one of them," Holly warned, "you will never see your kids again."

For once, he surrendered to reason, shoved the chair back, and backed off. He was out the door, gone for the night, to wherever night owls prowl.

Holly washed Valium down with a Tom Collins, and we went to the den to watch TV. The den was the best room in the house. An air-conditioner hummed in the window and one of the recliners rocked. Eric and I often fought over that recliner, although he didn't really care about rocking chairs. He sat on the ottoman, until Holly went to fix another Tom Collins. Suddenly, my brother propelled himself, as if from a cannon, onto my body. With the full force of his weight, he pressed his big-boy body on top of mine. "Get off me. You're crushing me. I am not a chair." At the sound of ice tinkling in a glass,

Eric relented. Holly returned from the kitchen with a fresh drink, unaware of Eric's malicious attempt to overpower me.

I wished I had a safe place to hide, but the house was especially eerie at night. There were attic doors and crawl spaces without locks. The locks were supposed to have skeleton keys to go with, but the keys were missing. My father *refused* to install a bolt on the bathroom door. He would use the toilet without closing the door. We would complain to each other, "Why won't he shut the door? P-U. He's stinking up the house!" I remembered that my mother had called my father an "exhibitionist." My father's room had a lock, but it was the slide-bar type that worked only from the inside. His closet had a dead bolt; I imagined a skeleton hidden behind the door.

Holly had decorated a cheerful nursery for a someday baby, with yellow curtains that puffed away from the open window. The other bedroom, the one with the ladder leaning to the window on the outside, had bunk beds and a dresser. I sometimes slept in the lower bunk. Holly used to make the couch in the living room into a bed for Eric, but now he slept in the basement.

"Why do you sleep down there?"

"It's my designated place. There's no room upstairs."

"Aren't you afraid?"

"No."

I got the feeling that my brother did not like sleeping in a cold, damp basement with cobwebs. There was one light bulb on a string, a lumpy cot, and a bathroom two flights up. He was putting on an act like when he used to wear his Superman pajamas and fancied he could leap tall buildings in a single bound.

As I tried to fall asleep, I was thinking about our father's side of the family. Eric and I had more relatives than we cared to count. Our favorite was Aunt Susie, my father's youngest sister. She was my brother's age, young enough to be our father's daughter and old enough to drive. Sometimes she took us to the Capitol Theater to see movies. Sometimes we cruised the streets, searching for record stores, singing along with Jim Morrison and The Doors', "Light My Fire."

Sometimes, my father invited the relatives over for barbeques. Holly and I would carry trays of condiments and soda to the picnic table on the patio. "Mix me a drink!" my father would yell. I was mixing lemons with sugar. "I'm busy," I yelled back. He barged into the kitchen: "Never, ever say no to your father." Holly showed me how to mix gin with tonic. After we shaped hamburger meat into patties, my father would douse the barbecue coals with lighter fluid. Sometimes, the extra squirts of flammable liquid would cause flames to escape the kettle. Sometimes, the wind carried sparks to the roof. "Get the hose! Get the ladder! Get a bucket! Turn on the faucet!"

To scratch his daredevil itch, my father was a volunteer firefighter and was on call for most of a weekend. A scanner squawked in the background: "200 block, Elm Street, 10-4." When his unit was called, he threw on his fire hat and rubber boots, orange-striped coat, and in a flash, he was out the door. When my father marched in the Independence Day parade with the fire department, my hand waved at him in a rare surge of pride. Didn't he look like a hero in his navy-blue uniform? Wasn't he a good man to contribute to his community?

Sometime in July, Eric decided to go back to the Poconos.

"Honey, why don't you stay here?" Holly suggested to me. "We could go to the mall for back-to-school clothes. Maybe we could drive into the city for a poetry reading in a coffee shop."

I imagined beatniks and bohemians with berets, snapping their fingers, chanting, "Cool, Daddio."

"Okay."

Susie drove Eric to Pennsylvania. Holly and I had a full day of hanging around the house, reading horoscopes and tarot cards, and eating peanut butter and jelly sandwiches. In the evening, we watched TV. I drank root beer. Holly drank wine with Valium chasers.

Holly was yawning. "Excuse me, honey. I don't know what got into me. I'm so tired. I told Manny I'd wait up for him, but I don't know where he is or when he's coming home. I have to go to bed."

"Me too." The bedtime routine included shutting off lights, locking doors, and closing windows. Rocking on the lower bunk, I listened as crickets and dogs made night noises, until I fell asleep.

In my sleep, I feel an ice-cold draft float over my torso and I am shivering. I must be dreaming. My pajama top is raised, baring my belly, giving me goose bumps. I try to raise my arms, but my body feels like it is frozen within an iceberg. A heavy block of ice is on top of my body, crushing the air out of my chest. There is no space, no room for air. I am too small, the glacier is too large, and my head hits the headboard. To catch a breath, I turn my face to the side. I look to see what I can see. I see feet in socks, toes down, heels up, hanging over the foot of the bed. I see glass doorknobs. I see the closet door. If only a skeleton would swing from the rod and chop up the ice with an ax. If only I could run out the bedroom door. If only I could turn on a light. If only I could yell. My mouth is blocked behind a smelly palm. A stinking voice whispers, "Be quiet. It's your duty as my daughter." I am not asleep. Wouldn't he prefer a woman with boobies? Where is my stepmother? What is the ice pick doing down there? I am too frozen to feel. This can't be happening. I pretend to be sleeping. I pretend to be dead. The block of ice is melting, leaving wet on the sheet under me, leaving my belly exposed, leaving messages in my ear. "You will remember...nothing." I am crying. Why can't I stop crying? I put the pillow over my mouth so no one can hear.

The next morning, I awoke to the radio playing, *"Hot town, summer in the city, back of my neck getting dirt and gritty."* The back of my neck was stiff and my skin was sticky. My eyelids were nearly stuck shut with sleep. How did they get so crusty? I didn't cry myself to sleep, did I? I smelled like a stagnant pond and felt as numb as a dead fish. The heavy odor of frying bacon led me to the kitchen, where Holly was spattering grease from the skillet. Holly bent over the stove and lit a cigarette with the flame of the gas burner, although she had several butts burning in the ashtray.

"I'm discombobulated," Holly said. "Manny has not shown up for breakfast yet. That's one thing I can count on, him wanting breakfast."

He would usually sleep late, walk past us in a huff, slouch at the table to eat eggs sunny-side up, and read the sports page. The cursing that always accompanied my father was noticeably absent, but he had to be home because his keys were on the counter. Except for the humming of the window air-conditioner, an ominous hush hung inside the house as thick as the humid air outside.

"Something doesn't feel right," Holly said.

"You got that right," I said. "Did you hear strange noises last night?"

"Honey, I was out like a light."

"It was creepy. Maybe a prowler came through the window. I felt a cold breeze over my body."

"I closed that window myself." Holly said. "Manny swears he is going to fix that leaky window, but he's waiting until it rains so he can see exactly where the leak is. He's a typical Aries, starting projects but never finishing."

"Maybe there was a man on the roof. That ladder has been leaning against the window for months."

"Maybe the room is haunted by a poltergeist."

"What's that?"

"It's a ghost that makes noises and moves things. Maybe something dreadful once happened in that room, like a murder or a suicide, and the ghost is hanging around. If only walls could talk. Is your father in the basement?"

I opened the basement door, saw that it was dark, and closed the door quick. "No, not there."

"Is he in the back yard?"

"Not there, either."

Maybe he was in the garage. Eric and I had peeked into the garage once. We saw gasoline cans, boxes of matches and bullets, girlie magazines, and a punching bag hanging from a beam. My father was furious that we had been curious. He boarded up the window and posted a sign: NO TRESPASSING! Often, we would hear him in the garage, swearing over the buzz of the chain saw.

Holly left her breakfast of cigarettes and coffee to look for him in the garage. I stood on a chair to watch from a kitchen window. "Oh, for crissake," she hollered from the garage. She ran back toward the kitchen, grabbed a knife, and ran back into the garage. I heard muffled noises, a thud, choking, and gasping. Holly sprinted back to the house. "I thought it was his corpse hanging from the beam," she said.

"What? What do you mean?"

Holly leaned forward, her hands to her knees. "Let me catch my breath." She wheezed, straightened, and lit a cigarette. "He stood on a chair, fashioned a noose and attached it to a rafter. Apparently, he kicked the chair out from under him. I cut the rope. He's on the floor of the garage."

"Is he alive?" I was afraid that he was and afraid that he was not.

"It's too soon to tell! I'd better call his brother," Holly said as she grabbed the phone. She was pacing onto the porch, back into the kitchen, over to the dining room. "Come on, Henry, answer the phone. Answer the damned phone! Hey! Henry! Manny has gone over the edge. Come knock some sense into the nutty bastard!"

Although he lived only a couple of blocks away, the wait for my uncle took an eternity. About ten minutes later, my uncle Henry arrived, hugging Holly as he entered the house. I noticed how he resembled my father in height but was slimmer. The main difference was the beard Henry wore to cover his acne scars. After he walked through the house, I could hear Henry and Manny quarreling by the garage. Their voices were sharply rising and falling like a roller coaster, with my father's voice peaking so that I could only hear his side of the exchange.

"Take me to the emergency room? Over my dead body!"

"Bellevue Hospital in New York? Not on your life!"

"Seventy-two hours! They'll never hold me that long!"

Standing on the chair, I could see my father's face flush red white red. His eye sockets were nothing but dark slits. His dingy, tattered T-shirt was soaked with sweat, and strangulation marks weaved around his neck like a purple snake tattoo.

"What the hell is the matter with you?" Manny asked Henry. "Can't you see nothing is the matter with me? Can't you take a joke?"

According to my father, it was not *he* who was crazy, but the rest of the world. He was the great Houdini, able to do a magic trick to convince his brother that he was okay. They left together without saying where they were going and Holly went back to bed, as if nothing had ever happened. I swept the kitchen floor, washed the breakfast dishes, and swatted at flies with a dishtowel. I left just a few live flies to keep me company.

Karen asked, "Who did you talk to about this? Did you and Eric discuss the summer?"

"There was an unspoken rule: DO NOT TELL, so Eric and I never talked."

"What did you tell your mother when she asked how your summer was?"

"I told her it was fine."

"Oh, Lynn. What an awful summer! You were not fine. Your father sexually molested you."

"What? That's what it's called?"

"Definitions vary by state in accordance with the law. Overall, child molestation is the sexual abuse of a child by an adult. Whatever the term, it's a trauma, a terrible hurt."

"Even the sound of its name hurts," I said with a heavy sigh.

"I know. Ugly, isn't it? Can you recall any feelings you had at the time?"

"I remember that I felt like an object. I felt like I had no personhood, no girlhood. My father just used me. I felt like nothing."

"I'm so sorry," Karen responded, extending the compassion I'd needed for so long.

I wondered, as I often did, exactly why my father ultimately committed suicide. Did he kill himself as atonement for abuse? There is no reprieve for perpetrating the unpardonable upon children. When he died, I deluded myself into thinking that ended the damage he had done. However, the ripple effect of his insanity formed emotional tidal waves that flooded out my will. Years later, I was still riding the crest of the wave.

Soap Operas and Sibling Rivalry

Though the past haunts me as a spirit, I do not ask to forget.

Felicia Hemans

"Your mother must have asked about the summer. What did you tell her?" Karen asked.

"I didn't, although we talked about my father. She asked me if he still went on 'those fishing trips.' 'Who knows what went on!' she said. She'd heard rumors about 'homosexual activities' occurring on the boat. She called my father an exhibitionist."

"What did you think about what she told you?" Karen asked.

"Well, her comments about his sexual conduct did not pertain to my relationship with him. Maybe it wasn't something I needed to know. I haven't come to any conclusions."

"That's okay for now. You had concurrent lives, one in New Jersey and another in Pennsylvania. What was life like in Pennsylvania?"

When I was twelve years old, my mother, stepfather, Eric, Rusty, and I lived in a ranch style house built on two acres of a dormant apple orchard. In the spring, the air was filled with the fragrance of the apple blossoms. Surrounding the orchard were upper-middle class houses. My mother pointed out the financial histories of the homeowners, whether they were "old-money" or "nouveau rich." Nouveau rich did not carry as much prestige with her as did old money. Although she never spoke to her neighbors, she knew which owned the car dealership, which owned land acreage, and which made her mark in real estate. My mother shopped for recreation; she liked the accoutrements of the fortunate, like fine furniture, porcelain statues, crystal vases, and the *good* silverware.

I was fortunate to have a room of my own. Wide windows opened to a view of the orchard. At night, I could see the constellations from my bed. Eric's room was across the hall, with a bathroom between us, and Rusty was next to Eric, across from our mother and stepfather.

Yet the house was filled with tension. All too often, I caught Eric peeking as I was changing clothes, so I locked my door and stood behind it as I dressed. At dinner, I would catch him looking at me.

"Mom, he's looking at me!"

"If you were not looking at your brother, you would not know that he was looking at you," she said.

Eric kicked me under the table.

"Ouch! He kicked me!"

"Stop kicking your sister!"

"It was an accident," Eric claimed.

"Lynn, stop making mountains out of mole hills," Dad said.

The bickering between my brother and I had escalated to hostile proportions. Our mother said we were merely engaging in "sibling rivalry" as if we were kids competing for the coveted prize from the Cracker Jack box. Actually, we were vying for attention in the way we knew best.

By that time, my body had bloomed to the measurements of some kids' mothers. My mother told me that Eric had told her that he was embarrassed at the way the boys checked me out on the school bus. He was embarrassed? What about me? It was embarrassing the way boys talked to my chest instead of my face. I wished for the flat-chested figure of a fashion model.

My stepfather had never been affectionate toward me, and our discomfort with each other widened as my body developed. One evening, I lay on the couch, watching *Shindig,* which featured the latest in rock and roll bands. After propping a pillow under my head, I raised my knees, and folded my hands over my belly. Just as I started snapping my fingers to the beat of the go-go-dancers, my stepfather walked through the family room, wearing only his boxer shorts.

"You look like a whore lying there like that! Sit up like a lady."

I did not even know what a whore was, yet felt the shame of doing something wrong. I was ashamed of myself even when I just said something stupid. Like the time my stepfather showed me his new car, a Pontiac Grand Prix.

"Look at our new car," Dad said.

I spelled the logo aloud and pronounced "P-R-I-C-K-S."

He shouted, "Don't ever say that word again."

"What word?"

"You know very well what word."

Perhaps I should have known, but I really didn't. As I told Karen, I lowered my eyes and hung my head in shame. Shame inhabited my heart like a squatter on abandoned land.

"There is nothing to be ashamed of," Karen said. "He was in the wrong. It is not uncommon for men to be uncomfortable around girls as they grow into womanhood. Your stepfather was projecting his discomfort onto you. He was accountable for his discomfort, not you. Of course, he was insensitive. How were your relationships to the rest of the family?"

When my brother Rusty was four and I was twelve, we shared a bathroom with Eric. Our bathroom looked like a section on function and taste from *Better Homes and Gardens*. It was equipped with separate sinks, wide mirrors, and a mauve tub and toilet. When Rusty was learning to brush his teeth, we brushed side-by-side, gargling, spitting, rinsing, and laughing until our sides ached.

I loved Rusty at that age, especially the way he voiced his observations in cute and concise sentences. He was thrilled about everything the world had to offer, and all he wanted was love and laughter. We did not look alike, with his olive complexion and brown eyes compared to my fair skin and green eyes, but we were brother and sister. He was older than a baby and I was younger than an adolescent so for a few years we had childhood in common despite the age difference.

One evening, as I was soaking in suds of bubble bath that concealed my body, Rusty was sitting on the toilet seat, swinging his legs. We were singing together, *"Hey, hey, we're the monkeys, and we don't monkey around, we're too busy singing, to put anybody down."* We sang louder, *"Hey, hey, we're the monkeys, and we don't monkey around."* Rusty stepped off the toilet, slipped on the wet tile, and hit his head on the heater vent. The singing and laughter turned to crying and bleeding.

Frank burst into the bathroom, picked Rusty up, and examined his little head. While I sat naked in the tub, lips quivering, he coddled his son and scolded his stepdaughter. "What did you do to him? You should know better than to splash water and cause a hazard. How could you be so careless? Little boys and big sisters should not be in the bathroom together. You should be ashamed of yourself."

As the water turned cold, my dignity disappeared with the suds, and my relationship with Rusty went down the drain. He was the favored child and I was the trouble-maker. My affection for Rusty was replaced with resentments that I harbored in orderly rows like boats at a dock.

"Look at the snowflakes," Rusty would say. "Did you know no two are alike?"

"Of course I know, stupid."

"Look at the shooting star," Rusty urged. "I'm going to make a wish."

"Don't count on it coming true."

"Look at the strawberry patch. Come on, Lynnie, let's go gather some."

"Don't be so silly," I'd say.

As we stood on the second-floor balcony over-looking the orchard, I threatened to throw him over.

"You wouldn't do that, would you?" he asked.

"You bet I would. I could pick you up and throw you over."

Of course, I wouldn't, but my threats and vicious tone of voice scared Rusty into silence.

On weekday mornings, our mother drove Rusty to kindergarten. I took the bus to middle school, and Eric drove himself to high school. Our grandmother had presented Eric with a Camaro for his sixteenth birthday.

One morning, our mother told us, "I'm taking Rusty to the pediatrician after school. We won't be home until five o'clock. You kids fend for yourself."

After school, Eric called to me from his room. "Hey, come here. I have something to show you."

"What something? Can it wait? I'm busy with a book report."

"I'll give you a brownie if you come here."

Although it was a sin to covet, I pictured those special chocolate fudge bars with thick frosting and walnuts, and my mouth drooled. Brownies were often used as barter between us for helping him with homework or trading off his housework. With the promise of those brownies, I went to his room. His curtains were closed, which seemed unusual for a sunny spring afternoon.

He turns and locks the door.

"Why are you locking your door?"

"Sit on the bed."

"What? No!"

He sits me on the edge of his bed. He gulps, and I see his Adam's apple bob. He has grown to man size and he has grown side-burns. My brother would not hurt me, would he?

"Let me go!"

He murmurs, "I want to show you what boys do to girls on a date. It's for your own good."

He knows that at thirteen I am not allowed to go on a date. Even when I am allowed, I don't ever want to date.

"Pull down your panties."

"No!" I try to get out, up, or away but he pushes me back onto the bed.

He lifts my blouse and fumbles with the fasteners on my bra. I try not to look at the bosom that overflows the bra. He yanks my underwear. I look down at the panties pulled to my hips. This cannot be happening!

What is he saying? "Spread your legs."

"No. I don't want to."

He forces his hand between my legs. He inserts his middle finger into the vagina. He wiggles his finger inside of my body.

"Ouch! That hurts! Stop it! Take it out!" I take in a breath. I can hardly hear him, but his mouth is moving.

"This is called a finger fuck," he says.

I feel him at my side, but there is no feeling. He is as rigid as a robot and I am stiff. I am thinking: If this is what boys do to girls on dates, I will be certain to join a convent, even if I do not have the calling, since I am no longer pure in body. Besides, what order of nuns would take me in?

Eric takes his finger out. I let out a breath. I look at him while he looks at his finger. He wipes his finger on the bedspread. I watch the door while he fiddles with the buttons on my blouse and the snaps on my bra. I try to be as remote as Eric. I stare straight ahead and beyond. If I do not look at him, I will not see what he is doing.

Maybe Mom will come home soon. I am afraid that she will, and afraid that she will not.

Eric stands up, leaving my panties down, and he is whispering, "You will remember...nothing."

Those words sound familiar. Where did he get those words? Is he done with me? I am in a daze. In slow motion, I stand up, on to shaky legs. I pull up the panties.

As if in slow motion, Eric moves to a corner, behind the locked door. I try to leave but he blocks the door. We stand face to face without looking eye to eye. His face looks twisted, as though he is wearing a rubber mask, like a costume of Satan on Halloween.

When he talks, his voice sounds like an egg cracking. "If you tell, it will kill Mom! Especially don't tell Mom. She'll go insane. Besides, no one will believe you! I will deny it! The whole family will hate you! You will be banished! Pretend this never happened. Forget this ever happened! You will remember nothing!"

I hear myself saying, "I will never forget this."

"You will. Train your mind. DON'T BE A RAT FINK!"

What did I do to deserve this? He hands me a brownie, as if to offer a token for a consenting trade. The brown square crumbles; it is dry and stale in my palm. Is this supposed to be a consolation prize for falling into a trap? Is the barter for my body a broken brownie?

"Keep your stinking brownie!"

He unlocks his door and dismisses me.

I studied the alarm clock on my nightstand, trying to learn to tell time all over again. The big hand is on the ten; the little hand is on the four. What's the time? Somebody, anybody, tell me what time it is! Time was standing still.

Fires of knots burned in my stomach. My body hugged the wall as I tiptoed from the bedroom to the kitchen. Where was Mom? I needed something simple, something filling, and something familiar. How about food? I scrambled two eggs in a skillet, just like my mother would, with butter, salt and pepper. As I put the fork to my mouth, the taste and soft texture repulsed me, and I threw up. After thirteen years of scrambled eggs and hard-boiled eggs and deviled eggs and Easter eggs, they suddenly made me nauseated.

I swept away the emotional garbage of the afternoon by operating as if conditions were normal. As I filled my insides with secrets, shame, guilt, and lies, I cleaned what was outside me. I scoured the skillet, wiped the counters, cleaned the stove, and picked at pimples. My mother came home to a house that looked like nothing had ever happened.

The next morning, the school bus picked up a different girl than I'd been the day before. Maybe I looked the same, but I was different. Before that day, I sat in that seat in that classroom and was able to concentrate. After that day, I could not count on my fingers or remember the days of the week. I was supposed to be taking a test in social studies, but I kept spacing out.

Each morning I would tell myself that I would tell my mother today. After school, my mother would ask, "How was your day?"

"Fine, thanks."

"Mom?"

"Can it wait a half hour? I'm watching *Another World*. I want to hear Rachel."

"But, Mom."

"Quiet. I'm watching."

As I was searching the cupboards for comfort, I must have been slamming the cabinet doors.

"Lynn, stop slamming things."

"I am not slamming things." SLAM!

"Lynn, what is wrong with you?"

"Nothing." SLAM!

"Lynn, you are acting out anger. What are you so angry about?"

"I don't know."

"Then let me watch my show in peace."

As I dunked chocolate-chip cookies in milk, I read the daily horoscopes and turned to Ann Landers for advice.

Not long after, Eric tried to entice me with money to enter his lair, which is liar spelled wrong. If that's what earning money entails, I would be certain not to have any. He never failed to reinforce his power. If we passed in the hall, he would punch my arm, with a glare in his eyes that threatened, "Don't tell or else!" Rather than risk being accosted, I would wait in my room until I heard him go in to or come out of his room. Or I would hiss at my brother, "I hate you."

I heard him in the kitchen using his righteous altar boy voice.

"Mom, what's for dinner?"

"Meatloaf with mashed potatoes and string beans."

"What's for dessert?"

"We'll have your favorite chocolate pudding banana pie."

"Mom, I have to tell you something."

When was he going to take off the persona of Saint Eric and reveal the Lucifer character?

"Lynnie said she hates me. What did I ever do to her?"

Was he testing to see if she knew?

"Lynn, come here," Mom demanded. "Did you say you hate Eric? It is not nice to use the word hate, especially toward your brother. Apologize to him."

"Yeah, sure."

"What kind of apology is that? What is going on between the two of you? If you only knew what I was going through, you wouldn't be acting like spoiled brats."

You don't really want to know, I thought. I sensed that my mother's nerves were as breakable as a jigsaw puzzle being moved from place to place. Forcing extra pieces of myself upon her might make her fall apart. So I deliberately kept certain pieces jumbled in a flimsy box behind my heart.

"Did you get the clothes out of the dryer like I asked you to?" Mom asked. "You can fold them and put them where they belong."

"Do I have to do his stuff, too?"

"Would it kill you to put Eric's underwear in his dresser?"

Opening the top dresser drawer, I noticed how his T-shirts and briefs were stacked in piles of three, placed in three rows across. Clip-on ties were lined in a single row in the second drawer. When I opened his closet, I saw that his oxfords and trousers were hanging at even lengths, in the same direction. He kept his outside world all neat and tidy to compensate for the chaos inside.

According to our mother, a toenail was the cause of Eric's moodiness. "Your brother has an ingrown toenail," Mom said. "He stubbed it again last night. It's so painful. I'm taking him to the podiatrist."

I wished there was a specialist who could dig out the source of my ingrown pain.

In his junior year, Eric ran away. He lived with our grandmother, going to school and working in the rink or driving the riding lawnmower on the golf course. Our mother did not understand what drove her son away, and she grieved his absence.

"Set a place for your brother," she would tell me.

"But it's been a year since he last ate dinner here."

"Do as I say. He might want to eat with the family tonight."

I never spoke of the secret in simple sentences. Instead, my nightmares spoke in symbolic images. *I dream I am swimming in the treacherous sea of life. I am treading salt water, wading in a swamp, knee deep in sludge, shoulders in slime, sinking in quicksand, swallowing pond scum. My body is engulfed, leaving only one forearm above the surface. Somebody, see me, somebody, save me. A young man comes to the edge of the thick water. Instead of pulling me out, he pushes me under, and I am drowning in an ocean of sorrow.* I awake and the sheets are soaked with sweat.

Karen was patting my hand, as if to wake me from a bad dream. "You are safe now." When I started to cry, she reached over to hold my hands. I was expecting judgment for the secrets I was giving away. Instead, I was receiving empathy. The touch of here and now surprised me. I had been in a time warp, unaware of how much time had passed, not only in hours and days, but also in years. "I feel so old."

"That is because you have been through ten times more in twenty-something years than ten others go through in a lifetime."

"Why did he do that? My own brother violated my privacy. He betrayed my trust. He molested me. He threatened me. Why? Why me? What did I do to him?"

"It happened to you, not because of you. You can't make sense of senseless acts. Molestation is usually a learned behavior. Molesters themselves have felt helpless, and as a cure for their own vulnerability, they molest to gain mastery over others. Also, the greatest fear of a sexual abuser is that of being exposed. That explains why he threatened you so vehemently."

"I am so very tired. Can I take a time out from life and hibernate for a decade? Or have I been sleepwalking through life for a decade? Where have I been all my life?"

"In deep denial. You can move through this. Tell me how you feel."

"Everything hurts! I already had open sores from my father picking at my heart. Eric rubbed salt on the wounds. When, how, will I ever heal from this?"

"Healing begins when we allow ourselves to acknowledge our wounds. You are doing that, so you are healing. Our wounds are not a measure of one individual's sad fate, but an indication of our unity with others."

"What do others have to do with my wounds?"

"Secrets isolate us. To reveal them is to share a genuine human condition. You have shared with me."

"Yes. Telling the real story makes me feel less like a fake," I said.

"Good! What else are you feeling?"

"I feel pissed off."

"Who are you angry with?"

"My stupid self."

"You focused quite enough anger on yourself. Anger is a valid emotion as a response to being endangered. Anger becomes negative when it is expressed in harmful ways. You found the real reasons for your anger, and anger must be directed at the appropriate offense and offenders."

"But it was inappropriate to express anger, especially to family. Besides, I saw my real father's anger as a reaction to anything and everything, or nothing at all. If I allowed my emotions to come undone, they would do me in."

"You took on your father's anger and added your own. That amounts to rage, which emerged as self-destruction. You also identified with your abusers, and continued to hurt yourself. What, if anything, did you tell your mother?" Karen asked.

"I played guessing games. I figured that if my mother guessed it, I would not deny it. If she could not guess what it was, I would not say it, because I did not have words for it. No words in my vocabulary sounded right for a violation so very wrong. She should have guessed. Perhaps I thought she should have *known*. And Eric had threatened me with her life: If she *knew*, it could kill her."

"You were attempting to communicate discomfort when you were saying that your brother was looking at you. Children do not have the capacity for clear communication to adults. It is the parents' responsibility to provide channels for communication. If the adults can not communicate, how can the children?"

I recalled how bouts of bronchitis kept me from breathing a word. How could I tell while hacking up phlegm? Once or twice a year, from the age of thirteen on, I stayed in bed with fevers and coughs that could kill. Death by pneumonia would be an acceptable way out, but it would take too long to wait for infected lungs to cooperate.

Eventually, the temptation to tell was replaced by the habit of not telling. Over the next couple of years, my mother and I exchanged words that never formed a fully coherent conversation. Or I'd provoke hostility. If I made her mad at me, it might mean that I mattered.

"Mom, will you always love me?"

"Of course, Lynnie, you are my daughter."

"Will you love me no matter what?"

"Yes. What is it? Is there something you want to tell me?"

"Can I tell you anything?"

"Yes, but you have to say it. I am not a mind reader."

"Mom, are you mad at me?"

"No, but Dad is getting impatient with all the time I spend with you. And I can't neglect Rusty."

"I'm sorry, Mom."

"Lynnie, why are you crying?"

"I thought you were mad at me."

"I'm not mad at you now, but I will be if you don't tell me what's bothering you."

Mood swings seized me with the tenacity of a terrier unwilling to release its target. I was either up and off the wall or down in the dumps, teetering on an emotional seesaw, unable to achieve a balance. One day, my mother said, "Lynn, I'm walking on eggshells, trying to guess what mood you are in."

I sighed. I must have sighed again.

"Lynn, why do you keep sighing?"

I could not even breathe right. "Mom, stop hassling me."

"What the hell is wrong with you?"

"Everything, Mom. Everything is wrong."

"Like what?"

"Nothing. Never mind."

"Is there anything you want to tell me?"

"I don't think so."

"Oh come on, Lynn, don't beat around the bush."

"Mom, why can't you just leave me alone?"

"What has gotten into you?"

You name it, I got it: evil spirits, alien beings, and foreign objects in my body. Yet my mother was demanding the daughter I no longer was.

"What has happened to my daughter? Whose daughter are you? Who made you this way?"

"I HATE MYSELF! I HATE MY FATHER! I HATE ERIC! I HATE YOU!"

My mother slapped me, asking, "Were you born just to make my life miserable?"

"I DID NOT ASK TO BE BORN. I WISH I HAD NEVER BEEN BORN. I WISH I WAS DEAD!"

"Oh, Lynn, spare me your self pity."

I tried to slap her back. I'd grown taller than her in the last couple of years, but my height gave me no advantage. As my mother, she'd always have more power over me. She grabbed my arm.

"Why are you making me give up on you?"

"I don't know, Mom. I'm sorry, I'm sorry. Please don't give up on me."

"Oh, I'm not going to give up on you. Just please stop antagonizing me."

My little brother took the brunt of my bitterness. When I was told to baby-sit, I neglected him while I listened to Big Brother and The Holding Company: Janis Joplin sang about a piece of her heart. At seven o'clock, I would say to Rusty, "It's time for you to go to bed."

"It is not. Mom said I can stay awake until nine o'clock."

"Stop crying like a ninny-baby and go to bed."

Our mother confronted me about my behavior toward Rusty. "What is the matter with you that I can't trust you to take care of your little brother?"

I stuck my head into his room and threatened, "You little tattle-tale. I'm going to get you!"

To keep himself safe from his sister, Rusty kept to himself. In the spring, he played with toy soldiers, building forts with dirt. In the summer, he rode his bicycle in the cul-de-sac, around and around. In the winter, he went sledding down the hill, walked back up the hill, and then slid down again. His time was spent all alone.

For my fourteenth birthday, my father sent me a dozen red roses, with a card that read, *"Long time no see."* My mother was arranging the flowers in a crystal vase. "These are beautiful! Your father never sent me roses. He didn't even give me so much as a corsage on our wedding day."

Whatever, any attention from my parents was better than cold rejection. "Mom, what do you think he wants?"

"There's no telling what he's up to."

"What should I do?"

"You're usually quite anxious to see Holly. I hear she is expecting a baby," Mom said.

Perhaps, I thought, I could tell Holly what Eric did to me before her baby arrived. Perhaps she could tell my mother. To tell or not to tell became synonymous with to be or not to be.

"You might as well see her," Mom said, "You've got time to kill this summer."

Could I kill time counterclockwise by turning the clock back to a time when time was merely a way to count the days? Time was just one monotonous moment after another that measured another dreary day.

Lynn C. Tolson

Bakeries and Beatings

Loneliness is never more cruel than when it is felt in close propinquity with someone who has ceased to communicate.

Germaine Greer

On the second Saturday in July, my father was scheduled to pick me up. My mother said, "Go wait outside for your father. The last thing I need is to see his good-for-nothing face."

My father pulled up and put my luggage in the trunk. "What's the matter with you, waiting outside?"

"Mom told me to."

"Is she in there breathing her rarified air or what?" He was in a rare good mood, which meant less cursing at the truck drivers and a stop at the bakery in Fairlawn for crumb cake.

"Hi, Honey. Like my dress?" Holly asked in greeting.

As we entered the living room, she added, "It's a maternity tent dress." Holly had traded in her hip-huggers for a sleeveless A-line dress that was hemmed to the middle of her chunky thighs.

"When is the baby due?"

"September. It's a Virgo."

"Will you two quit jabbering?" Manny said. "Could you make yourself useful? Can't you see that Holly could use some help around here? Your mother is such a clean freak. You think she might have taught you something. I've got a poker game."

While Manny was out playing cards with his brother and placing bets with his buddies, I had time alone with Holly. Was it time to tell?

I helped Holly clean tubs, sinks, and toilets. We washed dishes, clothes, and windows. In the nursery, we hung a wallpaper border and a mobile and folded blankets and diapers.

"I had a friend who had a baby in a toilet," Holly said. "She didn't even know she was pregnant."

"How could she not know she was pregnant?"

"She was really fat, like Mama Cass of the Mamas and the Pappas."

"Didn't her periods stop?

"She thought she was not regular."

"How come the baby came out in the toilet?"

"She thought she was having gas pains."

After we finished the chores, we rested at the kitchen table, and admired clear counters and shiny sinks.

"Holly, can I tell you something?"

"Sure, honey, you can tell me anything."

"Never mind. Can we call out for pizza?"

"Sure. Let's get delivery. What toppings do you want?"

Over slices of mushroom pizza, Holly asked, "What was it that you wanted to tell me?"

The mushrooms tasted less like a vegetable and more like fungus. I was about to tell my stepmother what I could not tell my mother.

"Holly, if you knew somebody did something really terrible and told you not to tell, would you tell?"

"Do you know somebody who did something terrible?"

"Well, let's not say who did what. Just say, if you knew, would you tell?"

"Did somebody do something terrible to you?"

"What if they did? Should I tell?"

"It depends. Honey, why don't you just tell me?"

"If I tell you, will you promise not to tell?"

"I promise."

"Well, my brother did something to me."

Holly listened to the details, and then asked, "Are you sure? Were you dreaming?"

"In his bedroom, in the middle of the afternoon, I was not dreaming."

Holly wrapped a hug of understanding around me, saying, "This is serious. I'm so sorry. I read about this kind of thing in the newspaper. It runs in families, from one generation to the next. We can't tell your father. I hope he never finds out. He'll kill your brother."

Holly consulted the astrology chart to illuminate the unthinkable. "You see?" She was pointing to zodiac symbols on the parchment paper. "Scorpios are ruled by the sex organs. They are also secretive. I always wondered about your brother. Still waters run deep. What have you told your mother?"

"I can't tell my mother. Will you tell her for me?"

"If you want me to. This will devastate your mother. She'll never get over it. Keep in mind that Eric is the golden child. He acts like such a good boy that your family may not believe you. Even if they do take your word for it, your grandmother will protect him."

"Protect him from what?"

"Considering his age, he could go to jail. Your family will do all they can to prevent that. Do you want to see your brother spend the rest of his life in jail?"

"No, I guess not."

"Your family expects Eric to go to college, and if he has a record, he won't get accepted. Eric plans on having a family and word of this will ruin his chances of having a wife and kids."

"What about me?"

"A girl's future is just not as important as a boy's future. Do you want me to tell your mother?"

"I don't know."

That summer, when other girls were planning picnics and swim parties, Holly and I practiced probable scenarios with my mother.

"When I drive you back to the Poconos, I'll tell her," Holly offered.

"What if she's having a bad day?"

"Let's have a signal. If you think it's not a good day to tell her once we get there, raise two fingers, like a peace sign."

"It's not like you're a regular visitor. She'll wonder what's up."

"I'll call Sophia, and tell her I need to talk to her about Manny. I don't know how to deal with him anyway."

"Are you sure? Do you really think that's okay?"

"Honey, you're not alone. When I was a teenager, I was raped. It was the worst experience and it took everything out of me. Maybe that had something to do with quitting school and being a runaway. Working the streets is no life for any girl, but what else could I do?"

That night, Manny came home with a face red with the rage of a mighty sore loser. I was backing up, into the den, as he hollered at Holly.

"You think I don't know what you've been up to, you fickle whore."

"What are you talking about?"

"You think I'm blind! You think I didn't see you flirting with him."

"Who?"

"My own brother, that's who!"

"I never did nothing with Henry."

"You must have done something."

The last I saw, Holly was crawling up the stairs as Manny was pulling her down. Huddling in the den, I heard the door to their bedroom slam shut and his tirade: "You're nothing but a worthless piece of shit. You ingrate. I took you in when you didn't have a pot to piss in, and this is how you repay me."

Thud. Thud. Thud. It sounded like he was hitting his fist into his punching bag.

"Look what you made me do, you bitch."

Holly was begging, "Stop, please, please stop. The baby. DON'T HURT MY BABY!"

Then, I heard his footsteps stomping down the stairs. I held my breath, afraid my father would rush into the room to use me as the next victim of his uncontrollable temper. My next breath came when I heard his car door slam, and he was driving away. When I thought it was safe, I followed the sounds of sobbing. "Holly? Holly?"

Holly was on her hands and knees, searching the bathroom cabinets. Was she looking for a gun?

"Holly, what are you looking for?"

"Sanitary napkins. I'm bleeding."

"Should I call an ambulance?"

"That will only make matters worse."

"Holly, what's the matter with calling a doctor?"

"Manny lost another job. We don't have insurance." Holly was leaning on me as she inched her way back to the bedroom.

"Crissake," Holly said. "It looks like a cyclone tore through the place." The room was littered with newspapers and beer cans, full ashtrays and dirty clothes. "Grab me a pillow, would you? I'm better off on the couch. Oh, and get my bottle of Valium and the Darvon."

Holly lay on the couch with washcloths on a bloody eye and a blanket over her swollen belly. "I swear," she said, "I saw the devil in his eyes. He is the devil incarnate. That son of a bitch is possessed. He thrives on evil. I wish he were dead."

"Be careful what you wish for, Holly. Isn't that what you always tell me?"

"I read an article about natives of Jamaica who make voodoo dolls. They use a rag doll that represents the evildoer and they stick pins in the doll to get revenge."

Even with pills to send away the pain and bring on sleep, she stayed awake to nurse wounds. In the pale light between night and dawn, when I was not quite asleep and not quite awake, my father stumbled into the house. He staggered up the stairs, swearing under his breath.

Bam! Bam! Bam! We heard what sounded like gunshots. Holly rose from the couch and folded her arms around her belly like a kangaroo protecting her pouch. With every step an effort, she wobbled up the stairs. I retreated to the den to wait for an answer to an inconceivable question. Did my father shoot himself? Was he dead? Through the floorboards, I heard the mumblings of an incoherent lunatic.

Holly came back down the stairs. "He's gone stark raving mad. He shot bullets into the ceiling. He said he wanted to see if anyone cared if he lived or died."

Did he care that he scared me to death? No. He never mentioned his rehearsal of suicide. He never knew that his play-acting haunted me with dread, as if it was real.

A couple of days later, as Holly was driving me to the Poconos, we stopped at a diner. Holly wore sunglasses even as she sat at the counter, scheming: "These bruises can be used to our advantage."

I looked at her swollen face and belly.

"Sophia will never guess that I have anything other than Manny to talk about," Holly said. She ordered a cup of tea instead of her usual black coffee.

"Holly, are you sure you want to do this today?"

"No time like the present. Are you sure?"

Woozy from worry, I was not even sure I could keep my balance on the counter stool.

My mother and my stepmother, two entirely different women, were sitting at our round dinner table, waiting for the coffee to brew. What they had in common was a man that caused so much misery.

"He's a crazy bastard," Holly said. "He better not cost me this baby."

"When I was pregnant," Sophia said, "he'd be gone all hours of the day and night. He'd come home with a mean streak a mile long. He goes on rampages with pregnant wives. Maybe it's because he was the oldest and his mother was always pregnant, so he didn't get all the attention he needed as a little boy."

My mother commiserated with Holly by using pseudo-psychoanalysis. Holly used the positions of the planets in retrograde to explain the absurd. This was not turning out to be a good day for telling truths. As I poured coffee for Holly, I signaled her, and a slight nod of her head responded. My mother's eyes met mine, as if I'd done something wrong. If looks could kill, I'd be incinerated alive in the searing glare of her eyes.

My mother wore a wardrobe of hats that afternoon, from perfect hostess to amateur psychiatrist, as well as two faces. As soon as Holly left, Mom said, "The gall of that woman to dump her problems on me. I don't know about your father. He's really gone and done it this time. What the hell was going on between you and Holly?"

"What? What do you mean?"

"Don't play stupid. Do you think I'm blind? I saw you two exchanging glances. Seems like you went behind my back about something."

"Nothing, Mom. There was nothing." To tell her the real reason for Holly's visit would require telling the whole truth. The knowing could make a mother go crazy.

Instinct and Survival

...just a tender sense of my own inner process, that holds something of my connection with the divine.

Percy Bysshe Shelley

Karen was trying to pass a box of tissues into my clenched fist. "What happened to all the emotions you were feeling during this time?" she asked.

"Nothing."

"Nothing? Not only did you have your feelings to deal with," she said, "but you also took on your parents' feelings. How did that make you feel?"

"What I felt was numb."

"Yes, you suppressed those feelings. So your emotions remained unexamined."

"Until now," I said. "You know, talking about my experiences and emotions doesn't *feel* good."

"I know. But putting words to it may dispel the hold it has on you. What else from your adolescence can you tell me?"

"You don't want to know."

"I do want to know. In order to help you, I have to know."

I recalled a particularly beautiful, sunny summer Saturday at Tanglewood Falls. The sky looked as though it had been painted on a post card in cerulean blue. My stepfather dropped me off at Tanglewood Falls when he went to work. I planned on skating at the indoor rink, so I hung my skating outfit in my grandmother's apartment. A tune by Otis Redding was sounding in my head, leading me to the lake to enjoy the weather before skating: *"Sitting in the morning sun, I will be sitting when the evening comes."*

Walking to the lake, I wandered under a shady grove of evergreen trees, inhaled the scent of pine, and listened to the trickle of the creek. How I loved the Poconos and Tanglewood Falls! A rustling sound in the brush made me wonder if a mule deer or a black bear was munching on mountain laurel.

Heading toward the swimming hole called Red Rocks, I glimpsed an unnatural red, the color of a T-shirt on a teenaged boy. I recognized him from the ice rink, where he played pinball machines in the lobby. As I turned in the other direction, he called, "Hey, I know you! Don't be so stuck up!"

Although I did not want to talk to him, I stalled to be polite. In an instant, instinct instructed me to run. *Run! Run!*

"Hey, where are you going? You think you're too good to talk to me?"

The boy is tackling me. Thud! Ow! I am stunned as the back of my head strikes a rock. The sky rotates in shades of gray with red and yellow stars. An ugly, pasty, pimpled face revolves around my head. I feel my shorts being pulled down my thighs. I am exposed in the daylight. This cannot be happening! The boy says, "You're nothing but a fucking tease."

I do not tease! I hate boys! I want boys to leave me alone! I fling my arms at a solid chest. I run my fingernails down a firm cheek. I grab at sand and throw. The boy pins me down with his whole body weight, like a boulder on my chest. My breasts are crushed. My breath is knocked out. He is yanking at my panties. "Stop! Stop! I have my period."

He invades my insides, fumbling with his grubby fingers. He rips the tampon out and throws it on the ground. A hard pressure pushes at my pelvis. As he tears my insides out with fire, I see red. Fire! Finally, he pulls the burning out and lifts the boulder off. Is he done with my body? "Go home to your big shot relatives, you fucking tease."

Thump! Thump! Thump! The thumping of my heart was so loud I could not hear myself think. I ran, but my legs felt like rubber. I ran while pulling up my shorts, holding back strands of hair, swatting gnats, and rubbing sand out of my eyes. The sand sticks to the sweat on my hand, and my fingers put sand in my eyes. Sand was shifting inside my panties and shorts, under my bra, rubbing my skin raw. Over creek pebbles and pine needles, I ran for my life. Thud! My face faced the grass, a sandal snagged on a rock. Where was the other sandal? Should I go back for the sandal? How would I explain losing my shoe? How would I explain this? What if my grandmother saw me? Surely, she's arguing with my stepfather in the hotel kitchen. What if my uncle saw me? Surely, he's in a meeting. What if my aunt saw me? Surely, she's shopping with Annie. Although I had been welcomed into Grandma's house a thousand times before, I felt like a sneak as I opened the screen door and turned the knob.

Inside her bathroom, I locked the door. What if my grandmother caught me taking a bath in the middle of the afternoon? What would I say? I fell? I fell in the creek? I fell in the creek and hit my head? I reached for a new bar of soap. What if my grandmother counts bars of soap like she kept inventory of canned vegetables? Not waiting for the bath water to fill the tub, I washed from the tub faucet. When I peeled my panties down, the blood scared me. I wondered if my grandmother had sanitary napkins.

My face stung from sunburn, sand, and tears, and the skin stretched over the cheekbones like a rubber mask. My hands were inflexible from scraped knuckles and clenched fists. My grandmother got her hair done at the beauty shop. I wondered if she had shampoo. My hair was too tangled, too wet with sweat, too covered with sand, but it covered the knot that throbbed at the back of my head. To prevent the towels from getting soggy, I barely blotted my body dry. I shook the sand from my bra and bundled up my clothes. After scrubbing and drying the tub and neatly hanging the towel, I packaged my panties in paper towels along with the used bar of soap and its wrapper.

As I put on the ice skating outfit, I panicked. How could I walk to the skating rink without panties or shoes? If I walked bare foot, my bottom would be exposed in the short skirt. Walking in tights would cause the knit fabric to tear. I tried to roll the tights over my feet and up my legs, but they keep twisting over moist skin. I used pads of toilet paper to make a napkin. I tied the sleeves of a sweater around my hips and stretched it to cover my bottom. As I walked barefoot to the rink, I threw my panties and the soap into a dumpster. Then, I willed myself to stop crying long enough to enter the ice rink, where Eric was working.

"You look like something the cat dragged in."

"Leave me alone! Where's Annie?"

"Aunt Ruthie took her to the doctor."

As I walked to the metal cabinet for a bandage, Eric asked, "What are you looking for?"

First aid, second aid, long-term care, what did he care? What if Eric found out? Would he tell? Would he turn it against me? Would he say it was my fault? Would anyone believe me? What if my mother or stepfather found out? I was out of my mind with worry about what others would think. I must have done something to deserve what happened. I must have been a tease so I better not tell. What if the boy comes into the ice rink? I could ignore him and pretend that nothing ever happened.

When my stepfather drove me home that evening, he asked, "What's wrong with you?"

"Nothing!" On the radio, The Beatles were singing, "Hey Jude."

"I hate that song," Frank said. "It doesn't make a bit of sense."

That's what he cared about? It did not matter if the song made sense; all I wanted was for Ringo Starr to drum out the din that was rattling my brains.

When I got home, my mother asked, "What happened to your hair?"

"Nothing!"

After slamming and locking the bathroom door, I saw the cuts that covered my body. There was a knock at the door. "Sweetheart, are you all right?"

"Fine, Mom, fine." I wanted to ask her if there was a salve for my burning vagina, but she would expect an explanation. I could not form an explanation because I had no name for the boy and no name for the episode. My mother had used Noxzema on sunburns, so I applied it to my vaginal area, only to experience the sting of mentholated camphor against tender, raw skin. A fresh pad protected my clean panties, but there was no relief for the pain that radiated from my pelvis.

What had that boy done to me? What would the Virgin Mother think? Was it like this for Mother Mary? Did I lose my virginity? What if I got pregnant? I lost a piece of myself that day, and it was not just a sandal. Ruined, ruined, everything was ruined.

After a few days, I returned to the skating rink, slipping through the back door with the EMPLOYEES ONLY sign. Walking past the blade-sharpening machine and the ice-resurfacing machine was one way to avoid the risk of running into the boy. "You're not supposed to come in that door," Eric scolded.

"So what?" In order to protect myself, I was growing eyes in the back of my head. As I put dimes into the vending machine for a hot chocolate, I felt someone staring. There he was, with scratches on his face and a buddy by his side, giving me the evil eye. If looks could kill, he was there to murder me. I considered throwing the steaming cup of cocoa into his eyes, but that would call attention to our acquaintance. As I switched the hot paper cup from hand to hand, the buddy moved toward me, until my back was against the knobs of the machine. "You sure did a number on him, you little tiger," he sneered. He positioned his hand in a claw and growled to imitate a tiger ready to pounce. Fortunately, honeymooners strolled by hand in hand.

My grandmother's advice reverberated in my brain. "Just put it out of your mind," she would say regarding whatever was too terrible. I trained my mind to not think about it.

I snapped out of this memory to hear Karen saying, "Lynn, are you listening?"

"What, what did you say?"

"I have been saying that you were a victim and rape is an act of violence. I don't think you heard me."

It was true that I often stopped listening, afraid of what I might hear. Reliving that experience was as treacherous as I thought it would be. I had spent more than a decade taming a wild tiger, whipping the cruel memory into its cage of suppression. Now I had allowed the episode to escape into the safe confines of a counseling session. Talk-therapy helped me to take back the power the rape had held over me. Talking was beginning to free me enough to begin to experience healing, not only the mind but also the body. Although I didn't fully realize it at the time, talking freely allowed the depression to decrease over time as well as reducing the pain of sexual assaults.

Genetic Codes and Cruel Jokes

Love is the emblem of eternity; it confounds all notion of time; effaces all memory of beginning, all fear of an end.

Mme. De Stael

"What else happened that summer?" Karen asked.

I recalled that Holly had her baby that summer. By then, Holly was in her thirties. I realized that at fourteen, I was old enough to conceive my own child.

Since the baby was the offspring of my real father and my stepmother, she was my half sister. Manny did his own calculations and determined that my new sibling was not his daughter. Although the infant was indeed the real daughter of my real father, he pretended she just was not real. The baby had one too many chromosomes, which caused the condition known as Down's syndrome. I was prepared with little knowledge of mental retardation, and was even less prepared for the defects of my family. I'd witnessed the devastating dysfunction of my family and it didn't stop with the birth of my half-sister, Heather.

Heather lay for hours with her tiny, weak body barely mobile. She was born with multiple needs and required constant care. I picked up the feeble infant and carried her to the rocking chair in the den. As the rocking lulled her to sleep, I studied her features. Her straight, dark hair stood up in a thin tuft, like a doll. Her paper white skin was so lucent that a faintly pulsating maze of blue veins was visible. Her blue-green eyes were fringed with lush lashes. Although Heather's eyes were slanted with the characteristic shape of Down's syndrome, her eyes were my eyes, an undeniable resemblance that overwhelmed me with a sacred connection to my sister.

I traced the jagged, vertical crease on the infant's torso. She had a scar as wide as her rib cage, where a plastic tube had been inserted to replace her ruptured esophagus. This was not premature infant conditions; these were injuries incurred in the womb when Holly had been beaten. Even with a fresh sprinkling of baby powder on her bottom, Heather smelled like the curdled milk that constantly spurted out of her mouth. Her tongue hung out of her mouth, another Down's syndrome characteristic. Her chin was covered with blisters where the flaccid tongue rested, and her miniature lips were chapped. I brushed her silky hair with a soft baby brush and combed a strand over the spot where she laid long enough to be bald. The infant with mental retardation and physical handicaps was the most beautiful baby I had ever seen.

Holly had no friends to discuss the tragic birth with, so she told me all about it. "I had pneumonia when the baby was born. I could barely breathe. But I knew something was wrong immediately after birth."

"How did you know?"

"The baby did not cry after it was slapped."

"The doctors slapped the baby?"

"Yeah, to see if the baby was alive. The baby was blue because the umbilical cord was tied around her neck. It's a miracle she's alive."

"It is?"

"Yeah, the doctors said that she was in critical condition and her chances for survival were slim. I wanted to hold her, especially if she was about to die, but the nurses whisked her away. According to the doctors, I was too sick, the baby was too sick, and it was best to just watch and wait. Later, the doctors told me that the baby had Down's syndrome, and that she was deaf. They tried to keep the baby from me. Can you imagine?"

"No."

"The doctors insisted that if the baby survived, she would have a better chance in an institution. Can you believe that?"

"No."

"The administrators brought me papers to sign the baby over to state guardians. I had to see my baby. When they finally let me hold her, I knew I had to keep her."

There were no cards of congratulations for Holly and no birth announcements for the baby. There were a few visits from relatives, who said, "Oh, what a shame!" The retarded baby was an embarrassment to Manny's own brothers and sisters.

Instead of a baby book to mark first sounds or smiles, Holly kept a journal to note the time and dose of pediatric antibiotics and medications. The baby's growth was measured in ounces of body weight and the amount of formula consumed. Many nights Holly bundled her baby and hurried to the hospital while Heather was choking on formula or gasping for air.

Holly's heart was torn, and Manny's attitude was enough to break her heart in two. He denied his participation in creating a "freak of nature," as he called his daughter. Holly tried to reason with him and to explain Down's syndrome in the only way she knew. The condition was not an issue of male ego; it was a matter of genetic code. No one was to blame. He refused to accept any responsibility. "I want no part of that imbecile!" His vehement denial of his own infant made me wonder: If it were so easy for him to despise this innocent baby, it would not be so hard for him to hate me.

One morning, when I went to pick up the infant, I noticed she was sleeping under a pillow with her head rolled to one side. Heather gasped as I lifted her. "Holly, how did a pillow get on Heather's head?"

"The pillow did not land on her by accident. I bet it was Manny, that ludicrous bastard."

While Heather was crying with urgency, my father was shouting: "Shut that idiot up! If you don't shut it up, I will! Shut it up! What are you? An unfit mother, that's what!"

Afraid of Manny's fit, Holly and I decided to take the baby for a ride in the car. It seemed safer to drive around with a sick baby than to stay in the house while he blew off steam. He threatened us: "Don't bother to come back with it, or else!"

As Holly drove around the neighborhood, I entertained Heather with the rabbit's foot that had broken from Holly's key chain. "Rub the rabbit's foot for good luck," Holly had said. Between puffs on cigarettes, Holly rambled, "I should have listened to the doctors. I could still give her up for adoption. I could get her in a state institution. That man is deplorable. He is the one who belongs in an institution. We would be better off without him. How could he put us out in the cold like this?"

Holly included me in her family circle as if she and I had a private connection. After driving around the block a couple of times, Holly parked in front of the house.

"We're on empty," she said. "I forgot my purse."

In the dark, we were deciding the lesser of two evils.

"Should we go inside?" I spoke in the direction of the red glowing ember of her cigarette.

"And face the wrath of that batty bastard?"

Out of the darkness, the night blazed with a single beam from the road ahead. I linked the light to a line from *Star Trek*: "Beam me up, Scottie." The transporter beam, a hazy blue and white streak coming from afar, carried civilians without a cumbersome vehicle. No matter how many trips the beam made to never-never land, it never ran out of gas or got a flat tire. The beam in front of Holly, Heather, and I headed into our eyes with a blinding vengeance. All around us were the roars of a motorcycle engine revved to unreasonable levels.

"It's him," Holly whispered. "What does he think he's doing?"

My father was driving his motorcycle, dead on, into the VW that carried his wife and daughters. "Don't look into the light," Holly yelled. "Duck."

Duck? I had an infant in my lap. I looked into the light that moved forward, toward us, until the light engulfed us. I closed my eyes immediately after my father swerved, only to hear his cycle rumble away.

We returned to the house with a hungry infant. Later that evening, as the baby slept, the sound of my father's motorcycle idling at the garage signaled his return. For the rest of the night, the house was unusually quiet. Holly napped on the couch while I watched television in the den. In an effort to protect myself from my father, I heightened my alert to his every move. For a while, he read the newspaper, drank wine, and smoked a pipe. Later, he sat silent, except for drumming his fingers on the arm of the chair as he preoccupied himself with some mental aberration. Who could comprehend the vast mystery of his warped mind?

The next day, I helped Holly wash diapers and dishes.

"Honey, you are such an angel. I'm glad you're here," Holly said.

I wished I wasn't here, here on earth. I wished I were an angel, invisible on earth but available for good deeds from heaven. In the spirit of the moment, I walked a couple of blocks to the corner store and bought a bottle of aspirin. My head hurt so bad that I took the entire bottle. I exchanged the pounding headache for a trembling body, burning stomach, and the runs. Someday I'd get something stronger than aspirin and rise to the calling of a real angel.

When I was alone with my father, driving back to the Poconos, I clung to the door on the passenger side. How far was it from the door to a ditch? Could I jump?

"Why are you sitting so close to the door? Are you afraid? How could you be afraid of your own father? Your mother turned you against me, didn't she? She makes me out to be some kind of ogre. I will never forgive her. And you! You are the reason I can't get back with her! If it were not for you, I would still be married to her. You are too close to your mother, and it's not natural. One of these days, you will have to untie those apron strings. You don't have to tell your mother every little thing. You talk too much, don't you?"

"I don't tell my mother everything!"

"Don't get defensive with me. I am your father. And move over, I'm not going to hurt you."

Karen was leaning forward, asking, "How were you feeling about your father at this time?"

"Isn't it obvious?"

"Yes, but I would like you to state your feelings."

"I hated him. Are you going to ask how I felt about feeling hatred? I felt like compost, with waste piled on bile, the stench rising from my rotten self."

"Even if you had acknowledged the hatred, you could not express it toward him, so you took it out on yourself. What else was going on at that time?"

In the Poconos, I was going to the public high school for ninth grade. Although it was academically easier than the parochial school, the inability to concentrate made it harder to get good grades. On a Monday, a slide of Leonardo DaVinci's Mona Lisa was flashed on the screen in art history; by Friday I could not remember the artist and his work for a test. My mind was like a pressure cooker. If I opened the lid to sneak a peek at short-term memory, long-term memory might escape like scalding steam.

Although I hated my father, a nagging obligation toward him made me agree to visit at Thanksgiving. Actually, I was interested in seeing Holly and Heather, and I was grateful for an uneventful drive to New Jersey. Once there, though, the holiday events were less than festive.

The baby lay in her crib with nothing to give or receive except love. But the battles to save Heather from her own endless handicaps and from the merciless hands of our father never ceased.

"Manny took the test," Holly said.

"What test?" Evidently, I had missed out on some vital information concerning my father.

"He took a paternity test to prove he isn't Holly's father. But the blood types match. He's the father. Of course, I knew that all along. Look at this book!" Holly was showing me an American Sign Language manual. "Heather will never learn to communicate, unless we learn to sign," Holly said. "Manny said he would not allow me to flap my fingers around like a freak."

"I'll learn to sign," I offered.

"That's sweet, honey, .but what's the use? The doctors said that Heather is barely educable."

While I was reading the book, my father was watching television, cracking his knuckles. Holly was heating a bottle of formula. Normally, silence was sweet, golden honey to my ears, but the quiet in my father's home was more like the deafening buzz of swarming bees. Suddenly, the sting of insanity penetrated the house.

Holly was shrieking, "She's gone! Where is my baby?" Heather was indeed missing, along with her crib. "Who stole the baby? Someone kidnapped my baby!"

Holly questioned Manny, "What did you do with Heather?"

"What makes you think I did anything to it?"

Holly bolted up the stairs, checking the closets. I grabbed my coat and dashed for the garage. On the way out the back door, I found my baby sister unclothed and uncovered in her crib on the porch. Heather shuddered as I swaddled her in pink thermal blankets; her pale white face had a blue tinge. The large, round thermometer on the porch pointed to thirty degrees. There was no telling how long she had been exposed to freezing temperatures. Did my father put the crib on the cold porch planning for the baby to freeze to death?

Holly's face was contorted with flared nostrils and lips curled in unrestrained anger. "Murderer, murderer, murder, premeditated even, how could you? I will never forgive you, you diabolical bastard. You'll live to regret this. I pray you burn in hell, you pervert."

"Just bury the dimwit in the back yard, dead or alive, who gives a shit, that retard is more trouble than it's worth. I can't get a decent meal out of you because of that goddamned idiot."

Holly was grabbing her keys.

"Where do you think you are going?" Manny growled.

"I'm taking my child to the emergency room."

"Oh no you are not! I won't let you air dirty laundry!"

Holly tried to pick up the phone, but Manny pulled it out of her hand. She picked up a pot and hurled it through the kitchen door, onto the back porch, at the thermometer, breaking its glass cover.

"You will rot in jail for trying to kill your own daughter, you despicable bastard."

"Either it goes, or I go!"

While holding Heather, I whispered, "Heather, Heather, Heather." She was two years old and would never hear her own name. But what if? What if she heard him? What if she thought her name were idiot, dimwit, and retard? She could not walk. She could not even crawl. She could not be toilet trained. But what if? What if she grew up to find out that her own father tried to kill her? How could she grow? The plastic esophagus failed to provide a pathway for nutrition. More food came up than went down. If she grew, she would need surgeries to increase the size of the esophagus. Her heart and lungs remained weak, and the risk of death was greater with each dose of anesthesia.

Holly was battle-weary and surrendered on the day after Thanksgiving. "Heather will never receive the kind of care only I can give her. I am her mother. If I put her in the institution, she would be a ward of the state. The costs for her operations would be covered. But I'll have to sign over parental rights. Manny said he'd gladly sign her over. Will you go with me to the institution, honey? I could use some moral support."

"Sure, Holly."

Heather was an adorable angel as I cradled her in the car. What did she do to deserve this? The brick building looked well-tended, with sprawling lawns inside stonewalls that went around for city blocks. Holly carried her baby, and I carried her bag to the admission sign. An odor of disinfectant mingled with dirty diapers, so sour it made my eyes water.

An officious nurse greeted Holly with a handshake and cooed inattentively toward Heather. We walked past children in cribs and wheelchairs, many in the crowded hall. A baby banged his head on metal crib rails. A child sat with his neck hanging to one side, resting it on his shoulder. I wanted to ask: What happened to him? What about her? There were too many to inquire about.

"What about my baby?" Holly asked.

"She'll be all right," the nurse assured Holly.

This was all right? Holly sobbed as the nurse took Heather and placed a plastic bracelet on the child's wrist. "Goodbye. I'll visit often." Of course, Holly couldn't because Manny wouldn't let her. My father won the war he'd started over his own defenseless little daughter.

When we arrived back at the house, Manny had a Beagle puppy. He had purchased all that a puppy would need to be healthy and happy. The puppy wagged its curled tail as his long ears dipped into the ceramic dog dish. How could I resist the wriggling black-and-tan dog? As I neared the puppy, it rolled over, exposing a fat pink belly with soft downy fur. When I picked it up, I reveled in the sweet puppy smell and the floppy ears that felt like velvet. The dog made peeping noises that sounded more like a pigeon than a pup.

"You like the puppy, don't you?" my father said. "What do you want to name him?"

Was that all he was worried about? Why bother to name a dog that would be discarded like spoiled meat? Usually, I loved dogs, but this puppy was no substitute for the lost love of a baby.

Karen stopped the story to say, “Love is never lost. Heather was here long enough to teach the lesson of unconditional love. The exchange of love experienced with her will never leave your heart.”

I would wonder what kind of care Heather had: Was she kept warm, was she well fed, were her wounds tended and mended? I would wonder how long she lived, if she made it to ten or thirteen. I would wonder what, if any, quality of life she had. I would always wonder what profound knowledge she had about the meaning of life. Why had she grappled so with a life not worth living?

Pseudo-Psychiatry and the Paranormal

The absurd duty, too often inculcated, of obeying a parent only on account of his being a parent, shackles the mind and prepares it for slavish submission to any power but reason.

Mary Wollstonecraft

Back in the Poconos, my bedroom was missing. "We made your old room into a guest room," my mother explained.

What guests? We never had sleep-over company.

"Since Eric went to college," she explained, "we thought you'd like to have his room in the front of the house. We fixed it up for you."

My new room was glowing with shades of red, yellow, and orange. A canvas-covered director's chair, a metal lamp, and a wicker wastebasket had vivid, warm hues. On the desk was a new Webster dictionary and Roget's thesaurus.

"Look, Lynnie, Dad built these bookshelves for you," my mother pointed out. The shelves displayed books by Kahlil Gibran: *Sand and Foam*, *Tears and Laughter*. I had read Gibran's *The Prophet* several times; now I had a whole set of his books.

"The curtains were custom-made," Mom explained. "See how the bedspread coordinates?" The room showed the bold geometric shapes and mod styles of the sixties.

"Dad and I got this Chagall print from a sidewalk sale in New York City. Do you like it?" It was a portrait of a flower child, with blonde hair, naturally.

The room was supposed to be a gift, but I forgot to say thank you. Instead, I asked, "Is that Eric's old bed?" The bed was positioned exactly as it was when he had placed me on it.

"No, Lynnie, we switched Eric's old bed with Rusty's newer mattress, so you have the one Rusty used to sleep on, and now Rusty has Eric's. Why do you ask?"

"No reason."

They had made these decisions for me and they'd assumed I'd go along. I felt pushed out of one room and forced into another. Eventually, the new room became a sanctuary of solitude. I withdrew into that room to listen to music and read poetry. The darker the subject, the more I delved into it, dropping Emily Dickinson to devour Edgar Allen Poe. Quotes, lyrics, definitions, and poetry conveyed more meaning to me than any verbal discourse.

Meanwhile, my chilly disposition dropped even colder until the deep freeze settled in like a long hard winter in the mountains. Apparently trying to transform her teenage daughter into a sunny disposition, my mother took me shopping at the best department store in Allentown.

"School is starting soon," Mom said. "You'll be a sophomore. I don't know what girls your age wear these days, but I know what looks good on you. Why don't you try on this jacket?"

"No, it's not me."

"Lower your voice. It carries. The clerks can hear you. What style do you think you are, anyway?"

"I like how Peggy Lipton dresses in *The Mod Squad*. She wears jeans and boots. And vests."

"That sounds like a hippie. That's not you. You're tailored. Just try on the jacket, will you?"

I tossed the plaid jacket over my shoulders.

"Lynn, let me see. Come on, put your arms in the sleeves so we can see how it fits. Try on the skirt while you're at it."

The hem of the green wool skirt touched above my knees.

"It looks too short. What size is it?" She looked at the tag: "9, junior. It looks tight. Walk down the aisle."

I walked barefoot on the industrial carpet.

"Your thighs jiggle," my mother said. "You can't wear that skirt. It's cut to fit a thinner body type than yours. The jacket fits fine. Look in the mirror."

The reflection was too close, distorting the image beyond recognition. Claustrophobia came down on me like cracked carnival glass. "I hate it. Let me out of here."

As we were walking through the store, Mom said, "Why do you have your arms across your chest like that? Everyone is looking at you. Are you sick?"

"No, I'm just cold."

"We should have bought that jacket."

On our way through the mall, we passed a pet store. I wished I had something soft to snuggle with, someone without the authority to argue.

"Mom? Can I ask you something?"

"Of course, what is it?"

"Please don't think it's stupid, okay, Mom?"

"Lynn, you know I don't like it when you beat around the bush."

"Well, I was wondering if we could get a puppy?"

"If you think that might make you happy. Sure, why not? We haven't had a dog around the house in a long time. Rusty would love it. We just have to ask Dad, and convince him that you'll be responsible."

Soon after, we got a twelve-week-old shepherd mix from the pound, and we named her Lulu. Her caramel-colored coat was short and coarse, and she smelled like graham crackers. Her pointed ears stood up like antenna, turning toward sound. The delight of having a dog offset the discomfort of housebreaking. An early winter arrived in the Poconos when the first snow of the season fell in October. Before school, after school, I stood in snow up to my knees. I trained that dog to sit and come; I brushed her in the garage and let her sleep on my bed. My mother was alarmed when the dog got loose one afternoon. But the dog returned soon after, sitting by the back door, proudly showing Mom the rabbit she had captured. Mom said she wasn't about to make rabbit stew for dinner. The dog was a steady companion for me, and the rest of the family liked her, too.

Meanwhile, my mother's personality became as unpredictable as the weather, shifting from a temperate disposition to a temper tantrum. Even a Doppler radar could not have warned of the late autumn tornados of temperament that drove her to depression.

The symptoms were apparent at dinnertime when she prepared packaged Hamburger Helper rather than broiled flank steak au jus with mashed potatoes and early peas. As we ate, she scolded, "Stop scraping your plates with the fork! My nerves are shot!" She often left the table during dinner to go back to bed. Some days my mother was still in bed when I got home from school. The drapes were drawn as she nursed her migraines and melancholy. "You kids will have to fend for yourself," she would say. Without Mom to glue us together with her mealtime rituals, we were only parts separate from the whole.

If Dad ate a sandwich with us, he would update us on Mom's condition. "Your mother is at wit's end."

"Will she get well soon?" Rusty asked.

"Does she need medicine?" I asked.

"What she needs," Dad said, "is a little appreciation. You kids take her for granted."

I *did* appreciate my mother, but I guess it was too little too late.

After school one afternoon, my mother left her room long enough to show me how to operate the washer and dryer. "Use this setting for towels and this dial for permanent press. Dad likes his shirts ironed. Don't forget to press the collar."

"Mom, how long should the sheets tumble dry?"

"This is not a good day. I'm croaking. I can't think straight. I can't take any more questions. Wait until Dad gets home."

Waiting for my stepfather to come home was like waiting to pass inspection with the drill sergeant.

"Why are the sheets still wet?" he asked. "You can't make a bed with damp sheets."

"I tried to ask Mom what setting I should use to dry them."

"Didn't I tell you not to upset your mother? Dry the damned sheets until they are dry! Just don't keep the dryer running longer than necessary. You should be grateful that you are living in a house with built-in appliances. Your ancestors didn't have a pot to piss in."

My thoughts were tumbling like the sheets in the dryer. I *was* grateful for the conveniences, I really was. But I was operating under less than ideal conditions, with a tyrant for a stepfather and an emotionally infirmed mother.

I showered my mother with appreciation for months. Her responses to "Thanks, Mom" were unconvincing. She'd smile small, and then sigh big. She went to see a psychiatrist to find a cure for whatever was ailing her. She had seen a psychiatrist before, between her first and second husbands, when I was five years old. We were living at Tanglewood Falls, and she would drive two-and-a-half hours each way to see a doctor in Philadelphia. Sometimes I went with her. I would wait with the receptionist while my mother went behind closed doors. Looking out the window from the 17th floor, I would examine the shingled roofs of lower buildings. After my mother's examination, the receptionist would say, "Your daughter is such a good girl." On the way home, we would stop at a diner for patty-melts and banana splits. "Thanks for being such a good girl," Mom would say. Now, about nine years later, during another depression and after sessions with another psychiatrist, my mother voluntarily committed herself to a psychiatric hospital.

While my mother was at the hospital, Frank brought food home from the kitchen at Tanglewood Falls. Sometimes we went to my grandmother's for dinner. As I chewed on my bottom lip, I lost interest in their conversation about whether or not it was time to close the golf course and open the ski lodge for the winter. I was losing interest in dinner itself. My grandmother dished out a serving of guilt. "In my day, during the Great Depression, food was hard to come by. I worked my fingers to the bone to put food on the table. You should count your blessings!"

After dinner, we watched *The Mod Squad.* Why wasn't I Peggy Lipton, with long blonde hair, doe eyes, a wide smile, and small breasts? I no longer wanted to be *like* somebody, I wanted to *be* somebody, anybody else.

Rusty asked, "When's Mom coming home?"

"When the psychiatrist says she's ready," Dad responded.

"What's a psychiatrist?"

"A doctor who heals the mind."

That blew my mind! Maybe I could get a psychiatrist. Perhaps I could *be* a psychiatrist. Then I could figure out my whole flipped-out family.

Before school, I made lumpy cream-of-wheat cereal for Rusty. After school, I made powdery macaroni and cheese, which he ate without complaint. Did he have to be so good?

"When is Mom coming home?" he asked again.

"Never." I could have comforted him, but I was too confused. We could have gotten close. But that would have taken some clear communication, something we were not accustomed to.

Television and radio included news reports of combat during the Vietnam War. High school assignments were essays about war and peace and the demilitarized zone. Conversations and controversy pertained to induction into the army, the draft, and ROTC. One classmate's brother was a conscientious objector and another left the country for asylum in Canada. Eric got a college deferment, which the whole family was grateful for.

The emotional tug-of-war with my real father never ceased. When he called to see if I wanted to visit him and Holly, I thought I had nothing better to do but to oblige. My stepfather said he could spare me for the weekend and would have Grandma take care of Rusty.

My father picked me up for the weekend, late as usual. He said it was due to heavy traffic and heavy rain. I gave him the benefit of the doubt because Route 80 was not finished and we traveled on the truck route. He must have shaved in a hurry because shreds of toilet paper were blotted with blood, sticking to his face like red and white polka dots. I tried to gauge his mood but it was like reading a crumpled map upside down in the dark. He immediately badgered me about my mother. "What's up with your mother? She can't bother to come to the phone when I call?"

"Mom is in the hospital."

"Your mother is some kind of hypochondriac. She would complain of some ailment if she lived in a bubble. I can't even see straight with this headache. It's killing me."

Although reading in a moving car gave me a headache, I buried my head in "Oliver Twist" to avoid conversation.

My father glanced over, "Who's Dickens?"

"He was an English writer."

"An English writer? Did Frank tell you to read that? Shouldn't you be reading something more suitable for a girl your age?"

"It's for school." Did he think I was incapable of choosing reading material?

His eyes darted from the rear-view mirror to the side mirror. What was he thinking? He was hot under the collar that morning, simmering over something, and I wanted to tell him to chill out. Suddenly, a few feet in front of us, a truck jack-knifed and the forty-foot trailer skidded, about to broadside our car. What if we died together in an accident on the slick New Jersey highway? I would not have minded, but how would my mother find out? My father managed to turn the wheel and missed the truck by inches. I turned to see the truck slide across four lanes in an L shape. My father pulled a cigarette from his pocket and tapped the cigarette on the dashboard. "I almost had a heart attack," he said.

My heart was fluttering like a bird with broken wings, halting my breath in mid-flight. Breath. Hiccup. Breath. Hiccup.

Normally, my father was exhilarated by imminent danger, but his pounding headache and heart must have gotten the best of him. He drove on as if nothing had happened. We might have made a mysterious connection, experiencing parallel fears in the face of real peril, but we did not express it.

"Do you mind?" he asked. "Stop that hiccupping!"

"I can't!"

"Hold your breath."

I inhaled the air that reeked of stale beer and cigarettes.

"Longer!" he ordered. "Hold it longer."

When we arrived at his house, it looked like a combat zone. On the average day, the house stood in various states of disarray, with unfinished projects littering every room. My father was unable to concentrate and complete any task, so several of his projects were pending, including the installation of a half-bath near the porch. The one working bathroom was littered with newspapers and the tub was ringed with scum. The washing machine had been overloaded and it had stopped in mid-cycle; the wet clothes were saturated with the smell of mold. My father said he was in the process of fixing it, but needed a part. A part? It looked like it needed an overhaul, not just the machine, but also the whole house.

Holly could barely speak without wheezing, her chest congested with bronchitis. Her hoarse voice greeted me with a weak and worn out, "Hi, Honey, how are you?" Usually, her hair was freshly dyed, but now the dark roots contrasted with the bleached blonde ends. She was sitting at the kitchen table with a pot of coffee and a framed picture. The picture was of a handsome young man wearing a white uniform and a hat.

"Who is in the picture?" I asked.

"My brother. He was a Green Beret."

"Holly, I never knew you had a brother."

"We were close as kids, but I haven't seen him in a while. I did not realize how much a part of me he was until now, now that he's gone."

"Gone?"

Holly was lighting one cigarette with another, and told me what had happened in stages. Earlier that month, two military officers came to the door and informed Holly that her younger brother had died in Vietnam. He was already buried because they were not readily able to locate his next-of-kin. Holly's mother was dead. Holly never knew who her father was or if her brother had the same father.

My father showed no support while Holly grieved. We were accustomed to his callous character, but that he was so cruel was beyond comprehension. He expected me to help while she shuffled around in her slippers. According to him, my value was measured in housework.

Of course, a weekend was not complete without some outburst from my father. When Holly carried the picture upstairs to their bedroom, my father threw a fit: "I'm sick and tired of your sulking. Sick, sick, sick of it. Snap out of it!" Then I heard glass shatter, and a succession of slamming doors as he left the house.

"He threw my brother's picture against the wall," Holly cried. She mentioned something about the Veterans cemetery in Jersey City. She threw on jeans and a T-shirt and jumped into her car.

Alone in my father's house, I went around to the porch door, the side door, the front door, and locked them tight. I made another round to make sure they were locked. I turned on every light, cleared the pizza boxes from the rocking chair in the den, and turned on the television, watching for shadows. What if my father came back before Holly? It would be worse to be alone with him in his house.

Hours later, the headlights of Holly's VW lit the driveway. She was breathless as she came into the house. She whispered, "Is he here?" I shook my head no.

"Good, let me tell you the most amazing story."

Holly had known which cemetery to go to, but once there, she saw rows and rows of identical white headstones. She had parked outside the gates to rest, wondering how she would ever find her brother's grave, and she fell asleep. When she awoke, she got out of her car and, as if under a spell, she was being led directly to her brother's grave. His tombstone was a few feet from her car, not visible from the road, but made visible to her. Holly left the cemetery feeling she had made peace with her brother.

Holly's experience impressed me enough to consider the existence of paranormal powers. When the weekend was drawing to a close, Holly felt good enough to drive me back to the Poconos.

Karen broke the spell of my stepmother's story. "Lynn, let's get back to you. After experiencing so much turmoil that year, how did you express all the emotions?"

I repressed feelings or was it that they were stuffed deep down inside? I substituted the need for emotional nourishment with food and went on a feeding frenzy. While watching TV, I ate ice cream. While doing homework, I ate cookies. While standing in the kitchen, I ate chocolate chip ice cream with chocolate chip cookies. Before school, I ate the single serving boxed breakfast cereals two or three at time, with extra sugar. After school, I ate frozen chocolate éclairs, frozen. I squirted whipped cream directly into my mouth, letting the sweet cream tease my tongue with solace. But I was never fully satisfied. After inhaling the whole enchilada, my finger would slide down my throat, forcing vomit until I was fully disgusted.

I watched the needle on the scale stall at higher numbers: 120, 130, 140. It was an out-of-body experience to see 156 pounds. Dragging myself around like the carcass of a dead cow, I wallowed in self-pity and waddled to the bus stop. I hid my obsession with food by buying snacks at school and hiding Twinkies in my pockets. I hid my body by wearing brown baggy pants with a loose flannel shirt.

"You look like a dyke," my stepfather said. "Don't you have something more feminine? Didn't your mother take you shopping for school clothes? She knows how to dress like a lady."

I didn't know what looking like a dyke meant, but his remark was obviously derogatory. So I decided to hide my body in a raincoat, wearing it like body armor indoors and out.

"Did you wear that coat in school all day?" my stepfather asked. "It's awful warm for a coat."

Rusty joined the conversation. "Yeah, the weatherman says it's just the January thaw."

Still the smart-ass sister, I asked, "Who asked you?"

"Your mother wants to see her family on her weekend pass," my stepfather said.

I thought he meant himself and Rusty.

"We'll all drive to the city and have dinner with your mother," he suggested.

Rusty's face lit up. "Really? I get to see Mom?" He leapt onto the couch to jump for joy.

"Get off the couch," Dad said.

"I don't think I should go," I said.

"Of course, you'll go."

"No, I better stay home. Somebody has to feed Lulu."

"I'll have an employee from Tanglewood Falls come by and care for the dog," Dad said. "Why won't you see your mother?"

"It's not that."

"What is it then?"

"I don't know." I did not want my mother to see me because she would be ashamed of me.

My stepfather raised his voice to a decibel I usually responded to. "What is it going to take to get through to you?" Then he lowered his voice, trying reverse psychology. "Your mother will be hurt if you don't go. She would love to see you."

As I was getting ready to see my mother, I made myself look into a mirror. My complexion looked like the bumpy terrain of a planet on *Star Trek*. After squeezing blackheads with my fingernails until they exploded, my face became blotched and bloated. To cover the craters and volcanoes, I borrowed my mother's make-up. As I tried on blouse after blouse, buttons popped open across my bust. A navy blue jumper stretched over my hippopotamus hips but the winter wool bunched at the waist. So, sucking in my stomach, I tugged at a girdle until I almost resembled a human female form. How was my mother going to recognize me?

Dad drove two-and-a-half hours to Philadelphia so we could have dinner with my mother in a restaurant on the Boulevard. Mom recognized me right away, commenting on what she called my beautiful eyes. Who was she seeing that I never saw? When Dad brought Mom back to her room, Rusty and I waited in a huge lobby with a grand staircase. Up those stairs, away from public domain, only psychiatrists were privy to the pieces of nervous breakdowns. As soon as we got home, as soon as Dad went to work, as soon as Rusty went to bed, I raided the refrigerator.

When my mother came home from the hospital, it seemed that she had experienced some kind of breakthrough. Spring arrived with her, the forsythia breaking through the thawing ground. Mom inhaled the aroma of apple blossoms. "Ah, it's so good to be home with my family."

I sensed I could spoil it rotten for her.

"I made so many friends in that place," Mom told me. "They all came to me to tell me their problems. I had them all solved. Sometimes they told me that I did them more good than the doctors."

Later, she confronted me with a creamy make-up compact that had a concave center. "How dare you use my make-up! I use this make-up only for special occasions. It's expensive."

Later, as I was tracing the beautiful faces in *Glamour*, Mom said, "Sweetheart, if you want make-up, we'll go to the drugstore."

"I couldn't care less if my face falls off!"

"You are behaving like a neurotic brat!"

My mother's psychiatrist, Charlie, was coming from Philadelphia to the Poconos to visit. My mother's crisis must have been so exclusive that she required house calls. Perhaps my mother's brain was as fragile as a light bulb, and required a continuous current of psychiatric power to keep from breaking down.

"Help your mother get the house in order," my stepfather ordered. "You'll have to share the bathroom with the guest. When you clean the tub, the faucet should be so shiny that you can see your face in it. This house is a reflection of the family. And don't forget to dust and vacuum the guest room."

My stepfather inspected the tub: "What kind of half-assed way is that to clean a tub? The porcelain should sparkle. Now do it again until you get it right."

I resented his dictatorship disguised as parenthood. The glass pitcher I was using to rinse the tub slipped from my hands. If I used the sharp pieces to slit my left wrist, I'd probably have to use my right hand afterwards to clean up.

"Why is the shrink coming here?" Rusty asked.

"She's a psychiatrist and she's taking a vacation," Mom said.

"Why can't she go to Florida, like everybody else?" I suggested.

"I want you kids to act right."

"How old is she?"

"She's in her thirties."

"Is she married?"

"No, she's too busy with her career. What makes you think this is any of your business?"

When her guest arrived, my mother's ability to change from a helpless patient to a capable hostess astounded me. She was serving a pitcher of iced-tea and a plate of lemon cookies, on the good dishes, on a silver platter. Charlie reminded me of a large bulldog, with a squashed face and a squared frame. Her physique was mannish, especially as compared to my mother's feminine figure. What did that woman want with my mother?

"Lynn, you can come sit with us if you want."

"Thanks, Mom, but I have to walk Lulu."

At night, I heard my mother, her husband, and her psychiatrist talking. Their voices carried to my room in hushed tones, like when one parishioner in a pew can hear another in the confessional.

The next morning, my mother knocked on my door before Lulu had a chance to lick me awake.

"Lynnie, can I come in? I want to talk to you."

"Sure."

"How are you, sweetheart?"

"Fine, Mom, just fine."

"I've noticed you've been stand-offish with my friend Charlie. Do you resent her for some reason?"

"I don't resent doctor so-and-so."

"Are you jealous of the time she and I spend together?"

"No."

"What are you feeling?"

"I don't know, Mom."

"I don't think you are in touch with your feelings. We'll have to work on that."

While eating an English muffin, I flipped through the books by Ruth Montgomery and Edgar Cayce that were on the coffee table. The chapters had titles about life after death. "Whose books are these?" I asked my mother.

"They belong to Charlie. She's teaching us about reincarnation. It's all about karma, which means that what goes around comes around. For instance, if you mistreated someone in an earlier life, you have to reincarnate to work on compassion in this life. Sometimes you reconnect with the same soul time after time until you learn the lesson. It turns out that Dad is able to go into a trance and determine karma. Want to hear about Dad's reading of your past life? You and Dad were seers in ancient Egypt. Although you were both able to predict the future and advise the pharaohs, you were rivals. When an advisement went wrong, there was a war in the land, and the rivalry worsened. You brought that rivalry into this life. You have to resolve the rivalry before your soul can be redeemed."

How did this explain all the other rivalries Frank had? Why couldn't he use his third eye to see what chance occurrences in this era changed me from who I had been before to who I was now? Since when were my parents the gatekeepers for my soul? Perhaps by concentrating on past lives, my parents could avoid and abdicate accountability for current ills. That left me not only responsible for all the problems in this life, but also for solving past life problems.

Shortly after her psychiatrist went home, my mother took me to see Dr. DeLuca, the family physician. This same doctor had treated the concussion, the bronchitis, and the strep throat. Maybe, my mother suggested, I had a tapeworm, and that's the reason I couldn't lose weight. The doctor diagnosed borderline low thyroid and detected the heart murmur again. "Best not prescribe diet pills," he said as he handed me a sensible but boring eating plan.

My mother persuaded me to attend Weight Watchers meetings. Women with flab that waggled under their chins talked about menus and measurements. In common was a cycle of obsessing about food each day and resolving to start a diet the next day. My notion of a diet was a magic potion that instantly dissolved the blubber.

Summer vacation with my mother was no picnic. The scale became a bone of contention between us as she forced me to weigh myself in front of her. She calculated the wins or losses from week to week: one pound gone, two pounds gained. She fixed small portions of lean meat and cottage cheese, with applesauce and gelatin for dessert. She delved into my diet rather than to deal with what was really eating me. How was I supposed to get through an entire summer without cream-filled coconut cakes? An invitation from Holly to visit in New Jersey for the month of August seemed just what the doctor ordered.

When my father saw me, he let me have it. He forced me to listen as he shaved in his boxer shorts, stretching one cheek, sliding the razor down his neck. "What is the matter with you? How could you let yourself go like that?" Shaving cream foamed around his mouth. He swished the razor in the water in the sink.

"I don't know." Didn't he know that fat was insulation that kept the cold wind from blowing cruel realities through my body?

"How could your mother let this happen? What kind of unfit mother is she?"

"I don't know."

"Bite your tongue. I don't know, I don't know, that's all you ever have to say. You sound like a broken record. Do I have to take matters into my own hands?" He left his whiskers in the sink.

He arranged an appointment with his doctor friend in Lyndhurst and Holly took me for a physical. After a cursory exam, the doctor prescribed diet pills called "Dexedrine." On the way to the pharmacy, Holly said, "I had a friend who drank nothing but coffee all day and smoked. She weighed 85 pounds. I guess cigarettes dull the appetite." For an afternoon snack, Holly and I smoked Virginia Slims over cups of black coffee.

The vial had "dextroamphetamine" printed on the label. In no time, I had less appetite and more energy to use to clean my father's house. After polishing the chrome on the dinette set, I scrubbed the crud off the vinyl seats, and stuffed the tufts of batting back into the cushions. I threw out ancient jars of jelly, moldy cheese, and rotten fruit. As I was cleaning the top of the refrigerator, I opened the cabinet above and found pistols, pills, and pot. I nearly fell off the stepladder.

Holly surveyed her sparkling clean house and said, "Honey, you are worth your weight in gold." That would be a lot of gold.

At the end of August, my father drove me back to the Poconos, expressing his pride in himself. "I'm proud of my girl. See how I know what's best?"

My mother was aghast at the amount of weight I had lost. "How did you lose so much weight so quickly?"

"Holly took me to my father's doctor friend in Lyndhurst. He told me about an all-protein diet." I neglected to mention that I had acquired a smoking habit, along with a tall container of diet pills.

"He took you to that quack? Does your father think I'm too stupid to know what is best for my daughter? You could get ketosis from that protein diet. Let's see if we can find a more balanced diet." She did not mind counting calories and cooking low-fat meals. Nourishing her children was her way of meeting needs. My mother had told me of how she had not been nurtured, had even been neglected by her mother while her mother ran a restaurant. My mother found the nurturing she needed in food.

It was far easier to focus on food than on feelings. If there's a feeling of discomfort, it's followed by food. If there's an empty conversation, it's filled with talk about food. While we were eating lunch, my mother talked about dinner. As she prepared the dinner, she examined ingredients like the health inspector at the hotel kitchen. Often, she consulted with Frank, "Come smell this steak! If it's not fresh, we could get parasites." Sophia was perfectly capable of determining the quality of groceries. It seemed she drew her husband in to collaborate on her decisions and enable her dependence. "Frank, does the well water taste contaminated? Is this pork loin cooked? If it's not cooked enough, we could get trichinosis. Does that can of tuna have a dent? Don't open it. We could get botulism." He was a mechanic or a manager; when did he become an expert on food or a diffuser for her fears? Sophia had been cooking since she was sixteen.

For my sixteenth birthday, my grandmother cashed a certificate-of-deposit so I could get a car. "It's a gift," she had said, "for sweet sixteen. Ask Frank to find a car for you."

My stepfather found a deal on a 1968 Mustang. But he had to look a gift horse in the mouth. "Gift, my ass," he said. "Your grandmother is not doing you any favors by giving you the money to buy this car. Those certificate-of-deposits are just tactics to avoid taxes. Children your age should be earning money for cars." Why did he have to taint my Mustang with cynicism?

After school, as summer turned to fall, I cruised the mountain curves at high speed, smoking and listening to Cat Stevens sing, *"Ooh, baby, baby, it's wild world."*

On weekends, I worked at Tanglewood Falls in the gift shop with my aunt or the hotel kitchen with my grandmother. While we were tagging the latest shipment of resort wear, Ruthie said, "A handsome young man would be more likely to flirt with you if were wearing this new halter top. Annie has two already."

When men came into the gift shop, they were searching for forgotten shave cream or condoms. Or they were passing through to the nightclub, with their wives on their arms. A souvenir shop at a honeymoon resort was an unlikely place to meet men, whether or not my cleavage spilled beyond spaghetti straps.

As we were arranging peach slices on pound cake one evening, Grandma said, "The way to a man's heart is through his stomach. I'd be happy to have you married and taken care of. I could introduce you to the new owners of the Alpine Inn. They have a son about your age. He's in business school so he can manage their resort when they retire. It's a good family. By the way, I'm short a hostess tonight. Would you like to fill in?"

"Do I have to, Grandma?" I'd rather work in the steamy hot kitchen, wearing an apron, hiding from strangers.

"No, you don't have to. But I did any job necessary to make a success of myself in the hotel business. Plus, I managed to raise a son and daughter. They never lacked for a thing, not a thing. I stood on my feet until it's a wonder I can still stand! The foot doctor had to pare the hammertoes. Anyway, I was thinking that maybe you could take over for me after you finish college. Maybe you can take courses and be a secretary in the office. Of course, we'd have to discuss it with Tony."

I realized that there was a patriarchal tradition that recognized a woman in terms of her relationships to men. But I was baffled by the mixed messages of career training and marriage planning. According to my family, it was acceptable for a woman to work until marriage. Or a woman could work while married, as long as she contributed to the family business. Even an education was considered a temporary endeavor until marriage, unless a college degree advanced the business. My mother, a woman of the 1950's, finished high school with typing and bookkeeping skills. She'd worked until she got married, then left her clerical jobs to raise a family. Women in the 1960's demanded equal pay for equal jobs in a male dominated society. By the early 1970's, when I was in high school, women were seeking law degrees rather than secretarial school certificates. All I was looking for was a sense of safety and approval working for the family. At the same time, I didn't plan more than which party I'd go to next.

Karen brought me back to the current counseling session. "You certainly had an awful lot to deal with. It doesn't sound like you had any role models or mentors to turn to, so you turned to pills. You were in survival mode, living day to day."

"Yeah, I lived one day at a time without making a plan. Whatever I did on any given day wasn't going to matter because I had no concept of a future."

Accidents and Amphetamines

When we are unable to find tranquility within ourselves, it is useless to seek it elsewhere.

La Rochefoucault

"You've covered the first couple of years of high school," Karen reminded me. "What happened during the next few years?"

I remembered Vicki, a friend I met in my sophomore year. She wore beaded necklaces, bell-bottom jeans, and tie-dyed T-shirts. Silver earrings dangled in her long blonde hair and silver rings adorned her fingers. When the winter weather moved in, she wore a wool coat with sheepskin cuffs and collar. As soon as we spoke to each other, I felt as if we had been friends forever.

"Maybe we were soul sisters in a previous life," I suggested.

"Wow, man, that sounds so far out!"

"Do you think we knew each other before?" I asked.

"Yeah, I knew you from when you took the bus. I thought you were Little Miss Perfect. You were always skinny, then you were, well, chubby, and now you're almost thin again. How did you lose it?"

"A doctor gave me diet pills. I don't know how to keep the weight off without them."

"Oh, yeah, Bennies and Dexxies. I know something else that will do the trick."

Following her into the girls' lavatory, I realized that I had never cut class. Vicki checked under each metal door, and then we crowded in a stall.

Vicki whispered, "This will cure even the most ravenous appetite in two seconds flat. It's methamphetamine, speed, crank, whatever you want to call it." She demonstrated how to snort the white powder through a straw and offered me a hit. "Sniff, don't make a noise, and whatever you do, don't sneeze."

The crystalline powder burned through my nostrils, and I coughed at the bitter taste as it went down my throat. Instantly, that hit of speed sent tingling sensations zipping like lightning through my body. "Wow, man, what hit me?"

Vicki nonchalantly explained, "You're really wired, aren't you? That's just the rush."

My heart pounded in random thunderbolts and the rush pulsed with electrical currents that brought me to life.

In 1969, the country was in the midst of a cultural revolution in protest of the Vietnam War, and to bring attention to civil rights and the women's movement. Social activists staged sit-ins and political militants motivated moratoriums. The mottoes were "Tune in, turn on, drop out," "Sex, drugs, and rock and roll," and "Don't trust anyone over thirty."

After school, at Vicki's house, we smoked pot from her ceramic pipe. The sweet smell of strawberry incense mingled with the scent of grass. We listened to The Byrds, The Band, the Grateful Dead, and Bob Dylan's, *"The times, they are a changing."* The beat of the music was enhanced with each inhalation.

"People in this town are so plastic. I can't wait for graduation. I'm going to art school in San Francisco." Vicki said. "I'm so stoned. What about you?"

"I'm stoned."

"No, I mean where are you going after graduation?"

"I like to read and write poetry. Maybe I'll major in English, but I don't know."

We engaged in intellectual ramblings about politics and intricate government conspiracy theories conducted by the Establishment. We concluded that a corporation had no conscience. We went off on cerebral tangents about outer space. "If infinity is this, then finite is that," and on and on. Meanwhile, I was out of touch with planet earth. There were news segments about men lost in space, the Apollo 13 mission, but I was too spaced out to comprehend it.

Sometimes we were more grounded and talked about boys. Except for me, the entire country was in the midst of a sexual revolution.

Vicki said, "Sex feels so good. You don't know what you're missing. You have too many hang-ups."

"Yeah, I guess. I'm just waiting for the right guy."

"You'll be waiting a long time. Get it on now, girl, before you're old and gray!"

Our circle of friends included the kids of business owners and their attorneys who lived large on the tourist trade. These fine families built custom homes on "Snob Hill," not far from where I lived. Frequently, their parents were either out of town at a conference or out for cocktails for the evening. With a stash of drugs in their every pocket, my friends were my sources.

"Come on Lynnie, it's coke. Try a hit."

"No, thanks."

"Don't be such a square."

"Oh, all right!"

Skipping school, assemblies, and pep rallies to get stoned, I would pick up friends and we'd drive from one party to the next. A neighbor and a schoolmate named Jason constructed a party place with a private entrance in the lower level of his parents' home. Complete with futons and fridge, stereo and TV, his pad had all that was needed to entertain in clandestine quarters. A secret code allowed only the coolest of the cool to enter.

As I entered with the password one evening, I waved my hand to clear the air of the muddy smell of musk oil. An arm with sterling silver bangles that jangled waved back, and through a cloud of smoke I saw my cousin Annie. She was wearing tall leather boots laced up over her jeans and a purple suede blazer, and her blonde hair spiraled past her shoulders.

"Hey, Annie, I like your glasses."

"Thanks, Lynnie. They're granny glasses, like John Lennon's."

Annie fired up a jumbo joint with a pewter lighter while I lit a Marlboro with a match. She took off her jacket to reveal a hot pink turtleneck sweater and a waif-like body of ninety-eight pounds. When I took off my coat, Annie whispered through a giggle, "You're Tits Laroo."

My shoulders slumped forward to conceal my bust.

"Lynnie, when you got it, flaunt it!"

Annie flaunted and flirted, collecting boyfriends like I collected books, reading them and shelving them when finished.

"Wish I had a boyfriend," I confessed.

"You're too much of a touch-me-not," Annie replied.

Annie and I partied until dawn, and then rolled into the resort with the headlights off to avoid alerting the security guard. Once inside her house, I raided the refrigerator stocked with foods from the hotel kitchen.

"I got the munchies bad," I admitted to a forkful of apple pie.

"Don't you have any will power?"

"I can't control myself unless I have speed."

"There's a doctor on the corner of Oak and Fifth. He'll fix you up with diet pills. No prescription, no appointment, and no questions asked, as long as you pay cash."

The next morning, visited the doctor in a residential office without much medical equipment. The doctor handed me plain white envelopes filled with pills. "Take a blue pill in the morning, and a pink pill in the evening." I didn't even have to endure an examination.

After school, Annie and I perused college brochures over glasses of rum and Coke. Annie applied to a liberal arts school in Ohio while I submitted admissions essays to colleges in Colorado. We listened to Annie's extensive record collection, from The Beatles to The Who.

"I can't wait to get away from this place," Annie said. "You know, I tried to run away when I was four. I'd run away again, if only I had a place to go."

I remembered Aunt Ruthie telling the story of how Annie had toddled four miles in the dark. Where was Annie running to then? Her father owned three hundred houses in the Poconos, but Annie had nowhere to go. What was she running from now? I'd overheard hotel employees gossip about Ruth, how she obtained multiple prescriptions from many different doctors. They complained about how she "talked a mile a minute" and "drove that Lincoln like a bat out of hell." Ruthie's moods would escalate to manic heights and then plunge to the depths of depression. Annie's mother had been hospitalized for a nervous breakdown, as had mine. And while Annie's father was working to accumulate more than he could ever need, Annie's needs went unmet.

I was admiring the evening gowns in Annie's closet.

"You can have all those silly dresses," Annie said. "My mother expects me to kiss up to those fat fart resort owners. Or those hypocritical church administrators. The only way I get through those dinners is with an appetizer of LSD. At least I get to sneak a whiskey sour every now and then."

At yet another party, with our own friends, Annie and I settled onto a futon with a couple of beers and heard Jimi Hendrix sing about a purple haze.

"Shit, I'm out of cigarettes," Annie complained. "Lynnie, will you go get a pack? You can take my car."

Eager to drive Annie's new Capri, I took the keys, a Quaalude, and a gulp of beer. The night was damp and foggy, so I drove slow as I adjusted the defrost dial. Suddenly, a black cat darted across the dark road. *Watch out! Don't let a black cat cross the path!* When I swerved to miss the cat, a tree hit the car, and the tree fell on top of the Capri. The front of the car was rammed into the base of the tree trunk and the upper branches of the tree rested on the roof of the car.

I sat dazed with my chin stuck to the steering wheel. An elderly couple was knocking at the window, "Oh dear, come inside, come inside." They led me into their kitchen. The old woman invited me to sit and her husband got on the phone.

My chin dripped blood onto their tablecloth.

"Are you all right, dear?" The woman gave me moist paper towels to compress the cut on my chin.

"I'm fine, thank you," I lied.

Her husband was talking to the cops. "One car, yes, just one. Young. Female. The tree."

"That's not necessary," I said, standing up, and then sitting down again because my forehead was throbbing to the beat of a lump.

The police arrived and asked me for the registration. As I was reaching into the glove compartment, my fingers brushed Annie's stash of pot. Quickly, I grabbed the registration and politely handed it over.

"This vehicle is registered to Tanglewood Falls. How did you get possession of it, Miss?"

"Well, sir, my cousin, I am my uncle's niece, and my grandmother, well, she's the owner, and my stepfather and my brother, you know."

"Oh! We know Tony. We still need to take you to the hospital to have a look see."

In the police car, on the way to the emergency room, I was worrying about a test that could determine drugs. The ER doc diagnosed no broken bones, just bruises and bumps, and a nasty chin laceration.

The cops continued their investigation: "It seems you were driving about eight miles per hour. How did this happen? Have you been drinking?"

"Well, sir, no, well, maybe just a little beer." I figured I could confess to a beer and avoid a blood test.

"Oh, we thought you were just in shock," the cop said. "You're underage."

So, I had inadvertently busted myself for drinking and driving, since their question had been routine for all automobile accidents. I'd have to pay a fine.

That weekend, Tony's secretary ushered me into his office. He sat behind a huge, highly polished mahogany desk, with his suit coat on the back of his leather chair. He gestured for me to come closer. Balancing on a high wire over an alligator swamp would be less nerve-racking than the walk from the door to the desk.

"How could you be so irresponsible?"

From his office I could see the lobby, where honeymoon guests were checking in. They were within earshot of Tony, who was hollering at me.

"When the owner of the tree found out you are related to the owners of Tanglewood Falls, they decided to sue."

They were suing for the tree, that tree, one tree in a million.

Uncle Tony was waving paper. "Do you expect me to pay your bills, too?"

The hospital bill had been sent to Tanglewood Falls, instead of to my parents.

"Instead of spending your weekends here," my uncle said, "you should go home to your own family."

When I got home, I was about to receive a lecture of another kind. My mother and stepfather were waiting for me in the kitchen, the heart of a family's home. A plate of wholesome oatmeal raisin cookies was within reach.

"Rusty, take some cookies with you to your room. I'll be in later," Frank said.

"Mom, what's going on?" I asked.

"We'll try to make this as pleasant as possible," Mom said.

"What?"

"This isn't easy," Mom said. "Frank, you go first."

My stepfather was looking at me, his eyes ablaze with anger. "What I want to know is why you insist on hanging out with Annie. She swears like a sailor. She's what? Fifteen? Sixteen? She has the reputation of a slut. She's nothing but trailer trash. Wait! I'm not finished yet. I've barely begun. The police know your car. That's right! They told me! What do you expect? You taxi hippie freaks around town. The cops are looking to make a solid bust. I told them to go ahead and arrest you if they see fit. Cast not your pearls before swine, young lady."

My mother took her turn with an improvised version of tough love intervention: "You have two choices. You can go live with your father. Or you can go to a psychiatric unit. I did a thorough investigation of a hospital in Philadelphia. It has a ward for troubled teens. The head psychiatrist is a specialist in adolescent behavior. It would be worth your while to delve into whatever it is that's causing your behavior."

"Mom, is it the hospital you were in when you had a nervous breakdown?"

"For your information, I didn't have a nervous breakdown. I was intending on a few weeks of rest. The hospital I am referring to at the moment is Friends Hospital, the same hospital Ruth was in."

"Mom, Aunt Ruthie has a mental illness! I'm not crazy, am I?"

"No, sweetheart, I don't think you're crazy, but you are getting more and more like your father every day. I can't condone your behavior. It's outrageous."

The word "outrageous" sounded like "rage out." I was feeling as fragile as a sand castle. One splash of seawater could sweep me away, into the abyss. I could disintegrate to an indiscernible grain of sand.

She picked up the phone. "I'm phoning your father."

"Mom, do you have to call him?"

"He's expecting my call."

This was unbelievable! They hadn't had a civil conversation in years. She had once told me that she "hated him, with every fiber of my being." And now she was calling him?

"Have you been talking about me with him already?" I asked.

"Of course. He's your father."

I turned toward my room.

"Don't you dare walk away!" my stepfather warned. "I'm telling you once and for all: straighten up and fly right."

My mother's nails sounded like galloping horses as she rapped them on the counter top. My stepfather turned to her. "It's okay, lovey. We'll deal with this mess together. If you don't need me for now, how about I go tuck Rusty into bed. He's been patiently waiting."

I listened to my mother's side of the conversation.

"Manny? Yes. I'm fine. Now, about your daughter. As you know, her behavior is appalling. She socializes with weirdoes, the bottom of the barrel. She gives in to peer pressure. She smokes pot, and who knows what else. She's defensive and defiant. She should see a psychiatrist. Excuse me? I'm her mother! What right do you have to tell me what I can and can't do with my own daughter?"

My mother held the phone at arm's length so I could hear my father saying, "What are you? Whacko? No daughter of mine needs a head shrinker."

My mother put her hand over the phone. "I don't know why I'm the one doing all the work," she said. Then she handed the phone to me: "You got us into this. The least you can do is talk to your father."

"What are you?" he was saying. "Some kind of head case? If you need a head shrink, it's your mother's fault. If you do see a shrink, consider yourself disowned!"

Disowned? When did he own me? What was there to disown me of? I put the phone on the counter as he continued his tirade. "If you insist on smoking pot, I would rather you come to me, and I'll get it for you. You never know what you get from those dope fiends. It could be laced with arsenic, for all you know. I know where to go. I'd rather you be safe than sorry. You hear me? Are you listening? Now put your mother back on the phone!"

"Yes," I heard my mother tell my father, "I'm fine, considering the circumstances. Yeah, she's a lost cause. Bye."

My parents generously gave me twenty-four hours to choose between an institutional nuthouse and my father's madhouse. At seventeen, what rights did I have? There was no adolescents' bill of rights for parents to abide by.

While they were driving me to Philadelphia, my stepfather said, "I love you as if you were my own flesh and blood."

I thought he must have been talking to the steering wheel. I'd never before heard him say he loved me. Why now? Was it a show of words for my mother's sake?

From the front seat, my mother explained the difference between a voluntary and involuntary commitment, suggesting that I cooperate rather than endure court proceedings. In the back seat, I watched as the well-known winter landscape of the country changed to a foreign, unwelcoming cityscape. Mom turned her head toward me; I turned toward the window.

"Are you all right?" she asked.

"Fine, thank you," I lied. I held the tears were welling up inside. If I shed a single tear the floodgates might burst open. I could start to cry and never stop.

"Think about how I feel," Mom said, "having to send my own daughter away. But I have your best interests in mind."

"Yeah," Dad began, "this hurts us as much as it must hurt you. We're just trying to make you a better person."

In the hospital admissions office, as we were signing insurance papers, Mom said, "I'm going to miss you. Call us if you need anything."

The office administrator showed us a form, which stated that no parental contact with a patient was allowed for the first two weeks.

"What? I can't speak to my own daughter? There must be some misunderstanding."

"No, it's here in black and white," the administrator explained.

Looking at my stepfather, my mother said, "I don't know if I can do this."

"It's for her own good," Dad said.

Mom turned to me, "I'm sorry, sweetheart. If only I had known about this."

I thought she had done a thorough investigation of the hospital. I thought she should have known more about the place that was taking her daughter. I thought we had been speaking all along, but not hearing each other. Our words had twisted into knots of misunderstanding until we couldn't speak to each other at all.

"I'll have an orderly take Lynn to her room," the administrator said. "Your name is Lynn, isn't it? Yes, yes, how careless of me. It's right here." She pointed at a piece of paper.

An ordinary looking young man in an orderly's uniform had been waiting outside the admissions office. As we were leaving, Mom took Dad's elbow for support. I watched their backs as they walked down the long hall. I was entrusted to a male orderly, who was leading me in the opposite direction. He had a key ring the size of a dinner plate, and used different keys to open first one locked door, then another. "There you go," he said, as he took me into a windowed office. Across a polished desk, I studied a man in a suit about twice my age who was supposed to be the psychiatrist, Dr. Griffon. He represented all that was anathema to my feminine psyche. Even if I knew what I was thinking, how could I speak my mind?

To determine my state of mind, the psychiatrist showed me irregular shapes of black ink on white paper. I was supposed to indicate what I thought the blobs represented. Weren't these the same inkblot tests that a psychiatrist had given my father? Didn't these tests determine that he was mentally ill? Were they thinking that I was a paranoid schizophrenic just like my father? My mind drew blanks; I couldn't crack the code of the inkblot tests.

After a cursory session, the psychiatrist diagnosed an adolescent adjustment disorder and prescribed Valium as an antidote. The rules of the ward were strict, such as lights out at ten o'clock, but patients were not ill-treated. In a hospital owned and operated by Quakers, many of the aides were conscientious objectors. These pacifists realized that the patients had survived enough battles with their parents. While I was on the ward, I made friends with other teenaged patients. They'd been prisoners of the war on drugs far longer than me.

Tonya was a heroin addict who came to the unit after detoxification. She pulled me into her room, which smelled like singed hair, and showed me the denim that was smoldering from the bottom hem to the knee. She had set fire to the jeans she was wearing.

"How did you get a light?" I asked.

"I stole a lighter from the nurse's station. Don't tell anyone, okay?"

A tall, handsome boy named Mark spoke to the radio. He claimed he was transmitting messages in response to the coded information only he could hear. He asked me to share the marijuana he had smuggled onto the ward. During a secret smoking session in the basement, he claimed to have taken hundreds of hits of LSD.

"How many hundreds?" I asked.

"At least five hundred. But don't tell anybody."

I spoke only when I was spoken to and listened to Don McLean singing, *"Bye Bye Miss American Pie, drove my Chevy to the levee but the levee was dry. Good ole boys drinking whiskey and rye, singing this will be the day that I die."*

My Aunt Ruthie sent me news from home and upbeat messages. Each contact took a special effort on her part: a trip to the florist or bookstore or card shop, a trip to the post office. She wrapped six small books of poetry, like Rod McKuen's "Caught in the Quiet," individually, with different paper. She inscribed each book differently: to my niece, to my goddaughter, to a special young lady. Although we never talked about it, I thought Ruthie could understand the indignity of banishment.

I felt like I had been banished by the rest of my family. Even after the enforced weeks without contact, I talked to my mother only infrequently and then briefly. My stepmother sent a dog-eared paperback copy of "Jonathan Livingston Seagull" by Richard Bach. Before I read it, I gave it away. That's what I felt like, a tattered book that had been thrown away before anyone bothered to read beyond the cover.

The ward was co-ed, but lavatories were segregated. The girls showered in a row of stalls without curtains and the toilets had doors without locks. As patients, we lived by a routine that was supposed to train us into good behavior. We ate the same seven-day rotation of meals at the same time each day. We had unisex uniforms of denim jeans and flannel shirts, made unique by the nametags sewn into the seams. It must have been the boredom that made us behave badly.

In the evenings, over card games in the recreation room, the lucid patients planned an escape. Brett was a reedy, restless adolescent. He nominated himself team leader, although he could not even focus on a card game long enough to win a hand.

"Go to the fire escape at seven," Brett instructed. "Run like hell through the tunnels, and meet on the east lawn. We can be back before lights out. Who is in? Let's see a show of hands."

Stoney, the boy with reddish-purple acne that migrated from his face to his neck, raised his hand as if we were in grade school.

"Lynn, where do you stand?" Brett asked. "Are you with us or not?"

"Yeah, but, which way is east?" I asked as I looked toward the long hall with rows of identical doors.

"Lynn, just stick with me," Peggy said. "I can work my way out of any maze."

Peggy was as ordinary as a field mouse, and her multi-braided hair hung down her back like rattails. I practically clung to her hair as I followed; she knew how to sniff her way through the underbelly of an old building. We ran over the grounds, climbed over the fence, and bounded down subway stairs.

As planned, we met Brett and Stoney at the subway stairs.

"Whew, we made it," I said. "I can't believe we made it!"

"Oh, Ye of little faith," Brett said. "Let's have some real fun!"

My conscience picked that moment to kick in. What the hell was I doing out on a dark winter night in Philadelphia with teenage lunatics? The near but distant lamplight on the hospital lawn looked softer than the harsh fluorescent bulbs on the subway platform. Could I retrace our steps, back toward the light, into the hospital? Not alone. My directional abilities were as impaired as my math skills.

The escapade included a stop at a hardware store. I was thinking of wood glue for an occupational therapy project, but Brett had aerosol spray in mind. After picking out a can or two, we mapped our route to the hospital grounds. Sitting in a circle, as if holding a pow-wow on hospital land, Brett passed the peace pipe, which was a paper bag filled with propellant.

"Hold the sack, cover your mouth and nose," he instructed. "Breathe in only once or twice."

Pressing the open bag over my face, I inhaled and inhaled and inhaled. Greedy for oblivion, I was unwilling to get my head out of the bag until hands took it off my face.

"I told you to stop!" Brett yelled.

"You scared us," Peggy said.

"Yeah," Stoney said. "You were huffing like there's no tomorrow."

Their voices sounded garbled. Had I been transported to another galaxy? My eyes fixed on the sky. The twinkling stars were whirling like Van Gogh's painted version. Poor Vincent. How could he get so out-of-touch with reality that he cut off his own ear?

We made it back to our rooms before lights out, undetected by hospital personnel.

While I was in the hospital, my father made no contact. My mother and stepfather came for a family conference that was supposed to open lines of communication. The psychiatrist had invited all family members to attend, including my older and younger brothers.

We met in the psychiatrist's office, which was lacking in family friendly atmosphere. The chairs that surrounded the desk were arranged for a meeting. Dr. Griffon sat behind his desk, my mother and stepfather sat together facing the desk, and I sat across from them. We were in an uneven triangle, and the balance was in my parents' favor. But the setting wasn't the problem. Apparently, *I* was the problem, and my stepfather wasn't about to overlook that.

"I was looking forward to meeting your older son, Eric," Dr. Griffon said to my mother.

"Oh, he's busy. Besides, I don't know what Lynn's behavior has to do with him."

"What about the younger son, Rusty?" the doctor asked.

"I'm not about to drag him into this," my stepfather said. "It's bad enough that we have to leave him with a baby-sitter, which, by the way, isn't cheap these days. Not to mention that I had to take a day off to drive all the way down here. What exactly is it that you have done to improve my stepdaughter's disposition?"

"According to the notes from the psychiatric aides, Lynn is making progress," Dr. Griffon said. "She's opening up to the staff and the other patients. Lynn is a likeable young lady. She makes friends easily."

"Oh, that's so nice," Mom said.

"I know exactly the kind of friends she makes," Dad said. "She attracts hoodlums and thugs."

My mother gave my stepfather a glance so full of frustration that it gave new meaning to the phrase "if looks could kill."

"You've always been too strict with the children," she told Frank.

"What do you think about what your wife just said?" the doctor asked Frank.

"Let me tell you a thing or two," Frank began. "First of all, Lynnie has always been high-strung. Second of all, she doesn't know how to listen."

"We're acting as if Lynn isn't in the room," Dr. Griffon said. "What would you like to say to her?"

Mom looked at me. "Did you hear what the doctor said, sweetheart? You're making progress."

"Lynn, what would you like to add?" Dr. Griffon asked.

"When I get out of here, where will I go? Mom, can I come home?"

"Of course. Right, Frank?"

"That depends entirely upon whether or not she can change her attitude," Dad said.

In the current counseling session with Karen, I realized that the family conference had had little chance of success. My stepfather had been like a Doberman protecting his turf, biting me with his sharp sarcasm. My mother had been like a dog with a bone, fiercely holding on to denial.

"What about you?" Karen asked. "You spent a large portion of your junior year on a psych ward. What were your overall feelings?"

"I felt like a bad puppy that had been abandoned at the pound, waiting in a cage for adoption or extermination."

"That's certainly understandable. What, if anything, did you learn while you were confined?"

"I learned new methods of escape: eluding authority, scaling walls, and sniffing propellants. I'd been medicated with tranquilizers and dominated by my stepfather's tyranny. I learned that communication could break down beyond repair."

Reincarnations and Ravioli

However confused the scene of our life appears, however torn we may be who now do face that scene, it can be faced, and we can go on to be whole.

Muriel Rukeyser

"How long were you in the hospital?" Karen asked.

"Three months."

"It must have been a difficult transition to return home and to go back to school. What happened when you were discharged?"

My mother, stepfather, and Rusty came for me on the day I was released. As we walked to the car, I noticed the signs of spring. The grounds-keepers had mowed the lawn I'd run across in the dead of winter. Orange and red tulips were blooming along the curbs. The forsythia bushes were stretching their golden-yellow branches toward the sun like they had just been awakened. I was anxious to get home, to be outside in the fresh spring air, with my dog Lulu.

I remembered how Lulu would plant her front paws to the ground and raise her hind end in the play position. She'd wag her tail in anticipation of playing ball. I'd missed the silent companionship of my pet while I was in the hospital.

"How's Lulu?" I asked once Dad was sailing on the freeway.

"I'm afraid I have bad news," Mom said. "After you left, Lulu got out of control. She dug up the carpet and she peed on your bed."

"Why would she pee on my bed?"

"She probably missed you. She ran away, looking for you," Mom said.

"Lulu ran away?"

"Several times. Oh, she returned. But I couldn't keep up with her. I had so much on my mind. So Dad and I were forced to make a decision. We took her to the pound. You understand, don't you?"

"Did somebody adopt her?"

"How would I know that?" Mom asked.

I looked at Rusty, who shrugged and looked out the window. After I'd been so mean to him, I couldn't expect that he would have been responsible for the dog that I'd cared for. I could understand if Mom couldn't look after the dog, having so much to worry about. We had the dog because of me, they got rid of it because of me, and I probably deserved it.

When we got home, my parents showed me around the house as if I was seeing it for the first time. They had converted the basement into a recreation room with a convertible ping-pong/billiards table and a sewing nook.

"You and Rusty can play pool," Mom said. "Just be careful not to tear the felt with the cue stick. Dad built the sewing nook for you. You did such a good job with that jumper you made in home economics. We thought you'd like a new hobby to occupy your time."

"Don't use the sewing machine when I'm watching TV," Dad ordered. "The power surge interferes with the satellite and we don't get a clear picture."

"How about we make ravioli tonight in honor of your homecoming?" Mom suggested. "I already made the marinara sauce. All I have to do is heat it up."

My mother had tried to teach me how to make her special sauce. "Enhance the flavor with fennel and bay leaves," she instructed while a pot of crushed Jersey tomatoes had simmered on the stove. "Add a pinch of oregano and a dash of salt. You can add a red pepper to taste." But cooking without a recipe was as complicated as a science experiment to me.

While I was setting the table for my homecoming dinner, my mother and stepfather were making balls of pasta dough, and then rolling it flat.

"Frank, do you think the dough is too soft?"

"No, lovey, I think it's firm enough."

They combined ricotta and Parmesan cheeses and spread it between layers of dough. Working in tandem, they cut the filled pasta into squares, pinching and flattening the sides to make pockets.

"Let's have a toast," Dad said as he poured red Bordeaux for himself and my mother.

"Can I have some?" I asked.

"Of course not," he said. "Raise your water glass! To Lynnie. Welcome back. We never thought you'd make it. We thought you were too far gone."

During dinner, Mom said, "I'm so glad to have you home."

"You are, really?" I couldn't be sure.

"Yes, of course. What do you mean, really?"

"I don't know."

"You know, Eric will be home from college next summer," Mom said.

"Did you know he came home for Thanksgiving?" Rusty asked.

How would I know? I was in a hospital cutting tough slices of cold turkey with plastic utensils.

"Eric looked wonderful!" Mom continued. "He worked at Tanglewood Falls during spring break. He's always studying. He made the dean's honor roll. Do you want more ravioli?"

"No thanks, Mom. I'm so stuffed I could throw up." Actually, I was so fed up with her tribute to my brother that I was afraid I'd spill my guts and make a mess on the white tablecloth.

"Frank, come help me with dessert," Mom said. She did not need help in the kitchen. She just wanted to talk to my stepfather in private.

Rusty and I sat at the dining room table without a thing to talk about. I wondered what our parents had said about me while I was gone. I wondered what my little brother thought about me. What did he think about his older sister being too far gone? To fill an empty silence between siblings, I took a sip of my mother's wine.

"You can't do that!" Rusty said.

"I can, too."

"I'm going to tell." Rusty ran to the kitchen. "Lynnie is drinking wine!"

"What is wrong with you?" my stepfather hollered. "We give you everything, and this is how you repay us? Why do you have to ruin everything? You are a lost cause."

"Frank, please, tone it down," my mother said. "Lynnie, I think it's time you go to your room. We'll talk about this later."

I went to my room, slamming the door to vent the anguish of being alive. Ruined, I ruined everything. Ruined, everything is ruined. They'd be better off without me.

Later, my mother talked with me, about me, well, almost.

"We'll have a couple of days together while Rusty is at school and Dad's working," Mom said. "We'll go shopping. I spotted a tailored yellow coat I think you'd like. I made an appointment for you with my hairdresser, Marianne. She'll know what to do with your hair. She's such a wonderful girl! She can teach you how to tweeze those eyebrows. You can go back to school with a clean slate."

I wouldn't make much of a fashion statement with plucked brows and short hair. Models were displaying bushy brows and long hair on the covers of the magazines. And they weren't wearing double-breasted, belted coats with wide notched collars. The ads showed them in unbuttoned designer jeans that were so low slung they exposed their midriffs.

"Can we shop for jeans?" I asked.

"I was hoping you'd try something more lady-like. By the way, the guidance counselor at school said you don't have to make up homework because your grades were so good."

"Do I have to go back to school?"

"What kind of question is that? You have only one more year of high school."

"What am I supposed to say if anyone asks where I've been?"

"Oh, you'll think of something," my mother said.

"Like an exotic disease? Malaria or Typhoid fever?"

"You'll be in the swing of things before you know it," Mom offered.

I'd been in the hospital, but I hadn't recovered from any illness I could speak of. I wouldn't mind being noticed by classmates, if it were for the right reasons, like being thin and pretty. After school, while students were in the glee club or on the soccer field, I walked to the public library. Sitting alone in a musty corner, I perused magazines, admiring the clothes modeled by Cheryl Tiegs. Perhaps if I wore the trendy styles I'd be in the "swing of things."

After dinner and before my stepfather's favorite TV shows, I designed fashions from intricate patterns, inserting sleeves, waistbands, and zippers. But as soon as a garment was nearly complete, I found fault with a tiny stitch, and trashed the whole thing.

"Where's the pink gabardine dress you were making?" Mom asked. "That black trim you added to the cuffs looked so chic, like something the first lady would wear."

"Oh, the seam frayed."

"You can fix that, can't you? Use the pinking shears."

"No, it's too ugly."

"That reminds me," Mom said, "Dad did another reading. He saw a vision of you in the 1800's. You were the daughter of an aristocrat in Europe, and an expert equestrian until a horse threw you. The fall left you disfigured, and in those days, there was no plastic surgery. Ashamed of your face, you spent your days in the scullery. You associated only with the servants. In this lifetime, you have to learn to get along with others. Maybe it's time you got out more instead of spending your time sewing all by yourself."

I was hemming an orange "tent" dress and the thread tangled, causing the knit to pucker. I yanked on the thread, which only tightened the knots.

"It isn't right!" I yelled.

"What's not right?" Mom asked.

"Look at this hem! I can't do anything right!"

What wasn't right was the pressure of pretend past lives compounding my already complicated current life. What wasn't right was how my mother chose my hobbies, and then told me when she thought it was time to abandon them. What wasn't right was the way the hem of the dress was unraveling as if to mock me. I was falling apart at the seams.

"Why don't you put the sewing aside and set the table?" my mother said.

At least I could set the table right.

Sometime later, the phone was ringing. My mother shouted, "Lynnie, will you get that? I'm sure it's your grandmother. I don't want to talk to my mother today."

"What should I tell her?"

"Tell her I'm sick with a virus. I'm sick and tired of hearing about her ailments."

That was one way to get along with others.

A sound like something sizzling drew me from my reverie. There was my counselor Karen, the patient listener, pouring from a can of Pepsi-Cola.

"What else do you remember from high school?"

After the psych ward, I resumed my friendships with Annie and Vicki. By that time, everyone I knew took Quaaludes, muscle relaxants that created a lightheaded feeling. We chanted a popular phrase, "Better living through chemistry," as we got spaced on Quaaludes, drunk on beer, stoned on pot, wasted on speed, zoned on psychedelics, or hooked on heroin. I experimented without regard to consequences but often with a guilty conscience.

For the most part, my high school years were a blur. I got high on whatever uppers I could beg, borrow, or buy: Black Beauties and White Crosses and unidentifiable junk. I owned no yearbooks or class rings, just vague memories of a mood of apathy and alienation.

My persistent self-consciousness expanded into full-blown paranoia. When I walked into a room, I thought my feet sounded like the clod, clod, clod of the enormous hooves of a team of Clydesdales on cobblestone roads. When people stopped speaking, I imagined they had been talking about me. When people whispered, I thought they were whispering about me: "Isn't she crazy? Ugly?"

I remembered a poem I wrote in high school:

The paranoid is caught in a whirlwind of fear,
Looking and listening for the narc to appear.
The senses are tuned in a fraction of time,
Watching and listening for the cop or the siren.
The fright sends the mind to a paralyzed trance,
The tension triggers her heart to a ceaseless dance.
The roach is doused in a rush of panic,
The tab is dropped in a motion so mechanic.
The art of alertness is well worth the cause,
To avoid the arms that capture outlaws.
For the paranoid well learned that she must beware,
Of the narc well trained to bust her unaware.

"What does that poem mean?" Karen asked.

"It means what it is about."

"It seems like it could have other interpretations," Karen suggested.

"I know! It's a metaphor doing double duty! The paranoid is my father or my brother and I could tell on them. Or I could be the one who is paranoid, having to watch out for them."

"Yes," Karen said, "poems may have more than one interpretation. What were you trying to express?"

"I was trying to express how I felt trapped in fear." I had not understood the symbolism of my own poem until Karen had asked me to read between the lines.

Regressions and Predictions

It is in the knowledge of the genuine condition of our lives that we must draw our strength to live and our reasons for living.

Simone De Beauvoir

"What else happened in high school?" Karen asked.

In my senior year, on New Year's Eve, the party crowd celebrated at Jason's pad with cases of sparkling Champagne. Half the crowd was making out, and the other half was passed out. Since Annie was between boyfriends and I was serially single, we left for our own homes after midnight. I slipped in through the back door, careful not to bump into the spinning walls. On New Year's Day, I lingered between sleep and waking, tucked in bed with a hangover. When Annie called, it was not to say "Happy New Year" but to tell me that Jason's brother found him choked to death from his own vomit. The calendar marked another morbid anniversary.

In spring, Annie and Vicki surprised me with a birthday party. Instead of the customary candles, the cake had seventeen marijuana joints sunk into the icing. For birthday presents, my friends gave me silver earrings, bags of pot, and a pipe.

Before the school year ended, Vicki said, "I'm pregnant. I'm going to California to stay with relatives until the baby is born."

"Will you finish high school?"

"I'll give the baby up for adoption. But I don't know if I can come back to graduate."

Close to my high school graduation, my mother said, "Dad did another reading."

"Why?"

"Why what?" Mom asked me.

I wanted to say: Instead of reading past lives, *why* couldn't my stepfather read science fiction? Instead of arranging my life, *why* couldn't my mother arrange flowers? What I said was: "Why did Dad do another reading?"

"Because we are concerned about your lack of ambition."

"Oh. So Dad went into a trance?"

"Yes. He saw you as a princess in the ancient city of Atlantis. The people were highly evolved, and able to use telepathic communication. You were a popular princess, so people gave you presents. Servants handed you whatever you needed, without you even having to ask. Then you lost your position and all your possessions. In this lifetime, you have to learn to work hard for what you want. Nothing is going to be handed to you on a silver platter."

A vision of Atlantis swam in my head, with high-rise buildings standing firmly on sand under the sea. In the real world, Miami was made of massive buildings on sand. What if the city slipped into the Atlantic Ocean?

My mother and stepfather assumed myths as facts with their karmic pastime. Not only did they believe that Dad had extra-sensory abilities, but they also believed he could read past lives, and they believed that people had previous lives. Their theory was that people had evolved enough to breathe under water and communicate without language. They supposed that the mythical city of Atlantis existed. They never asked me what I believed. What I assumed was that in order to be accepted by my parents, I'd have to believe what they believed. They assumed that I could use their nonsense to make sense of my past and my future at the same time.

My parents had a formula for the stories of my past lives. In the beginning, I am prosperous and important: a seer, an aristocrat, and a princess. In the middle, there is a tragedy: a war, an accident, and a demotion. The story ends with an adversity that serves as a karmic lesson for reincarnation.

One spring evening, after Rusty went to bed, my mother, stepfather, and I were watching TV. In a rare relaxed tone, my stepfather asked, "Lynn, what are you going to do after high school?"

Wasn't he a self-professed guru? Couldn't he levitate and predict the future? Why didn't Dad peer into his crystal ball and tell me what I was going to be when I grew up, if I grew up?

"I like to read and write. I like art. But, I don't know."

"I admire your free spirit, but you won't make a living on the Left Bank of Paris writing poetry. It would behoove you to have a career you could fall back on. Did you decide on a college?"

Who said anything about Paris? What does he mean by *behoove*? It sounded like he was saying, "Behave, go to college."

"I don't know, maybe Colorado."

"Have you sent out the invitations to the graduation ceremony?" Mom asked.

I didn't want to attend my own graduation, much less ask anyone else. I hadn't seen or heard from my father since I'd been admitted to the psych ward. I wondered if I should be a good daughter, let him see me graduate, and maybe even make him proud.

"Mom, should I invite my father? If I invite him, will he show up? If he shows up, will I have to see him?"

"If you want to see your father, I can't stop you," she said. "Do what you want to do. Just make sure you don't invite him to the house."

"I don't know what to do. Why won't you help me?"

"Don't raise your voice to your mother," Dad ordered. "It's time you show her respect."

"Stop yelling," Mom said. "Rusty is sleeping."

"I don't belong here. I never belonged."

"Why are you antagonizing us?" Mom asked. "I can see that you won't be happy until you make us really mad."

"Why can't you ever be on my side?"

"I'm warning you, Lynn. I'll give you one last chance to quit while you are ahead."

"Then what? You'll banish me to an insane asylum?" The build up of tension was intolerable, and unrestrained anger was one way to tear it down. Despite all efforts to restrain tears, I began to cry.

"Keep that up, and I'll give you something to cry about."

"Here's a news flash for you. I'm not going to live long enough to make it to college. So what difference does it make what you do to me?"

My stepfather was standing. My mother couldn't stand up to him when he pulled me off the couch. He was spanking me, holding my left arm behind my back as I tried running to the back door. My body fell on the heater vent, the edges cutting into my butt, my face facing him as he slapped it, shouting, "Either shape up or ship out."

I felt like the snared rabbit I'd once found. When walking in the woods, I came upon a cottontail rabbit with its hind leg caught in a trap. I released that bunny, and it hopped into the brush. Although the rabbit had been freed from the metal clamps, the injuries were evident with each uneven hop.

The next morning, my mother was making my favorite, French toast, for breakfast. "I'm sorry Dad went overboard. But you insisted on provoking us."

"Okay, Mom." Okay, Mom, I thought, you don't have to be responsible. I concede; it's my fault.

After I had sent the invitation to my father, I got scared. Rather than face him, I planned on running away.

Sitting on the tiled floor of the girl's room, I smoked Marlboros with a classmate named Jenny. She was not the smartest girl in class, nor was she popular, but she was there. Although I barely knew her, I mentioned that I had to get away.

"Why would you run away two days before graduation? Is it that bad with your parents?"

"Yeah, but I can't explain it."

"I didn't know pretty people had problems," Jenny said. "I have a car, so I can help you."

"I have a car, but I don't want to use it."

"You have a car and you don't want it?"

"No, they'll send the cops to look for the car and they'll find me."

"Okay. I'll pick you up at dawn. You can stay with my boyfriend, Glen. He graduated last year. He has his own home. Sometimes I stay with him. We're engaged. See?" She lifted her left hand, fingers spread, to show off a thin band with a garnet chip. "It's my birthstone."

At dawn, I crawled out my bedroom window into Jenny's car with just enough luggage to hold a nightgown, underwear, jeans and T-shirts.

"I don't get it," Jenny said. "If I lived in a house like that, I would never leave."

"It's not the house I'm running from."

After school, Jenny took me to Glen's singlewide mobile home in a trailer park. In the narrow living room, we sat on a corduroy couch with cushions striped in earth tones. A planter suspended by beaded macramé swayed in the summer breeze as we got acquainted over a joint.

"So you had to fly the coop?" Glen asked.

I wondered how much information I should share for small talk with a stranger. I took a drag to fill an awkward moment. "Yeah, I'm like a bird without wings. I didn't get very far."

"Man," he said, "parents breathing down your neck can be such a bummer. Wouldn't it be great to hitchhike to California or Mexico? Someplace exotic."

"Yeah, anywhere but here."

Later, at nightfall, Jenny left.

"I thought Jenny was going to stay."

"Jenny's father is an old fuddy-duddy about the curfew," Glen complained. He lit candles, turned the lamps off, and took his T-shirt off.

"What are you doing?"

"I'm getting ready for bed. You don't mind, do you? You look tense. How about a massage?"

"No, thanks. Is Jenny coming back?"

"Not until tomorrow."

As I sat on the rough corduroy, Glen poured oil from a blue bottle into his palms and briskly rubbed them together.

"The friction warms the oil," he explained. "Here, smell this." The bottle smelled like fresh brewed coffee. Sitting too close for comfort, he smoothed the scented oil on my forearms and reached for my shoulders. Did he think that I was promiscuous because I partied?

"Please don't. What about Jenny?"

"What she doesn't know won't hurt her," he said. "You look so luscious and voluptuous in the candle light." He tried to kiss me with lips as slimy as his hands, but then stopped. "You're stiff as a board. You really don't want this, do you?"

"No. Please leave me alone."

"If that's the way you want it, you can sleep on the bed, and I'll sleep on the couch."

He let me go! I locked myself in his bedroom, which was sparse, clean, and quiet, perfect for a prayer. *Let me die tonight. Let me fall asleep and never wake up.* I slept in my clothes so my body would be dressed in case God granted my wish.

The next morning, Glen called out, "I'm going to work. You can use the shower if you want."

Standing in the shower, I rinsed off the stale coffee smell and wished the drain would suck me down to the sewer.

When Jenny picked me up, she asked, "Are you all right?"

"Fine, thank you."

"You don't look fine. Did something happen?"

"I didn't sleep well last night." How could I tell her that the man she was engaged to hit on me?

I followed other seniors to the auditorium for the graduation ceremony rehearsal. Sunshine lit the bleachers and reflected from the waxed hardwood floors. Graduating seniors giggled and joked with each other. When the principal assigned seats, I ambled through the rows of folding chairs to find my section. I'd been assigned a seat next to Katie because we were National Honor Society award recipients. Katie, a cheerful girl with curly blonde hair and brown eyes, waved at her classmates.

"Hi Lynn," Katie began, "how are you doing?"

"I'm fine, thank you."

"We were in German together," she said.

"We were?" My recognition of Katie had been lost in a long-term memory fog. All that I could recall of German class was Herr Frankl. He was the coach of the soccer team and a dedicated teacher. In my sophomore year, he had been concerned because my grades had dropped and he had asked me in plain English about my family life. I told him then that everything was just fine. Now, at commencement rehearsal, Herr Frankl was the high school principal. As if he were speaking a foreign language, I struggled to interpret his instructions for obtaining and returning caps and gowns.

"What? What did he say?" I asked Katie. "What are we supposed to do with the tassels?"

In response she asked, "Why are you crying?"

I hadn't realized that telltale tears had been peeking through a thin veil of "fine." "I ran away from home," I whispered. "I had to. My parents, they don't understand. They don't care. I don't know where to go."

"Wow! It must be awful. You can come to my house to get ready for the graduation ceremony," Katie offered.

"Really?"

"Yeah, really. I have friends over all the time. We have lots of room. I'm sure it will be okay with my parents."

After school, she drove us in a blue Volkswagen Beetle to a secluded area of the Poconos. Her ivy-covered brick home looked like a gingerbread house from a fairytale. A blonde Cocker Spaniel puppy romped through the tall grass to greet us. Katie introduced me to her father, who was a slight man in khaki shorts and a blue chambray shirt. He was lettering a board on the porch. I'd been accustomed to abrupt men who acted as if I were invisible, so his warm welcome surprised me. He extended his hand to me.

"You don't have to be formal here," he said. "Just call me Joel."

"Can Lynn get ready at our house?" Katie asked.

"Of course," Joel replied. "Are you going to meet your family at the auditorium?"

"Well, I don't think they're going to my graduation."

"How can your parents *not* go?"

"We're not on good terms right now," I explained.

Joel paused with paintbrush in hand. "I don't mean to pry," Joel said, "but I'd like to ask a couple of questions. Okay?"

My cheeks were hot with embarrassment as I awaited his questions. How could I explain that I was merely a remnant of an uncommon family unable to pull itself together for a common event?

"Who are your parents?" he asked.

I told him who my mother and stepfather were and where they lived.

"I know that name," he said. "Just give me a minute. It's on the tip of my tongue. I know! Are you related to the owners of Tanglewood Falls?"

I would have preferred to remain anonymous, but I confessed to the relationship.

"I'm a sign painter," he said. "I did the signs at that resort. Pretty posh place." He put his finger to his lips as if contemplating some absurdity.

"Did you run away?" he asked.

"I left. I had to leave."

"Why? What's wrong?"

I couldn't make a list at that moment, so I just shrugged in sad silence.

"It just goes to show you," he said, "you never know what's going on behind the scenes, family troubles and all. Let me know if there's anything you need."

What I needed was a safe place to stay. When Katie's mother, Megan, came home from work, she wanted to know more about Katie's new friend. Explaining my situation a third time was no less embarrassing than the first. As I spoke about having nowhere to go, Megan stopped putting groceries away to look directly at me. Megan's brown eyes were identical to Katie's; there was no mistaking the mother-daughter connection. But eye contact made me even more nervous. My gaze shifted around the kitchen. A small table had piles of papers, magazines and mail, condiments and cereal boxes. I could see that Megan had her hands full with children, a puppy, a full-time job, cooking, and laundry galore. Seeing potential for earning my keep, I said, "I can clean. I'll help you with the dishes." I felt like an orphan anxiously awaiting adoption.

"You don't have to clean to be accepted," Megan said with a sweetness that I hadn't experienced from my own mother in years. "I'm a social worker," Megan continued. "I understand that family conditions must be unbearable for you to run away from home so close to graduation. How old are you?"

I told her that I had just turned eighteen.

"Well," she said, "you're not a minor. Do you have any other relatives you can live with?"

I told her I couldn't think of any.

"Okay, then, you can stay here, but you have to call your mother to say that you're okay."

"Do I have to?"

"Do you want me to call her for you?" Megan asked.

"No, that would just make my mother mad. Can I wait until after the graduation ceremony?"

"What if I call her while you kids get ready for the ceremony? I want her to know you are safe. I'll tell her you'll call in the morning."

While we dressed for graduation, I confided to Katie, "I wish I didn't have to go."

"You have to go!" Katie encouraged. "We'll come back here after and celebrate."

What was she so gleeful about? It was just a silly, stupid ceremony. I felt so gloomy it seemed as if I were facing a funeral.

Before we left, Megan reported her conversation with my mother. "She's glad to know you are okay." That was all? The brevity of the call disappointed me; didn't my mother ask if I wanted to come home? I'd call Megan's house "home" for now. The comforts and conveniences of my mother's house were missing in Megan's: there was no automatic dishwasher, the rooms were small and cramped, and bathrooms were shared. But I sensed that privacy and safety would not be compromised. Home was where I felt worthy of respect.

"If you ever want to talk, I'll be glad to listen," Megan offered. "Anything you tell me will be confidential. Okay?"

"Anything?" I stood before Megan, my heart heavy with secrets, and wondered what was okay to talk about.

"Yes, anything. Is there something I can help you with now?"

"No, thank you." I couldn't bring myself to tell her anything.

During the graduation ceremony, every student's handshake with the principal caused a round of applause from relatives in the bleachers. I wondered who would clap for me. What if the entire auditorium remained silent? The cardboard cap kept slipping off my smooth hair, and I was sweating with self-consciousness as I marched to the platform. I appreciated the obligatory sprinkling of applause that accompanied me as I took the roll of parchment paper from Herr Frankl.

When the ceremony was over, I rushed from the auditorium rather than bear witness to parents hugging and congratulating their kids. I nearly collided with my grandmother in the parking lot.

"Lynnie, you seemed surprised to see me. I'm so proud of you."

"How did you get here? I know you don't like to drive at night."

"Your mother said she wasn't feeling well enough to come tonight, so I drove myself. At least the roads are dry."

A classmate called to me: "Hey, Lynn, wanna party? Let's celebrate!"

"It sounds like your friends want to get together with you. Take care of yourself and stop by when you want."

The next day, I called my mother, who said, "The family you're staying with are not saints. But I hope you're happy there. By the way, your brother is back from college and working at the resort. You know, your father showed up at the house after your graduation."

"He was at the graduation ceremony?" I asked.

"You invited him, didn't you?"

I felt accused of a crime, and defended myself accordingly: I didn't think he would come." I redirected the conversation: "By the way, I ran into Grandma in the parking lot."

"She was there? I told her we weren't going. She's seventy-something years old and she can't even drive herself to the hairdresser's. Half the time, I have to take her. She drove to your graduation at night? Boy, you must think you're something special. Anyway, imagine how I felt when I saw your father at my front door! He was expecting a celebration. You know, we heard you climbing out the window the morning you ran away. Dad had an ulcer attack and I had the worst migraine."

My mother's concern for everyone and everything other than me made me feel as rotten as any fallen apple in the orchard.

"By the way," Mom said, "Dad sold your car."

"Already?" I wondered if they'd already gotten rid of pictures of me.

"He sold it for $650.00, as is. He's keeping the money," she said.

"But it was my Mustang. Grandma helped me buy it."

"Too bad your grandmother didn't pay the insurance. Your stepfather did."

"You never mentioned insurance before," I retorted.

"Do you think money grows on trees? Dad supported you for ten years. And this is how you repay us? You know, you cut off your nose to spite your face."

Clichés tore at the meaning of words like cats tearing curtains, their claws ripping cloth to shreds. Understanding was left hanging like frayed fabric, and we hung up on each other.

I stayed with Katie's family all summer, occasionally visiting my grandmother or partying with my cousin. Once in a while, longing for connection, I'd call my mother, only to be discouraged by our inability to communicate.

Katie worked at a children's center for the summer, saving her money to supplement her school scholarships. At the end of the summer, Katie left for nursing school, full of the excitement of a college-bound freshman.

Meanwhile, I used my savings to purchase a blue Chevy Nova from a used car lot. The Nova had none of the appeal of the Mustang, but it served as a reliable vehicle for bar hopping.

One weekend morning, after Katie had been gone for a month, Megan asked me, "What are your plans, dear?"

"I don't know." I helped myself to an English muffin that had just popped up from the toaster.

"Why don't you call your grandmother? I'm sure you could get work at the resort," Megan suggested.

"I can't go to Tanglewood Falls." I buttered the muffin. Suddenly, I felt like a beggar and refrained from taking a bite.

Joel said, "Your grandmother would be happy to see you."

"You don't understand," I practically pleaded. "My whole family is there."

"I realize that," Joel said. "You'll be all right. I took the liberty to call your grandmother. She wants you to work at the resort and live near her. She's waiting for you."

"In the meantime," Megan said, "you're welcome to stay here until you're all set. Go ahead, eat the muffin!"

I was surprised that Joel had called my grandmother on my behalf, but he was probably right. I made plans to leave the family that had so kindly provided me with comfort. After spending a September Saturday packing my few belongings, I said goodbye as if I were going to my grandmother's. I took a couple of diet pills to fortify myself for what the future held.

That Saturday evening in September, a chilly autumn storm marked the end of summer. I'd intended to postpone my arrival at Tanglewood Falls until I felt strong enough to answer inevitable questions. "How was your summer?" my grandmother might ask. "Why don't you try to get along with your mother?" But I was strung out on speed, so I drove around the mountain passes in circles and ended up in Allentown. It must have taken me hours to go forty-five miles. Night had fallen, the gas tank was nearly empty, and so was my purse.

Katie was in nursing college in Allentown. Perhaps she could help me out again. As I drove, I searched the signs until the school came into view. I knocked and knocked on the door to the dorm, impatient for someone to answer. Finally, the lights came on and an older woman wearing a nightgown opened the door.

"What do you want?" the dorm mother asked.

"Can I see Katie?"

"Visiting hours were over long ago."

"I have to see Katie."

"You have to leave."

"Please let me see Katie!"

Finally, the woman went to wake Katie, who also appeared in a nightgown.

"What are you doing here?" Katie asked. She looked at me with sleepy eyes that easily expressed her annoyance.

"I ran out of gas. I need a place to stay."

"You can't stay here," Katie said. "You'll get me in trouble."

The dorm mother was standing behind Katie. "This is not a motel," the woman said. "If you do not leave immediately, I'll call the police."

"Oh, don't call the police," Katie said. "She's harmless. Oh, Lynn, how about if I give you a couple of dollars for gas so you can get back home?"

"You wait right here," the woman said to me.

I stood shaking and shivering in the doorway while I waited for Katie to get some cash. Katie returned with a couple of dollar bills and shook her head. "You're so wasted. Why are you doing this to yourself? Try to get some help."

I sat in my car in the dark, watching rain on the windshield. I was coming down from the high. Remorse was creeping into the mental places that had been occupied by speed. I'd been pleading for a place to stay, begging for some cash. I hadn't considered the consequences of my arbitrary actions. I blew a friendship because of an irresponsible midnight intrusion.

Dawn arrived through a dense fog that shrouded the streets. On a Sunday morning during the gas shortage, I drove around looking for an open station. Signs pasted on pumps said "No Gas." My car died at a stop light that blinked green yellow red green yellow red.

Suddenly, a man was tapping on my window. "Hi, can I help you? Roll down the window!"

Did he think I was crazy enough to open the window to a perfect stranger?

"Please, let me help you."

He looked like any ordinary middle-aged man of average height and weight, except he wasn't wearing a coat on this cold morning.

"Are you out of gas?" he asked with a smile. I nodded.

"I'll take care of it," he offered. "It's okay. You can trust me."

"But there are no gas stations open," I explained through an inch of open window. I buttoned my jacket and shoved my hands in the pockets.

"I know of one," he said.

"But I have no way to carry the gas."

"I can get a gas can," he offered.

"But I have only two dollars."

"That will be plenty."

The stranger pushed the car over to the side, walked into the mist, and then returned. After he filled the tank, he winked and waved, and vanished as suddenly as he had appeared. Was he a mere mortal, a Good Samaritan, or was he an angel?

I headed toward Tanglewood Falls. I was only a day late. Pulling up to my grandmother's apartment, I could see her watching through the storm door.

"Lynnie, it's so good to see you!" my grandmother exclaimed. "I was worried. I thought you'd be here last night. Wasn't the weather terrible?"

"Yeah, so I thought I should stay at Megan's one more night," I lied.

"You don't look so good. Are you all right? How about I fix you something to eat."

My grandmother bustled about in her apartment kitchen, reaching for milk and cereal. "Tony said he could use you in the office. That man works so hard." She peeled a banana. "I have to have a banana every day. It keeps me regular," she explained. "Oh, I can't wait until you see your brother. He looks so good. He graduated from college, you know. I'm so proud of him."

Like black magic, as soon as she said that, Eric appeared. Shocked to see me, he faltered in the doorway. "Come on in," Grandma said. "Give your brother a hug for God's sake." In front of our grandmother, we hugged like stiff stick figures drawn simply for effect. "Whatever it is between you two," Grandma said, "you should forgive and forget."

Whatever it was, he'd forgotten. I'd pushed it toward the back of my mind.

My grandmother set me up in a cottage no longer suitable for guests. The cozy cottage smelled moldy from the flood fifteen years earlier, and swarms of gypsy moths rushed in when I opened the windows. The whole of the hut was smaller than a roadside motel room, but it stood alone in peace and privacy.

During the day, I operated the switchboard with three hundred connections. "Good morning, Tanglewood Falls." Tony was a barracuda to work for, saying, "Is that any way to answer the phone? You don't sound cheerful. Put a smile on your face when you take a call." Nobody trained me for these tasks. I was sent to sink or swim with the sharks when what I needed was a life raft.

My brother also worked for our uncle and grandmother. We worked at the same place, in a family business, yet Eric refused to acknowledge me. Once, when we literally bumped into each other, he said, "I am ashamed that you are my sister. You hang out with low-life, the bottom of the barrel. When others notice our same last name, I tell them we are not related. As far as I am concerned, you do not exist."

After he'd said that, I stayed awake all night, jotting down thoughts on hotel stationery. *My brother's words spread through me, staining my spirit with shame. A vision of dark, syrupy Port wine spilled on white satin comes to mind. No amount of scrubbing or solution can remove the stigma. Eric set me up for shame by using me sexually, and then self-righteously said he was ashamed of me. He disowned his shame and his crime and projected them onto me.* In the dim light of a small lamp, I re-read what I'd written: *using me sexually*. What? Afraid of the indelible words, I burned the paper with my cigarette lighter.

Sleepless nights were routine for me. Thoughts raced around my mind like a car competing at the Pocono 500 racetrack. Zoom! Zoom! Zoom! With all the knowledge of one high-school psychology class, I analyzed what it must have been like for my brother when I was born. He was three years old. He had witnessed the madness of our father and the sadness of our mother. Then I was born. He may have been afraid his baby sister would rob him of a precious resource: love. Maybe he even wished she had never been born so he could have all the love for himself. Of course, his hostility was subconscious. It manifested in accidental acts of aggression, like pushing and shoving. Eventually, his desire to do away with his sister culminated in a deliberate act of cruelty. He did do away with me. He caused me many emotional and psychological deaths, until my only desire was to die. Didn't I have a stash of sleeping pills somewhere?

One evening after work, I wanted to skate, but Eric was working the rink. When I saw him behind the counter, I almost fled from the building like a cockroach caught in the light. But why would I let him keep me from skating, I thought. Like so many times before, I reached to the top shelf for the box marked "Lynn's skates. DO NOT TOUCH." The box was missing.

"Eric, where are my skates?

"On the rack with the rental skates."

"What? Why?"

"I didn't think you wanted them anymore."

Wasn't that my decision? Amidst hundreds of pairs of ladies' figure skates, there was no way to tell which pair was mine. Had he been so jealous of my ability that he destroyed my skates? Or was this another power play? Did he take it upon himself to punish me? I must have deserved it, so I simply accepted the punishment. Besides, I told myself, skating was for kids.

Now that we were adults, Annie and I would drive to pool halls and band halls in Port Jervis, New York on the weekends. We'd meet our older party chums who could get us into the bars. *Cheers*! After shots of Tequila with beer chasers, Tequila Sunrises, and pitchers of beer, or shots of Wild Turkey or Southern Comfort or Jack Daniels, we were seeing double. After hours of partying, Annie or I navigated the mountain curves in her new Mercury.

One Saturday morning after one of those Friday nights, I cured a liquor-laden, sleep-deprived hangover with a hit of speed. At the gift shop, the cuckoo clocks were driving me crazy: cuckoo, cuckoo, cuckoo. No one ever left the Poconos with a cuckoo clock. I was sorting souvenir T-shirts by size when a woman in a coral-colored pants suit walked in. A coordinating silk scarf was draped around the head. I did a double take to see that it was Annie.

"Hey Annie, why are you dressed like that?"

"I'm on my way to work."

"Since when do you work?"

"My father is putting me to work in the office."

"Why? What happened?"

"Look, look." Annie slowly slipped the scarf off to show a black and blue welt the size of a baseball. "My father cornered me when I was barfing in the bathroom. He beat the shit out of me. I couldn't get away. He said that I was a disgrace. He tore my jeans off. He said I have to dress like a lady, not like a low-life. He said you were a bad influence. He said we can't be friends anymore."

"But how can we avoid each other?"

"I'm supposed to act like I don't see you," she responded.

"But we were supposed to be friends for life."

"I tried to leave you out of it, Lynnie, I really did. I even told him that I'm capable of going to hell in a bucket all by myself."

Her self-evident humor made me smile.

The next day, as I was dusting junk in the gift shop, the in-house phone rang. "Gift shop, this is Lynn."

"Hi Lynnie."

"Annie, where are you?"

"I'm in the stupid reservations office, stuffing stupid brochures."

I could almost see Annie stuffed under a counter with boxes of number 10 envelopes, sneaking a call to her cousin.

"Guess what, Lynnie. I'm getting married. Will you be my maid-of-honor?"

Annie got engaged to Phil. He was the son of the owner of a major tourist attraction. Phil was an entrepreneur, filling his nights with negotiations for kilos of marijuana.

Ruthie defied Tony's forced dissolution of the friendship of her only daughter and goddaughter. We took day trips to New York City so Annie could register for gifts. Even if Ruthie had no cash of her own, she had enough spite. "Up the ying yang," she said gleefully as she charged the shopping sprees to her husband's accounts.

One autumn evening, after the social-event-of-the-year engagement party but before the wedding-of-the-decade, a police cruiser pulled into Tanglewood Falls. Annie and Phil sat in the back seat, behind the bars. Apparently, the cops had seen a Corvette driving erratically. When they stopped the car, the cops saw the driver and his passenger were the grown children of important business owners. The cops took the tipsy lovebirds home.

My uncle blamed me for influencing his daughter. He forbade me to be Annie's maid-of-honor, no matter what the bride wanted. Annie and Phil married as soon as she graduated from high school. They honeymooned in Europe for three months. The newlyweds returned to the states in time for the holidays.

A couple of days before Christmas, Phil told Annie he was going to New York City to buy presents. A couple of days after Christmas, Phil was returned in a hearse. He had died of a heroin overdose on Christmas Eve on the streets of New York.

When I called to console Annie, my aunt said, "She's napping. The tranquilizers the doctor gave her knocked her out." My grandmother got on the line, "Isn't it terrible? She's a widow at such a young age. What a terrible tragedy."

Not much had been said during that call, but its terseness told a lot about the strategy for dealing with death. Take tranquilizers to avoid sorrow. Isolate instead of seeking support. Romanticize widowhood.

Deny, deny, deny. My family used Mass cards and Rosaries to pray for the dead, and then they invested their emotional energy in the funeral. However, no matter how close we had been to deceased relatives, they were never spoken of again, almost as if they had never lived.

After Phil died, my friendship with Annie was sporadic. She fancied herself a model and actress, having her hair styled like *Vogue* cover girls. Local photography agencies used her for brochure ads; she'd be dressed like a ski-bunny for winter promotions or undressed in a bikini for summer shoots. She had a series of bad boyfriends, broken engagements, and abortions. She never went to college. She never even left the Poconos, except to shop for fashions in Manhattan. I missed my cousin but kept my distance to avoid being the scapegoat for her malfunctioning spirit.

As Annie's life fell apart, so did her parents' marriage. Ruthie and Tony became embroiled in a bitter divorce battle. She demanded the house. He said she could not have it. She said that if she couldn't have it, no one could. The house, once featured in magazines, stood empty in the ruins of spite and greed. Roof tiles littered the veranda. Bricks loosened from exterior walls, leaving gaping holes. The hot tub was overturned in the yard. No maintenance company was called in for repair; nobody cared. My aunt moved to a house in town, and I didn't see her much after that.

Meanwhile, my mother and stepfather sold the house in the apple orchard. They planned on moving to Phoenix and starting a business. Before they left, they discussed it with me at Tanglewood Falls.

"We want Rusty to grow up in a normal environment," Mom said. "I don't want you to feel left out. You can come with us if you want."

"It's beautiful there," Dad said. "The desert reminds me of Egypt."

"When were you in Egypt?" I asked.

"You know, in an earlier life when I was a seer to a Pharaoh."

"No, thanks. I'll stay here."

Mom, Dad, and Rusty were a trio tied up in a neat little package, and I was out of the box. I felt left out, but had affairs of my own to sort out. The pill doctor had taken an early retirement, so I hung out with some unsavory characters to score speed. After cashing my paychecks, I got glassine envelopes of crank from dealers loitering on Main Street.

I snorted speed, its bitter taste lingering in the back of my throat, causing a constant sore throat. Sometimes my nose bled into the straw even as I was snorting the stuff. That scared me into shooting the speed straight into my veins. The pharmacist bought it when I told him that I was diabetic and needed a case of insulin needles, thirty-six to a case. I always used a new needle, because old dull needles took more time to get through the skin. I would never want to share with some strange street junkie and end up with a deadly virus, would I? I was a fiend for speed, using it like high-octane fuel to blast my body out of bed. Most mornings I got off on speed before getting up, leaving droplets of blood in trails on the sheets.

The crystal meth is shaped like tiny icebergs and I shave off slivers with a razor blade. How much? This much, that much? More? I measure a hit onto a small round mirror to see and save every white speck. So as not to waste any, I run a finger across the blade and the mirror and lick the microscopic granules. A teaspoon is a mixing bowl, and drops of water moisten the white rock into an odorless liquid. I attach the needle to the barrel and load the liquid meth into the syringe. With a flick of the index finger, I tap, tap, tap the syringe to dislodge the air bubbles. I would not want an air bubble to kill me, would I? I cap the needle, rinse the spoon, and pour alcohol onto a cotton ball. The clean, strong smell of the alcohol associates with speed. I hide the speed, so that no one would find the stash even if they find me dead. I listen. Is anyone coming? Who? My grandmother? Sitting on the toilet lid, I wrap a belt around my upper right arm like a tourniquet, and that purple vein plumps up ready for blast off. With my teeth, I remove the cap and then slip the needle into the vein. Ah, relief. I push the plunger in ever so slightly with the left hand, until blood mixes with the cloudy fluid in the syringe. I slowly push the plunger again, until the barrel empties. After loosening the belt with the teeth, the belt falls. I withdraw the needle, and then hold the alcohol swab to the crook of the arm. What a rush! Into orbit! I savor the sensations that burn through the limbs and chest and prickle the scalp. My heart is pounding like Mickey Hart of the Grateful Dead is using it for a drum. Hot. Dizzy. Dazed. I return the paraphernalia to its hiding place.

I turned the record player on and listened to Linda Ronstadt sing about *"Weeds, whites, and wine, show me a sign"* and lay down so as to not pass out. All of a sudden, I was ready, primed for anything. Lunch hour was over and it was time to go back to the office. Although it was ninety degrees and ninety percent humidity, I put on a sweater to hide my arms. The tracks were not tiny puncture wounds, but bruises upon bruises where the abused veins had collapsed. In the office, I was eager and efficient.

I'd seen what drugs could do to someone. I'd seen Smiley hanging out on Main Street, with a grin affixed to his face. He'd smile even when the cops handcuffed him for urinating in public. Too much crank turned him into a vegetable, void of inhibitions and emotion. There was his ex-girlfriend Birdie, whose arm hung like a piece of string, withering with uselessness. Her boyfriend was shooting heroin into her vein and missed, piercing a nerve. There was Bones, the former varsity football player. He'd had a stroke after a hit of cocaine. I'd pass his house and see him on the porch, a skeleton propped in a wheelchair. I thought it was cruel that his former classmates had nicknamed him Bones. In denial of my addiction, I rationalized that nothing like *that* could happen to me.

To cure my migraines, I used heroin, strictly for medicinal purposes, of course. Why did God make me suffer from these excruciating headaches, anyway? Theories crawled out from the rock of my subconscious: Perhaps the pain was fair punishment for my foolishness. Perhaps the headaches replaced the psychic pain. Maybe the migraines gave an outer reason for inner pain. Maybe they represented a need to release the pressure of pure rage. Suppose the pain was a cry for help? Whatever, I would put an end to the suffering myself. I injected the junk to ease the intense pain and anticipated the euphoria associated with heroin. That treacherous narcotic alleviated a migraine instantly when administered directly into a vein. But euphoria was a mental state I never achieved, naturally or chemically.

Speed was a way to avoid sleep. Nasty nightmares shook me from sleep with screams that had no sound. I'd run from my room to a labyrinth of moon shadows, pacing outdoors at midnight. Sometimes I stayed awake for seventy-two hours straight, chain smoking, and writing poetry. At two in the morning, phrases flew into my brain like brilliant June bugs, but by nine, those same words seemed incoherent or insipid.

I cannot be free, nor be myself,
Without this speed, I belong on a shelf.
No more can I laugh, there's no reason to smile,
Only this dope eases the pain for a while.

Glancing in a mirror, the sight of me as a walking cadaver scared me. The whites of my eyes were yellow, my pupils were dilated, and vacant black pools reflected from where the blue-green color used to be. There were tiny bruises on my forearms, like dots of ink on brittle parchment paper.

My grandmother noticed that I never ate anything other than ice cream cones from the snack bar. When she was working, which was six nights a week, my grandmother would set a table in the storeroom of the hotel kitchen. It must have been lonely for her, dining with cans of beans and bags of rice. Stacked cans of albacore tuna kept her company.

"Ask Craig the cook to fix you a plate of the special," my grandmother said one evening. I felt so hyper I could hardly sit still across from her. She'd known me all my life, but I didn't know what to say. If I said anything, who knew what secret might accidentally spill out?

"The weather has been terrible," Grandma complained. "Everybody's sick with a virus. Even your brother has a sinus infection. He is such a hard worker. That poor boy, he works day and night. I couldn't help but notice that you two don't spend any time together. Did you and your brother have a falling out?"

"Not really. I suppose we're both busy."

"It's unnatural for a brother and sister to not be on speaking terms. I practically raised you two. You were so close as kids. He's grown into such a fine young man. I'm so proud of him."

Her alliance to her grandson was stronger than her bond with me, just like she favored her own son over her own daughter, my mother. I picked at sliced turkey and cold broccoli, feeling a chill of resentment as she praised Eric. Should I tell Grandma that it was not natural for a brother to sexually abuse his sister? I covered my food with a napkin, as if I could smother secrets under table linens. It was useless to tell her the truth, I thought, as I scraped leftovers into the trash.

I went to my tiny cottage to crash, using willpower to refrain from getting off on speed again. Maybe tomorrow I would try to quit a drug I knew was killing me. But the next morning, I couldn't function without a fix, and I accelerated through yet another day on fast-forward.

Tarot and Testimony

Love is the only thing that we can carry with us when we go, and it makes the end so easy.

Louisa May Alcott

In the resort office one morning, I plugged in a cord to answer another call, "Tanglewood Falls. Can I help you?"

"Hi, honey. How are you?"

"Oh, Holly. I'm surprised to hear from you."

"Long time no see. Why don't you come down here?"

I hadn't seen Holly since before I'd gone to the psych ward two years earlier. I wasn't sure if I wanted to see my stepmother or why she'd want to see me.

"Tanglewood Falls is busy making reservations for the upcoming fall season," I explained. "I don't think it's a good time to ask for time off."

"Oh, honey, we haven't talked in ages. I'm sure you could use some time off. Why don't you ask your uncle for some time off?"

Asking my uncle for anything was worse than not having whatever it was that I wanted, even if I knew what I wanted. He was liable to yell at me in front of staff and guests, making me feel mortified.

"You've been working all summer," Holly said. "You must be exhausted. It won't hurt you to ask. Tell him it's a matter of life-and-death."

"Life and death?"

"Yeah, you know your father and I are getting divorced. I could sure use some of your moral support."

"Oh, all right."

That evening, I asked his secretary to ask Tony to give me some time off. The next afternoon, she reported that he said he would think about it. For the next couple of days, Holly kept calling. "Did you get the time off? When will you visit?

I was honest with her: "I don't know. Besides, the battery in my car is dead."

"Just get it jumped and take it to a mechanic and come on down. I'll help you pay for gas."

When I asked the secretary to ask Tony again, she said, "Let's wait until he's in a better mood."

Holly called again. "You're his family," she said. "I can't believe you can't get time off."

Although I'd been working at Tanglewood Falls for nearly a year, it took a couple of weeks to get my uncle's permission for a few days off. I almost wished he'd said no. The plan to revisit New Jersey filled me with trepidation. But I made the long drive on a late summer day, when the leaves of the elm trees were about to take on their autumn hues.

When I arrived at my father's and stepmother's house, a dead rat served as a welcome mat.

"Holly, why is that dead rodent there?"

"Nice, huh? Your father put it there."

In the process of divorce, he had moved out. Pastel paper littered the kitchen counters, blue for overdue utilities, pink for cancelled services.

"He won't make the mortgage payments and the house is in foreclosure. I curse the day I met the crazy bastard. I curse the day he was born."

At the kitchen sink, I chased silverfish with the sprayer until they scrambled down the drain. I cupped my hand under the faucet for a sip of gritty city water. "I'm in a bit of crisis myself," I told Holly. "I think I got hooked on speed. It started with those diet pills, and now I can't stop."

"Yeah, you are really skinny. You better kick the habit. I went to a funeral recently. The daughter of a friend of mine overdosed. She was your age. She looked like she was ninety years old in that coffin, and weighed about ninety pounds. You hang in there, honey."

"Holly, do you think my father is on drugs?"

"Why do you ask that?"

"Well, he offered to score drugs for me."

"He did? When?"

"The summer I got those diet pills from his doctor friend."

"Really? What exactly did Manny say?"

"He told me that if I ever experimented with drugs, he would rather I get them from him than some scum bag on the streets."

"Yeah, the streets are not safe. But Manny could inject cyanide into an artery for all I care. I hate him." Holly lit a cigarette butt retrieved from an overflowing ashtray. "Honey, could you come to divorce court and testify on my behalf?"

"What would I say?"

"Tell the judge that your father encouraged you to use drugs. You were a minor then. They ought to get him for corrupting the morals of a minor. Or child endangerment. Do you have any cigarettes?"

I handed her a Marlboro.

"It's not menthol," she said. "But thanks, honey. Beggars can't be choosers. Look, look what that psycho did!" She showed me a long white box with one dozen dead black rose buds on long stems. The card read, "Till death do us part."

"What sort of florist sent dead black roses?"

"Oh, honey, you are so naive. Could you wait in the den while I place a call to my lawyer?"

I tried to watch *I Love Lucy*, but the TV picture was nothing but snow. My thoughts were accompanied by Ethel and Fred's banter. It finally dawned on me that my father had used black spray paint on the roses to convey his message of hate.

"It's all set," Holly said later.

"What is?"

"The court date. It's tomorrow. You'll go with me, right? I sure need your moral support."

I did not want to go to divorce court. "I don't have anything to wear," I replied.

"I'll loan you a dress. Listen, honey, I really need an ally. Will you testify? I *need* you."

I needed to be needed, so I agreed. "I'll go, but I don't want to be up on the witness stand."

I borrowed a dress, and the tri-colored earth toned suede pumps I had loaned her two years earlier. I wobbled up the courthouse stairs because her big feet had stretched my small shoes. Holly told me to

"Act natural." Natural? I was on the verge of breaking down from nervous energy. Holly anxiously paced the hall, chain smoking, and muttering, "Demented son of a bitch. Deranged bastard."

As we walked into the courtroom, the sight of my father already sitting on the witness stand caught me off guard. I tried to avert my eyes, but was unable to ignore how the side of his face lifted in a half smile to greet me. It was one of the few times in my life when my eyes met his, and in that fleeting moment, I felt sorry for him. Evidently, he thought I was there on his behalf.

The judge asked him, "Where is your counsel, sir?"

"I represent myself. I know my rights." My father's face wore a cloak of confidence.

Holly's lawyer questioned him: "Is it true that you offered drugs to you daughter?"

"I was trying to protect her."

"That could be construed as corrupting the morals of a minor," the lawyer said.

My father rose, and with an incredulous expression he shouted directly at me: "Tell the judge you know that I meant it for your own good. How could you tell Holly? How could you betray me? Holly conspired against me. She taught you to hate me. Do you hate me?"

Manny yelled at Holly: "You made your bed, you goddamned slut. Now lay in it."

"I hope they lock you up for life!" Holly shouted.

The judge was shouting as he pounded his gavel. "Order in the court! You're in contempt."

My father slumped back in the chair, and with a lowered voice, appealed to me: "Lynnie, do you hate me? Do you hate your own father? How could you hate me? You have always been Daddy's little girl. It hurts me that you hate me. Whatever made you hate me, I am sorry. Tell me that you don't hate me."

The divorce proceedings were as much about love gone wrong between a father and a daughter as they were about irreconcilable differences between a husband and wife. It was all so twisted, and my head reacted with the pulsing of constricted veins that felt like barbed wire inside my brain. It took all the strength I had to raise from the seat and leave the courtroom. I waited by Holly's car. When she appeared an hour later, her hands were shaking so that the match would not meet with the end of the cigarette she was trying to light. I lit cigarettes for both of us. "I'm drained," she complained.

"I'm shocked, Holly. Did you hear him say he was sorry? My father never said he was sorry for anything."

"He's just a sorry son of a bitch. I'm sorry I ever laid eyes on him. After all he's done to me I should spit on his grave."

"Where is he?"

"He's probably trying to weasel out of paying alimony."

At the house that once belonged to my father, I surveyed the fragments of a family not yet dead but no more living. The bunk beds where I laid with eyes wide open were stripped to bare striped mattresses. An infant's mobile hung in the nursery over an invisible crib. My father's room was perforated with bullet holes; a window was shattered in the shape of a spider's web. Vials of drugs laid askew on the dresser: some contained Phenobarbital or Thorazine from a pharmacy, and others, without labels, contained powders or pills that even I could not identify. The phantom torment of incomprehensible schizophrenia seemed to echo within the four walls. What if my father showed up? How could I face him after I'd turned my back on him? In the kitchen, cabinets and drawers hung open, curtains hung awry, and boxes spilled over with junk. This was the wreckage of life gone crazy. Holly was squatting and smoking on a packed cardboard box, using a fry pan for an ashtray. I was ready to leave. "Do you need anything before I go?" I asked Holly.

"I needed you to testify for me against your father. There's not a thing you can do for me now."

I felt like crying from confusion, but her eyes, which were red with fury and burning with hate, kept me from showing her my vulnerability.

"I read your astrology chart," Holly sneered. "I double-checked the tarot cards. You will be lucky if you don't end up just like your father."

She zapped me with her witch's brew of bad luck and ill will. She took my worst fear and threw it back in my face. She turned a friend into an enemy. For nearly a decade, we had been allies as we witnessed the worst together. With her attack on me, the daughter of my father, she was ending our enigmatic relationship as adversaries.

As I walked through the dilapidated back porch, I froze, like the smashed thermometer that was stuck at thirty degrees. I wondered about my half-sister Heather, the baby who was put on the porch to perish. I heard Holly's raspy voice call out to me. "Honey?" For a second, I thought she might apologize. I turned toward her voice.

"Honey, there's something you should know." Perhaps she had a secret to share that would clear the air.

"What is it Holly?"

"Once a junkie, always a junkie."

She added insult to injury, and then and there I swore I would never see my stepmother again.

At the counseling center, the cotton curtains beckoned the breeze through an open window. The high-pitched sounds of children playing outside brought me back to the present. I looked out. Children were at a party in the park, playing with colorful crepe streamers and balloons. "Tag, you're it!" a child squealed. I turned back to see Karen, her blue eyes riveted in my direction. She tended to my emotional growth like a scientist searching for a cancer cure. She asked, "Did you see Holly again?"

"No. When the marriage was over, she no longer needed me to side with her against my father. I guessed it was all about her greed for alimony."

"Your family was not good at gracious goodbyes. Did you see your father again?"

"No. The courtroom was the last time I saw him."

"Are you able to answer his question?"

"What question?"

"Did you love your father?"

"That was not his question, since he asked from fear and not love. He asked if I hated him."

Whether I loved or hated him, or both, was an abstract piece of heart subject to interpretation. It depended on how I looked at it. My instinct was to love him and expect him to love me in return. That was natural. Perhaps if he had loved me it would have been easier to love him. But he did not nurture love. Instead, he provoked hatred. Love was defeated by fear until I hated him with a passion, which was what he'd asked about. I wrote one line to describe how I felt: *It saddens me beyond my tears that love was lost within the fears.*

To resolve the tumultuous relationship with my father meant recognizing that he could not be separated from his mental illness. It takes forever to find the scattered shards of the broken heart of a little girl. Yet I was certain that he offered an apology in spirit.

Choice and Control

The strongest principle of growth lies in human choice.

George Eliot

Looking out the window of the counseling center, I was watching a child blow out seven candles on a birthday cake. "Those children at the birthday party remind me of how I used to party."

"Why don't you tell me about it," Karen invited.

I worked at Tanglewood Falls by day and partied with colorful characters at night. At least on the party circuit, I was popular. There were lots of party friends, but no real friends to speak of, or to, because we were too loaded to carry on a conversation. Typically, I partied with my new friend Lisa, who partied with her brother Leo, who partied with his girlfriend who often flirted with other guys. With several kegs of beer and kilos of pot, sometimes the parties got out of control.

On one occasion, which could have been any night of any week, I picked up Lisa. She was tall and thin, with spiked and streaked blonde hair. She wore bell-bottom jeans that hugged her waist just below her round belly and a tube top that stretched across her small breasts. "Hey, Lynnie, let's go downtown. Andy just moved into an apartment. He's having a party."

"Who is Andy?"

"Leo's friend."

Leo and his girlfriend were already at Andy's apartment, fighting in the kitchen. From the living room, I heard Leo shouting: "Were you trying to make me jealous?"

It was all too familiar, like the fights my father had with Holly.

"Lisa, I'm out of here," I decided.

"Don't be such a party pooper. Relax." She patted the slick fake leather couch, and I sat with a throw pillow pressed to my torso. We were watching The Rolling Stones with Mick Jagger mouthing the microphone with his inflated lips. Lisa passed a joint.

"I'll give you something to be jealous about," Leo was shouting. His six-foot frame loomed over his petite girlfriend.

I was waiting for the fighting to stop, just like I had waited in my father's den. Without warning, the pillow flew from my lap.

Leo grabs me by the arm and hauls me to the bathroom.

"Stop. Let me go!"

He pushes me down on my knees.

"Help!"

No one can hear me above the blaring stereo. He pulls a string to turn on a bare light bulb, then cranks open a window. To my left is a porcelain pedestal, to my right is a wall, and in front of me, between my body and the toilet, an erection emerges.

"Stop. Let me go!" This can't be happening.

He holds a chunk of my hair, presses on my head, and rams my face onto his penis.

Ow! My jaw cracks with the pressure. I try to raise my hand but my elbow is lodged perpendicular with the wall. With my forehead against his crotch, I am suffocating in his rank odor.

A voice growls, "Suck suck harder suck suck suck swallow swallow bitch swallow." I hear banging on the door. "What are you doing in there?" I hear yelling from what seemed like outside. "Look through the window. That slut is in there with my boyfriend. That uppity bitch is sucking his dick."

He shoves me away and flings open the door, done with me.

As I was heaving into the toilet, I heard Lisa shouting: "How could you, how could you? That is no way to make your girlfriend jealous." Andy was shouting: "Shut your old lady up before the neighbors call the cops."

Lisa came into the bathroom. "I'm taking you home," she said. As we were walking out, Andy shrugged and said, "Guess this party is over."

Lisa hissed at her brother, "You Neanderthal!"

"Why didn't she defend herself?" Andy asked in accusation.

"This was not her fault. My brother did this."

Her words were reverberating in my mind: "My brother did this, my brother did this" along with self-recriminations: Maybe it was my fault. Perhaps I was a slut and a fucking bitch, or nobody at all.

I was an accident waiting to happen as I was driving Lisa home. The noise in my head was louder than traffic in gridlock with multiple drivers honking horns. Like cars ignoring lanes, my thoughts lacked order.

"Stop!" Lisa shouted. "You almost went through the red light. Have you heard a word I've been saying?

Disrupted from my carelessness, I asked Lisa, "What is it?"

"I have a problem," Lisa said. "But you have to promise you won't say a word about it."

I was almost glad that she had a problem to preempt mine. "Whatever it is, I won't tell anyone," I said.

"I'm pregnant," Lisa announced.

"Are you sure?"

"Yes, I'm sure I'm pregnant but I'm not sure who the father is. I have to go to New York City."

"Why the city?"

"I have to see a specialist. But he's expensive. Can you loan me some cash? I promise I'll pay you back."

The next day, I cashed my paycheck for Lisa. But I never saw that money again. Somebody told me she moved to Florida after getting an abortion.

At some of the parties, where speed freaks and heroin addicts mingled with nothing more than a needle in common, there was a junkie named Christopher. He had shoulder-length, curly blonde hair, a stocky build that filled out a tie-dyed T-shirt, skin scarred from burns, and magnetic blue eyes. He was a casualty of the Vietnam War, a shell of a man with a wounded body and a soul missing in action. We were drawn to each other, kindred spirits ship wrecked on an inhospitable island, searching for signs of rescue.

"You make me wonder," he mused. "You are the wonder chick." I wondered about him, too, pondering our peculiar affinity for each other.

We had no conversations beyond a shared interest in rock and roll and lukewarm bottles of Cold Duck. Sitting on a porch swing on a chilly summer night, Christopher wrapped me in his fringed blanket. When I plowed through his neighbor's fence with my car, he took the rap, paying for the property damage. Other than that, we just hung out.

In June, Christopher started seeing a psychiatrist, courtesy of the Veterans Administration. Since he had joined the Army, he was eligible to join a free methadone program. Seeking rescue from the same system that had thrown him over board, he traded a street habit for a clinic prescription. In July, his brother got him a job in construction. Christopher was going off to work instead of getting off on heroin. In August, the psychiatrist ran off with a patient. Christopher predicted, "I don't think I can make it without the shrink." He scored Seconals and Nembutals to soothe his stressed-out mind, strung out on reds and yellows instead of monitored on methadone.

In September, I went to Christopher's house to idle away an early autumn afternoon. Christopher was passed out on the couch with his camouflage pants loose at the waist, his belt on the floor.

"Chris said he was feeling down," his best friend Bo claimed. Bo was sitting backwards on a kitchen chair, his legs straddling the back, reaching into a bag of fries from a fast-food place. "He kept asking to get high. So he took a hit."

"You mean you gave him a hit," someone shouted from the living room.

As I walked toward the sink, Bo pulled me to his lap. "Where do you think you're going?"

"To get a wash cloth."

"Oh, just don't use the phone," Bo ordered. He was looking pale. His skin had not been tanned by a summer job and his belly was soft from too much beer. Bo's brown, wiry hair hung below the seat of the chair, nearly sweeping the floor. Looking at his hair made me feel sweaty and scratchy, as if a wet wool blanket had been thrown over my shoulders.

Christopher's scarred skin was a mottled blue-green shade and his chest was barely rising. I could feel the cold flesh of his forehead, but sweat streamed from beneath his sideburns. Dabbing his face with a moist dishtowel, I asked, "Should we take him to the emergency room?"

"Duh. Does anything register?" Bo said. "We'll all be busted for guilt-by-association. His mom will take care of him. We'd better hustle out of here."

That evening, while these friends were getting drunk and laughing hysterically over *All in the Family*, I worried.

"Hey, get over it. Chris was hard-core. He can handle it," Bo said. "Here's his number if you insist on checking up on him."

I cautiously dialed and asked for Christopher. His mother said, "He's sleeping on the couch." That's all. He's sleeping. Still, I worried.

The next morning, the phone rang in my cottage and before I answered, I knew the reason for the call. Bo explained that earlier that morning, Christopher's brother went to pick him up for work and found Christopher with a syringe in his arm. It appeared that Christopher woke in the middle of the night, did another hit of heroin, and since he had been clean for a while, it was too much. His brother had taken Christopher to the hospital, where he was pronounced dead on arrival. Twenty-six years old.

That night, I awoke from dreaming that Christopher was on the rocking chair in my cottage. At first, I was afraid of what I was seeing as my eyes adjusted. A figure of light, wearing a gauzy robe of white and framed by a golden halo, appeared to be sitting in the dark. The hazy form was in the chair, as if looking at me, as if talking to me. I sensed a warning, but the apparition was silent. No longer afraid, I fell back to sleep comforted by the apparition. Or was it real?

My sole objective the following day was to get a hit of heroin. At eighteen, I had no aspiration to live to the ripe old age of twenty-six. My ambition was to join Christopher in heaven, or was that hell?

"Bo, lay a hit on me," I begged.

"I'm out."

"Come on, don't hold out on me now!"

"I know what you are thinking. I won't help you with that."

No matter who I asked, the market for heroin had crashed. Like cockroaches scurrying for cover, dope dealers go into hiding after an obvious overdose in a small town.

"You were Chris's favorite chick. You should go to the wake with me," Bo urged.

"What am I supposed to do at his funeral?"

"Just go with the flow."

"I don't want to."

"Christopher would be glad to see you pay your last respect."

"Oh, all right."

As we walked into the funeral home, Bo linked his arm to mine, as if the wake was an ordinary social event. Naturally, the somber sight of Christopher lying in a satin lined casket took me aback.

Someone whispered, "Why isn't he dressed in jeans?"

When Christopher's mother thanked us for coming, I imagined her pain: realizing her child died of an overdose after surviving a war, buying her son a suit so he could be buried in dignity, purchasing his plot before her own.

I must have been dreaming. There was Christopher, his form like a star with a luminous essence yet without a surface. I was there, too, sitting with him on his fringed blanket, which was spread over his casket. It was a beautiful warm day, and we were watching his funeral together as if on a three-dimensional, high-definition screen. The sky was bluer and the grass greener than any artist's brush stroke of vivid color on a painted canvas. The air had the pungent smell of fresh earth at a newly dug gravesite. There were not many people at the funeral, but those who were there were sad. Christopher and I were having the most pleasant time, sitting cross-legged and facing each other. He plucked blades of grass and put one in his mouth, letting it perch on his lips, and handed a blade to me. When I pressed the green grass between my lips, I had a taste of something sumptuous, both sweet and salty at the same time. We were playing the childhood game of patty-cake. We were touching palm-to-palm, lifeline-to-lifeline, and with each press of our palms, I intensely felt the giving and receiving of love. All the while, I was hearing the melody to "He's got the whole world in his hands. He's got the whole wide world in his hands." Christopher was talking as we kept the rhythm of patty-cake. "Don't be so sad. I know I am dead. I'm not in any pain. You are not to come to me. I will be with you, for a while." All my senses were engaged: sight, sound, smell, touch, and taste. But I must have been dreaming.

I wrote a letter to Christopher, as if I could send it through space and time.

I feel the absence of you as strongly as I feel the presence of you. For no matter how far apart, you are still very close. When you were around, I was never alone. Yet, I am not alone for you are still around. You are nowhere to be seen with eyes that look for you here and there and everywhere. I sense your being near to me breathing at my side. Your being encircles me still, your arms embrace me yet, your wisdom enlightens me as ever, and your love enfolds me forever. The image of you is imprinted indelibly upon my mind; within my heart too, you are here.

Several days later, my grandmother handed me an envelope from University of Colorado, Boulder. “It’s thick! It must be good news! All your expenses are covered by your college trust fund. Travel, tuition, room and board, books, everything.”

I didn’t think I was worthy of such a wealth of opportunity. “Thanks, Grandma, but I don’t think I can go.”

“Why not?”

“I’d be alone. I won’t know how to make my way around campus.”

“You’ll make friends! You can join clubs. You’ll be studying for tests. You can come home for Christmas and spring breaks.”

Strangers, tests, and travel all sounded so overwhelming. I’d rather crawl into a cocoon and lay dormant until spring. “I can’t go!”

“Well, I’d love to have you here, with your mother so far away in Arizona.”

“What would I do here?”

“I could train you to manage the hotel kitchen.”

I didn’t think I could manage to avoid my brother on a daily basis.

“I don’t know, Grandma. Maybe I should go to Phoenix.”

“If that’s what you want, I won’t come between you and your mother. Maybe you should go to Phoenix and be with her. I’ll make the arrangements with my travel agent, and I’ll have Eric drive you to the airport.”

A couple of days later, Eric drove the two hours from the Poconos to the Newark airport. So close in the cramped car, I couldn’t help but notice the similarities of skin between siblings. Neither one of us had an olive-complexion like our Southern Italian mother; we were both fair-skinned like our Northern Italian father. Eric's flesh was as translucent as mine, showing blue-gray veins bulging with tension. His left hand on the wheel made me steady because he was taking me away. His right hand on his knee made me uneasy. What might he take away from me with that inactive hand? I tried to make small talk about his 8-track cassette tapes of Richard and Karen Carpenter. Why couldn't we be like a brother/sister band? His taste was different from mine; I was silently reciting the lyrics to Neil Young's "The Needle and the Damage Done." As my brother was driving, he concentrated on the road with his lips sealed in sanctimonious silence. He was probably glad to get rid of the body of evidence of adolescence gone awry.

"I hope you can get your life straightened out," he said as we parted.

It's a six-hour flight from Newark to Phoenix. My grandmother had packed snacks, good wishes, and magazines in my carry-on bag. Perhaps I could carry on with a normal life in Phoenix. As I looked over the clouds, I recalled the dream about Christopher. I sensed him comforting me at 36,000 feet above the earth.

"Look at me, Lynn," Karen was saying.

My eyes were focused on the carpet in the counseling center. When I lifted my head, Karen met me eye to eye: "You had a soul connection with Christopher, didn't you? That he was a drug addict, as you said, did not make the connection any less important. His death had quite an impact on you."

"I was obsessed with thoughts about him. Why did it take me such a long time to get over his death?"

"You were grieving. Mourning doesn't come with a stopwatch; it takes time. Grief is a powerful emotion with many layers, like denial, anger, and acceptance. His death represented the other losses inherent in trauma. Focusing on his death allowed you to grieve the loss of your childhood, the loss of protection by parents, the loss of your sense of self."

"I was grieving accumulated losses that I hadn't acknowledged before."

"That sounds about right," Karen agreed.

Excited by insight, my arms flew up as if participating in a wave at a baseball game. "I just hit on something," I interrupted.

"What?"

"I couldn't control Christopher's death, just like I couldn't control Heather's life. I couldn't even control the loss of my own virginity. So I was also grieving the loss of control."

"So much in your life was beyond your control. What do you think you could have controlled?"

"My friends," I realized. "I befriended everyone who seemed to like me, or I did anything to get him or her to like me. It did not matter if I liked them, as long as they showed me some sign of the affection and acceptance I craved."

"What does that remind you of?"

"My own family. I was used to a family out of control, a family that took control of my body. My so-called friends used me in ways that I was accustomed to, physically and emotionally. It's like I automatically put myself in harm's way."

"Yes," Karen nodded. "The early episodes of sexual abuse set the stage for subsequent assaults. That does not mean it was your fault."

"What now?"

"You have the ability to assess your surroundings and the power to control your activities. When you meet people, you have the right to ask yourself whether you like them. When you are asked for a favor, ask yourself if you want to do it, or if you are doing it to avoid confrontation or out of a misplaced sense of duty."

"But if I don't do things for people, I won't have any friends."

"Choose your friends based on healthy common interests. True friends bring out the best in us. Be true to yourself by acting according to your own values."

I'd been allowing bits and pieces of myself to be swept away. I was learning that the whole of life was more about how I shaped it, day by day, by making good decisions and better choices.

Stress and Desensitization

I cannot believe that the inscrutable universe turns on an axis of suffering; surely the strange beauty of the world must somewhere rest on pure joy.

Louise Bogan

I'd been coming to the counseling center for months. One summer afternoon, I was early. It's not like I was eager to expose more of my past. But talk-therapy was challenging me to create myself and I couldn't wait for the finished product. While I sat in the small waiting room, I watched a distant date palm waving in the breeze. The brownish-green fronds spread over the top, protecting the fruit from the scorching sun. A couple of clients came and went, and when Karen arrived, I gave her barely enough time to settle into her chair. "When do you think I'll be finished?" I practically demanded.

"With what?"

"Counseling. I feel like all I do is talk about my problems."

"We talk about trauma and recovery, your strengths and your development," Karen said. "Recovery is a process, a work in progress, like making a piece of art. You don't want to force an end product."

That's true, I thought. It's like baking a cake. The process of measuring and mixing ingredients, greasing and flouring pans, was as important as the finished product. If the process was rushed and an ingredient missed, the whole cake could flop.

"Let's begin where you left off," Karen suggested. "After Christopher died, after the prescription scam, you moved to Phoenix. Your mother, stepfather, and half-brother were living there. What happened when you arrived in Phoenix?"

I felt like an outsider when I got to my parents' house. They seemed like such a close-knit family. What with all my troubles, my mother, stepfather, and my brother Rusty had been better off without me.

The house in Phoenix backed up to an orange orchard. An oasis of hibiscus and oleander bushes surrounded the pool in the back yard, and a pitcher of tea brewed in the sun. My mother had a room ready in their four-bedroom house, using the furniture from my high school bedroom.

"You can stay here for a while," my mother said. "When you start college, maybe you can rent a room from a nice family near the school."

Why would I rent a room from a family when I supposedly had a family and my own room? How would we know if they were nice? I wouldn't be able to discern a mild-mannered monk from an ax murderer.

My suitcase was stored on the top shelf of the closet as a reminder that my visit was as temporary as a city slicker at a dude ranch. I organized and reorganized my scant wardrobe in a dresser occupied by my mother's dated *Ladies Home Journal* and *Redbook* magazines. The captions on the cover made promises that the articles failed to deliver. "Can this marriage be saved?" Another drawer was filled with fliers from health food stores; the informative text was actually advertisement for vitamins. "Cure the common cold with vitamin C." A third drawer contained a shoebox of trial and error supplements from the latest trend in alternative healing. My mother stashed quick fixes that were no solution for her complex problems.

Reading *The Phoenix Gazette*, I wondered if I was good at any job listed under "female help wanted." Maybe I could be a dancer in a club. Girls dance *naked*? Maybe I could sell carnations on a street corner. Maybe I could clean rooms at a hotel. Maybe I could bathe dogs at a pet shop. Maybe I could waitress at Cork and Cleaver. Or maybe not. I would not wear that uniform with the micro-mini skirt and the blouse that revealed cleavage. Over a bowl of cereal each morning, I continued to read the want ads.

I made myself useful to ensure a place to stay. When my mother needed a chiropractor or a health food store, chelation therapy or a colon cleansing, I drove her downtown to the dubious treatment centers. When Rusty came home from school, I baked chocolate brownies or yellow cake with chocolate icing. "Oh, Lynnie, you outdid yourself this time. This cake has such a tender texture. It's delicious."

"Really? Thanks, Mom."

When my stepfather came home from work, I served him Earl Grey tea.

"Dad loves for you to make him tea," Mom said. "It's nice that you bake. But sometimes it sounds like a bomb going off in the kitchen. Could you cook a little quieter?"

Meanwhile, I stopped using street drugs. My second car had been sold before I left Pennsylvania. In Phoenix, it seemed like too much trouble to ride a bicycle along squares of unfamiliar streets to search for dope. Besides, who knew what strange stuff dealers might sell? It could be some toxic substance, one hit of which could cause a permanent case of psychosis or paralysis. I'm sure my mother and stepfather had not known the depths of my addictions.

My cousin Annie was addicted. She sent me a postcard from an alcohol detoxification unit in Pennsylvania. "Guess what," she wrote. "I learned in therapy that I'm actually worth a shit." I wondered who or what made her think otherwise. My parents and I didn't talk about Annie, except when they said, "Oh, what a shame," in reference to the life they judged as wasted.

After living with my mother and stepfather for a couple of months, I got a job as a waitress at Howard Johnson's. I was good at serving food and mopping spills. A couple of blocks away from my parents' house, I rented a studio apartment. That's when I met Todd.

"You met Todd about four years ago," Karen was stating. "Let's talk about what's happening with you and Todd today. You've been financially dependent on him for quite a while. Have you thought about getting a job?"

"A job? But it's been years since my last job."

"I realize that. You're healthier now, emotionally and physically. How do you feel about getting a job?"

"Scared. What if? What if I get sick? What if I can't work? What if I can't think?"

"One thing I know you can do is think."

"Yeah, there are too many thoughts. They seem jumbled like puzzle pieces. I can't fit the pieces together in a pattern. My mind roars with complete nonsense, without rhyme or reason or rational conclusion. Sometimes I think I could scream out loud for inner silence."

"When did this confusion last occur?" Karen asked.

"A couple of days ago, a trip to the grocery store for a few items seized me with terror, so I decided to do without. The next day, I forced myself to shop, but once inside the store, my palms perspired and my heart palpitated. The choices overwhelmed me: this bread, that size, this price, that amount, double coupons and fat content. My mind was like an archery target, with arrows of disconnected thoughts misfiring *what ifs*. All of the thoughts missed the bull's eye of a rational connection. What if I went berserk? What if I fainted? What if I threw up? What if I dropped a carton of eggs? What if I bought round steak and Todd really wanted ground round? What if I forgot something? In the checkout line, I was crowded, even with only one person ahead and another behind. The cashiers seemed to take hours to bag groceries, chatting about the weather. I felt as though the customers and cashiers were watching me, but I could not make eye contact. I scurried from the store and rushed to the car. How could I get a job when I could not even get groceries?"

"What you describe are panic attacks, a common reaction related to anxiety. There is a physiological connection between the mind and the body. One way to relax is to concentrate on breathing. Deep breathing allows calmness to enter the body. Breathe in, hold to the count of four, breathe out to the count of four, inhale, hold, exhale, take it all in, let it all out. With every concentrated breath, you can experience peace of mind."

"You make it sound easy."

"You make it too hard. The inner silence you cry out for is a search for inner peace. Try repeating affirmations as you breathe: 'I am submerged in peace. I am immersed in peace. There is nothing but peace.'"

"I thought peace pertained only to political issues such as war and peace and peace treaties."

"Peace is also achievable from within. You can tap into that peace at any time by breathing deep. You know what Ralph Waldo Emerson said?

"What?"

"He wrote: *Nothing can bring you peace but yourself.*"

Before I left for the day, Karen gave me another homework assignment: "I'd like you to list ten things that interest you."

"Ten? But I can't think of ten." I had lost interest in books and music, or thought that those interests were not important. I paused to censor my thoughts.

"Lynn, stop thinking. Just name one thing."

"House plants."

"Good. Let's go on an outing. We'll go shopping for house plants."

It seemed so silly, but Karen seriously planned our excursion as a desensitization technique.

"We'll drive in separate cars," Karen suggested. "We can take the Superstition freeway to the Extension Road exit."

"But I don't drive on the highway. What if I miss an exit or run out of gas?"

"You can follow me."

"But what if I lose sight of you?"

"I'll drive slowly," Karen promised.

I followed closely behind her gray Honda; she seemed like a safety net in an unsafe world. "Congratulations!" Karen said when we arrived at the nursery. "You ventured into the unknown without hyperventilating!"

We meandered through the aisles of ferns, ficus, and flowers. As soon as I picked out a plant to purchase, I put it down again. What if it was the wrong kind for dark corners? Breathe! Relax! If I did not choose one plant, another plant was available. There were plenty to choose from, and the choice was mine. Pick one! How about a sanseveria? With minimal light and water, it would survive.

Afterward, Karen was laughing: "I had fun on our outing. How about you?"

"I'm having a revelation! Fun can be experienced in everyday errands. But, why can't I be happy?"

"You *can* be happy! I'd like to explain the effects of a certain condition," Karen started.

"You mean I have a condition?"

"You experienced profound trauma. Have you ever heard of post-traumatic stress disorder?"

"I heard of post-traumatic stress syndrome as it pertains to those who have been exposed to war. My great-uncle was a medic on the front lines in France during World War II. My relatives say he was "shell-shocked" when he returned because he suffered from flashbacks and night sweats. My stepfather spent his childhood in war-torn England and then served in the Korean War. Even the normal sounds of children playing knocked him off his rocker, and he reacted with wrath to any disturbance."

"Yes, post-traumatic stress disorder is a result of profound trauma. Even witnessing a traumatic event may cause symptoms, including nightmares and nausea, headaches and stomachaches, the depression and anxiety. Your body registered the truth of the memories even if the mind repressed them. You experienced threats to your well-being, to your *very* being. You are constantly in an alert mode."

"It's like the traffic light of life is constantly flashing the caution signal. I don't know whether or when to proceed through the crossroads. Something terrible may happen no matter which direction I turn to."

"Exactly," Karen said. "How can you experience pleasure when your inner alarms are blaring? Happiness evolves from a love of life perspective. Remember when you watched the chipmunks play and smelled the Pocono pine? You tuned out the negative chatter and tuned into the positive vibrations of that moment. With all your senses, use that memory as a seed to cultivate contentment again. And the recollection of contentment will grow into a garden of happiness in your everyday life. Happiness flourishes in a moment of good feeling."

"But do I even *deserve* to be happy? After all, I was a drug addict. I attempted suicide."

"Everyone deserves happiness and good things in life," Karen said.

"Isn't it selfish to be happy when so many others are suffering?"

"No, on the contrary. To carry happiness into the world is a gift to others, who can then experience God's great gifts of love and light."

"Happy. I like the word. Happy *sounds* happy," I laughed.

"It helps you to play with the word, doesn't it? That's quite all right! Let's plan another outing. I'd like you to prepare."

"Are we going far? Should I put gas in the car?"

"No, silly, I want you to prepare by visualizing yourself strolling up and down the aisles of the grocery store with a smile on your face."

It was a stretch but I did as she instructed: sit quietly, open my fists, breathe in, breathe out, count down ten to one, imagine a feather floating from the sky, imagine confidently choosing favorite foods, comfortably paying for them, calm and relaxed. Breathe, breathe, breathe. We repeated this guided visualization several times.

At the grocery store, the doors whooshed closed behind us. Feeling enclosed, I sucked in my breath, holding it tight in my chest. The black and white linoleum floor swirled beneath my feet. "Karen, wait, I have to go back to the car. I forgot my list."

"You don't need a list. You're getting only one item, remember? Cereal. You are in control here. Take a deep breath. Look how the items are in order. Your mind and body are in perfect order, too. Breathe."

In the cereal aisle, I felt overwhelmed by choices. Hot cereal? Cold cereal? Cereal bars? Wheat flakes? Wheat germ? Bran flakes? No, they taste like cardboard. Granola? No, too many calories. What would Todd like? Kicks? What would my mother have on hand? Oatmeal? Variety pack? No, that costs too much. What should I pick? Years of making poor choices with my life-at-large rendered me unable to decide on the smallest of things.

A mother strolled down the aisle. Her child was swinging his legs in the cart, pointing at cartoon characters, and she put a jumbo box in her cart. I felt embarrassed by how long it was taking me to pick cereal.

Karen nudged me. "Lynn, what are you thinking?"

"What if the boxes fall on my head?"

"Wouldn't that be a hoot," Karen laughed. "Pick any kind of cereal you like."

My sweaty palm put a box of cereal flakes with raisins into my cart without causing an avalanche.

"Great! How do you feel?" Karen asked.

"I feel paranoid. What if that woman thinks I'm mentally ill?"

"Look at the other shoppers," Karen instructed. "See? No one is watching you."

Everyone was in her own world, mothers taming toddlers, cashiers counting change. A Randy Newman song was playing: *"In America, you get food to eat, don't have to run through the jungle and scuff up your feet."* Perhaps I could release the awful hold anxiety had on me. Maybe I would reduce grocery shopping to the simple errand that it really was. Maybe if I could manage this task, I could manage a job.

Freedom and Faith

To enjoy freedom we have to control ourselves.

Virginia Woolf

Meanwhile, Todd was holding me hostage, at least financially. He exercised a false image of power with his week-to-week paycheck, doling out a stingy portion for groceries. Letting him support me reinforced his image of me as needy. My payoff was a false sense of security. The marriage of convenience, with him paying bills while I kept house, made us merely unfriendly roommates with the same last name. The efforts I made, like doing laundry, maintained the status quo until I was ready to be independent.

"Karen, I've been wondering what it would be like to live without Todd. But to leave him, I need money. I need a job, but he won't let me get a job."

"His control of the household income is economic abuse, as were his prior attempts to keep you from getting a job."

"I don't have any skills. How could I support myself?"

"You are capable of earning your own living. After all, that's what you were doing when you met Todd."

"But what about interviews? What if they ask me to explain the years of not working? What if they find out I spent months in a psychiatric ward?"

"Just answer one question at a time. You are a young married woman who chose to be a homemaker. Now you choose to get back to work. That's all that's necessary to say. A potential employer cannot determine that you were hospitalized."

We role-played interviews: Karen would ask about my strengths and weaknesses until I could answer with relative ease. Karen also recommended visualization. I pictured myself at the bank, smiling at the teller, depositing a paycheck paid to the order of *me*. As I visualized, I repeated an affirmation: "I am guided to the job where I am joyful and where my financial needs are met."

Still, I procrastinated by taking mid-morning naps instead of interviewing. As I fell asleep, I heard the words “the good earth” whispering to me. When I awoke, the words “the good earth” shouted at me. I heard “the good earth” as I laid my head on the pillow for an afternoon nap. Compelled to decipher this message, I asked Karen, “What do you suppose ‘the good earth’ means?”

“It’s a book by Pearl Buck.”

The book made no match to the message in my mind. However, the white pages listed a restaurant in Tempe called “The Good Earth.” I was amazed to hear myself on the phone asking directions.

As I began to enter the restaurant, I studied the small stucco building with foliage surrounding the arched door. When I walked in, I again surprised myself by asking for a job application. The prospect of serving customers filled me with apprehension. What if I had a colitis attack while taking an order? Meanwhile, the hostess and bartender engaged me in conversation and wished me good luck. At least the staff was friendly. The manager conducted the interview:

“Any experience?”

“Yes.”

“Where?”

“Howard Johnson’s.”

“How long?”

“Six months.”

“You’re hired.”

I dreaded telling Todd. The last time I thought I wanted a job, he had said, “No wife of mine will sling hash in some dive.” This time, he just shrugged: “Don’t let the door hit you on the ass on the way out.” He was inconsistent with his craziness, or was it the craziness that made him inconsistent?

I fit in at the Good Earth from the first day. My co-workers were teachers supplementing their income, art students in need of supplies. With people my own age, I expressed a friendlier personality. When I was overwhelmed with customers, other servers helped. The kitchen was in an uproar, with din and clatter and dishes breaking. The server aisle was noisy and hectic, with a playful kind of chaos and confusion. Line cooks cursed and servers swore, but no one took it seriously. The young men were unique characters, and I no longer viewed all men as alike. One waiter leaped and bounded like a jackrabbit, bursting with the energy of youth. Another waiter strode through the server aisle peaceful and poised as if he were meditating on a mountain instead of waiting on the hungry masses. Their ad-lib antics made me laugh out loud. It was a loony bin disguised as a restaurant, and we were loony tunes having a good time at work.

I worked in the mornings and afternoons while Todd slept, and he worked at night while I slept. Once a week, I would meet Karen after my lunch shift, sometimes bringing her a honey-walnut sticky bun from the bakery.

"How's you new job going?" she asked, licking the glaze off her fingers.

"Better than I expected. Todd doesn't control the tips I make. And I have a convenient schedule for avoiding him."

"What are you doing with your evenings?"

"Sometimes I read or watch TV."

"Those activities are good ways to relax. But there are other ways to use your time that may be more fulfilling."

"Like what?"

"Have you considered going back to college? You did so well your first two years. The personal enrichment classes at the community college provide the resources necessary to prepare for independence. How about a homework assignment? Get a schedule, okay?"

With the assistance of the "non-traditional student" service, I signed up for courses such as "New Horizons for Women" and "Personal Finances Made Simple." The classes were a cornerstone to reestablishing my values and autonomy.

Meanwhile, Todd remained unable to fit within the circle of civility. When a neighbor was blaring Bob Seeger's, "Like a Rock" Todd confronted him. Unable to quietly discuss the loud music, it came to a shouting match in the doorway, with Todd threatening to "tear a new asshole." I felt alone even in an apartment complex with five hundred residents, avoiding neighbors because I was ashamed of the behavior of my spouse. As I grew less tolerant of Todd's crass comments, I interrupted him or talked over him to cover what came out of his mouth.

I wondered if it was worse to be married and lonely than single and alone. People can be happy in a relationship, but relationships cannot make them happy. I looked straight into the mirror, and a healthy reflection smiled back. I saw that I had what it takes to be secure: courage, integrity, and faith. I recognized myself for who I was, and that was good enough. I'd be better off by myself.

A TV commercial prompted me to file for divorce. After paying a five-hundred-dollar retainer, I met my lawyer, Mr. Jaworski. The scrawny young attorney with unkempt hair resembled Mick Jagger with a tattered briefcase. He was not like the polished TV representative of the firm. According to Jaworski's legal expertise, I was entitled to this and that, which amounted to a lot of nothing but debt. After the meeting, he asked me to dinner. Thinking there was important information to discuss, I agreed to a cup of coffee at Denny's. Once there, the lawyer complained about his own pending divorce, the high cost of alimony and child support, and the lonely nights without his wife. I felt swindled by the attorney. I deliberated with myself regarding who was at fault; perhaps I'd led him on. No, he didn't deliver on divorce proceedings. I phoned the firm's secretary.

"Mr. Jaworski met me briefly to discuss my divorce, but I haven't heard from him. I'd like a refund of the retainer, please."

"Why do you want a refund?" she asked. Her question was an unexpected cross-examination.

"Mr. Jaworski, well, he." I lost all semblance of assertiveness, and withheld the facts, so the request was denied. Would it have been different if I had the wherewithal to threaten to sue the attorney for harassment?

From the yellow pages, I located another attorney who charged ninety dollars for uncontested divorces.

"You won't contest, will you, Todd? All I want is my life."

"You won't get diddley squat," Todd announced.

Sally was more than supportive of my plans for divorce. She and her husband had recently bought a home, and they offered me a place to stay, a place to store my stuff, and a truck to haul it in. Todd would never know where to find me. What we did not know was that I needed to get away sooner rather than later.

I am dreaming. *Ten Todds form a circle around me. One Todd after another rapes my body while it lays naked in bed. I am screaming, but guttural sounds stick in my throat. I am powerless. Let me go!* When I awoke, I realized that I was in an undeniable danger zone, and it was time to get out.

Early on a Saturday morning, when Todd was expected to be working over-time, Sally and George planned to help me move. But Todd did not schedule overtime that weekend. Instead, he brought glazed doughnuts and coffee home after his graveyard shift, intending to share in pretend domestic bliss. Should I dare piss him off by packing right in front of his face? I started to pile my books in boxes.

Todd grew angrier with me as I wrapped and packed. "My heart is in my throat," he said. "Where do you think you are going? Your heart is as cold as ice. It's colder than a witch's tit." Didn't he already have another helpless victim to humiliate? As I was wrapping a baking dish in newspaper, he yelled, "You can't take that. Put that pot back!"

"Give me a break! My mother gave me this baking dish."

As we grappled over who bought what when, Todd grabbed my throat with one hand. He pushed me into a corner and aimed a fist with his other hand, about to break my nose. Staring at his knuckles, I wondered if this juncture was worth the whole journey. I took a deep breath. Todd passed on the punch when Sally and George arrived as planned, letting themselves in to help me pack.

"Do you want me to call the police?" George asked. "Do you want to press charges?"

Todd backed off. "She's still my wife. Mind your own business."

"Her safety is our business," Sally said.

"So, now you need security guards?" Todd sneered. "Like I said, you can't take care of yourself."

"Hey, Todd, why don't you and I talk outside?" George suggested.

"Why don't you kiss my royal red ass?" Todd left in a huff. My friends and I stood looking at each other, realizing the close encounter with domestic violence.

"Let's get moving," Sally said.

We quickly loaded the boxes without taking time to wrap and pack. I was leaving with all that I needed, including a warm heart. As I left, I looked back into the apartment to see a vacant shell of a living room. Todd would come home to nothing to show for a life with his eighth wife. Rather than feeling free, I was feeling edgy, like a fugitive. Todd was a snake that slithered unseen through the grass or coiled under a rock until he was ready to strike.

In George and Sally's guest room, I shared accommodations with the boa constrictor George kept in an aquarium.

"You're not afraid of snakes, are you?" George asked.

"Only in my nightmares."

One evening, while we were playing Scrabble and making plans for apartment shopping, we heard a knock. Three pairs of eyes looked at the door as if we had x-ray vision through the wood. We looked at each other.

"George, you get it," Sally suggested.

"If it's Todd, I'll let the boa loose to strangle him," George warned.

"I'll get it," I answered, nervy enough to face the enemy. Instead, a police officer showed me his badge. "Please identify yourself, Miss."

Did Todd send a posse to hinder my independence?

"The vehicle in the driveway was reported stolen."

My license and registration proved legal possession.

"Sorry to bother you, Miss."

Evidently, Todd was playing cops and robbers by reporting the car stolen. The cops were obligated to report to him the location of the car, and with that my whereabouts.

With pride, pleasure, and a measure of self-esteem, I moved into a brand new apartment of my own. It was close to my job and the college, and far from Todd's territory, or so I thought. I had leased the apartment with my own money, earned day by day in waitress tips. "I Will Survive" by Gloria Gaynor played repeatedly on the radio, serving as an anthem for divorced women: *"As long as I know how to love I'll know how to be alive."*

My apartment was furnished with surplus marriage goods and found objects. Sally was carrying a Boston fern around, looking for a place to plant her housewarming gift. "This is so nice," she said. "I wish I had an apartment like this."

"Sally, that's silly, you're married and pregnant. This apartment is too small for a family."

"We're getting divorced. I'm moving to my mother's in Nebraska this weekend."

"Why didn't you tell me?"

"George and I wanted to wait until you were settled."

"What can I do for you? You and George gave me asylum from abuse. I'm so grateful."

Even as my friend and I said goodbye, I realized that there was much to be grateful for: the music that lifted my spirits, the books that enriched my mind, and the plants that adorned the apartment. There was so much to be grateful for that I was even glad to be alive.

Standing on the balcony of my apartment, I took in the turquoise twilight of the desert. The sky was shimmering with slender, silvery clouds. A seventy-degree air temperature smoothed my skin like luxurious lotion. Retirees from the north were called "snowbirds" and they flocked to Phoenix for this ideal climate. Photographers commemorated evenings like this in *Arizona Highways* magazine. This breathtaking nightfall made me believe in everyday miracles.

That night, I dreamt of mystical green pastures and rolling hills, with blue sky ongoing to infinity. The landscape clearly depicted the world as a friendly place. In this scene, I found the clarity and peace I'd been seeking, and a positive perception of the future.

One day, I strolled around a nursery selecting plants for the patio. Purple and yellow pansies popped up as if to greet me. Rows and rows of vivid colors vibrated with energy. Was this a flashback to an acid trip? Actually, it was the life force flowing through me, the cumulative effects of meditation made visible in a spring afternoon.

It was time to mark the calendar with an occasion to celebrate. The hole in my heart was filled with hope, returning my will to live along with the ways to bring about a better life. I finally figured out what made me happy: faith, friends, freedom, forgiveness, harmony, health, honesty, and peace. These values fulfilled my life and sustained my sanity.

The divorce was final five years from the day that I had married Todd. As the final curtain closed in divorce court, my real self entered center stage. As if to copyright my own identity, I wasted no time in dropping Todd's last name for my maiden name. I felt fully relieved of the man and the marriage that had nearly been my finale.

A month later, as I looked out the window of my apartment, I saw Todd entering the laundry room. Next to him, a young woman was carrying a load of laundry. She was the image of an earlier me, full-figured, with long brown hair, denim overalls, and a red flannel shirt. Out of all the apartment communities in Mesa, Tempe, Chandler, and Phoenix, he picked the one where I lived to live with his new girlfriend.

For a few days I was unnerved and thought about moving. I even called the rental office to cancel my lease. But I liked where I lived. So I chose to ignore him. After all, there were several hundred units in this complex, and my world had expanded beyond my ex-spouse. With this decision, I realized that I had made a major shift in how I let others affect my life.

After I'd worked a lunch shift one afternoon, I happened upon my brother Rusty near Arizona State University. It had been nearly two years since I'd last seen him. I barely recognized him now that he was nearly six feet tall, wearing shorts and a Polo shirt, a baseball cap, and loafers. He put his backpack on the hot cement and we sat under a stately palm.

"Thanks to Grandma," he said, "I'm using the trust fund and majoring in computer science. Would you believe I'm in a fraternity? Did you know that I'm engaged? Do you want to meet my fiancé?"

He was eager to talk, so we talked about what we had in common: our relatives. I told him that I'd heard from Annie; she was getting married again. Rusty told me that he had flown back to Pennsylvania with Mom and Dad to go to Eric's wedding. I said I'd been invited, but had been too desperate with my own divorce to consider attending.

"Rusty, I am so sorry I was such a wretched sister!" I blurted. "Can you ever forgive me?"

"I can't say your behavior didn't have an impact on me because it did. I have a hard time trusting people. But it wasn't all you. Even when you weren't around, I was miserable. Mom has a terrible temper sometimes, and Dad can be so cynical. But you had my forgiveness all the while."

"Wow. Thank you. You don't know how much I appreciate that."

"Have you talked to Mom and Dad lately?" Rusty asked. "It seemed like you cut them off so abruptly. I don't know what went on, but Mom told me she was always stressed after she talked to you. I wish you and Mom could have a normal, natural mother/daughter relationship."

"I don't know what that is."

"I have to get to class," he said. "Keep in touch."

When we parted, I thought about how Rusty had done all the right things at the right time. He seemed so *normal.* I couldn't help but identify his firm position in the family, which seemed to center around protecting our mother.

Later, as I was pulling up to the counseling center, I saw Karen sitting under the canopy of a maple tree, eating a burger and fries. "Want some?" she offered.

"No thanks. Guess what? I bumped into my younger brother today."

"How did that go?"

"He was friendly. For years I mistreated him, but he said he forgives me. How is that possible?"

"You were a child yourself, weren't you? As a child, you were not responsible for what happened to you."

"Yeah, but, that doesn't relieve me of the responsibility for hurting him."

"Yes, we are accountable for our actions," Karen said. "And you are responsible for what you do now. Still, try to forgive yourself."

"Forgive myself?"

"Yes. God forgives us before we forgive ourselves."

"Oh, Karen, that sounds so cliché."

"The phrase is repeated because it's true," she responded.

"How do I forgive myself?"

"Forgive yourself by not condemning who you were and by celebrating who you are becoming."

"I'm a waitress. I'm getting my real estate license. I'm taking more college courses. What else am I becoming?"

"A survivor. Your sense of self was violated along with your body. Now you're gaining mastery over trauma and taking control. When you lose your identity as a victim, you gain an identity as a survivor."

I thought about what it meant to be a survivor. I had overcome adversity and endured dysfunction. I lived through ordeals, faced demons and death, and reconstructed myself. I was a survivor.

Once in a while, my mother would call. One afternoon she told me that my cousin Annie was widowed again. Annie's second husband had been driving while intoxicated and his car dove down a mountain. "What a shame," my mother said. "She's still in her twenties and she's been a widow two times. Her father had to put her in rehab again."

My heart went out to Annie. I wished we could have a sleep-over in our pajamas with hot chocolate and popcorn. But that was for kids and we were grown, gone in different directions. Maybe someday Annie and I could get together for a long talk.

"How are you doing, Mom?"

"I'm managing. I have toxic levels of mercury in my system so the dentist is replacing all my old fillings. You should check into that, too."

"My fillings are fine. I got my real estate license. I received the 'Lister of the Month Award' already."

"I always thought you'd be good in sales. But don't get any grandiose ideas. Real estate is a very competitive business. With your intelligence and good looks, you could compete with anybody."

"Thanks, Mom."

I thought about how ambiguous my relationship with my mother was. We *appeared* to be close by showing affection and appreciation. But we avoided talking about what really mattered. How close could we be under an umbrella of denial?

One evening, my stepfather called. "Your mother is not up to talking," he began. He told me that three weeks after Annie had been released from the latest rehabilitation center, her car crashed into a pine tree. Despite efforts to save her, including air ambulance to the best hospital in Philadelphia, Annie died. "You know, Lynnie," he said, "you two were wild girls hell-bent on destruction. I thought you'd be the one to go first. I never thought you'd make it."

I'd heard the term "blaming the victim" and that's what his obtuse statements sounded like. My reaction to him felt different; instead of being intimidated, I realized how ignorant and arrogant he was.

Using my work schedule and final exams as reasons, I didn't go to the funeral. My grandmother said she'd put yellow roses, the symbol of friendship, on the coffin for me. I envisioned the burial: first the family would murmur empty endearments, followed by that worthless phrase, "What a shame." Then they would avoid talking about Annie for the rest of their lives. I wanted to avoid my anger at being cheated out of a friendship for life. Annie and I still had secrets to share and I wanted to share with her all that I'd been learning. All I could think to do for her was to live what I'd learned the best way I knew how, for the both of us. And I vowed to undertake the creative endeavors that had given her pleasure, like painting and poetry. I wrote a poem:

Be sorry, for a friend has gone from the earthly plane,
Be sorry, with her passing on, we are left in pain.
Be glad, she has left behind the hardships we endure,
Be glad, she is free now to have her soul be pure.

I dreamt about Annie. We were six or seven years old, dressed alike in lacy white frocks and white veils of tulle that draped to our shoulders. We wore white patent leather Mary Jane style shoes with white ankle socks. Her curly blonde hair glowed beneath the veil, and my own hair was shining like golden-brown strands of silk. It was our First Holy Communion, and we faced each other with our hands folded in prayer and our foreheads touching. We bowed our heads to pray like little angels. The dream spoke of the purity and the love we'd once felt as children.

My grandmother called me more often after Annie died. She'd report the weather, the business, and the obituaries. She would let me know about the last time she had talked with my mother; Grandma confided in me about how hard it was to get along with her own daughter. Meanwhile, all but one of Grandma's brothers and sisters had died. Aunt Ruthie died during hip-replacement surgery and even the family physician, Dr. DeLuca, had died. The ice rink was closed and the roofs of the honeymoon cottages were caving in. No matter the news, I was grateful for our cross-country, cross-generational connection. Our relationship was a solid tie that I treasured.

Transformations and Destinations

When you can't remember why you're hurt, that's when you're healed. When you have to work real hard to re-create the pain, and you can't quite get there, that's when you're better.

Jane Fonda

I was driving on the same streets toward the same motel where I had suffered in suicidal silence two-and-a-half years earlier. The peace that had eluded me in that final gesture now filled my soul. Saguaro cactus bloomed with spring flowers that looked like orange artichokes open to the sun. In the desert, seasons turn with subtlety. Nature paces its change in gradual steps, and in this time of renewal, I danced in sync to the rhythm of life.

I'd been seeing Karen less often. The foundation formed by therapy was strong enough that my insight was standing on its own. More and more, I was able to figure my life out by myself, thinking for myself. This afternoon Karen had asked me to meet her at a coffee shop instead of the counseling center. When my vision adjusted to the change from the bright sunlight to a dimmed diner, I saw Karen sitting in a booth. Her hair had grown, and blonde curls puffed around her head like a pampered poodle.

"Your hair looks good," I said as I slid into the opposite seat. "When did you get your hair cut?"

"Several weeks ago," she said with a smile. "Do you want some pie?"

"Sure. I'm sorry I didn't notice your hair sooner. I'm so self-centered."

"You are also more centered in your own sense of self." She ordered pie and ice water from a waitress who seemed bored with short orders during long afternoons.

"I remember when I met you," Karen began. "You were abused, addicted, and destructive. You were ravaged by that suicide attempt."

"Don't remind me. I almost died. I *did* die."

"What died in that suicide attempt were the false values and attitudes that no longer served your life. In their place, love and wisdom were born to guide you. You survived, and now you thrive. I'm so proud of you!"

"Thanks, Karen. I couldn't have done it without you."

"You did the work. It took acts of courage and leaps of faith to make a comeback from traumatic experiences."

"But, what if I go crazy again?"

"You were never crazy. You were born sane to an insane family." We paused over a plate of apple pie, sharing a piece in wholesome friendship.

"I have something to tell you. I'm getting a divorce," Karen said. My mouth dropped open, and my fork fell to the floor.

"I accepted an offer for a position in Utah," she explained. "I'll be better able to provide for my daughters. The rest of my family is there."

"How can I carry on without you?"

"I can refer you to a colleague for further counseling."

"I'm sorry you're leaving, Karen. Is there anything I can do?"

"Yes. Write your story of transformation."

"But!"

"You have a way with words and words are powerful instruments. Use your ability to share the way back to hope, health, love, and peace. Healing in the world begins with us."

"But!"

"Lynn, don't deny your gift."

"I don't have anything to give."

"Of course you do," Karen said. "Giving to others is as simple as a smile, and there's so much to smile about!"

I reflected on how Karen had led me on a clear path to discover my true self over the last couple of years. She showed the way with practical explanations, achievable destinations, affirmations, meditations, and celebrations. Her compassion shed light on a dark trail, so I could carry on in safety.

But it was another two decades before I was ready to write the first word. Light-years had passed before I realized that I had lost track of time. Had I really survived for over two decades since that suicide attempt? During those years, I returned to college, worked in real estate, made good friends, and sustained some semblance of family relations. I felt like I'd been on an emotional roller coaster ride with long rises and deep plunges. I'd been steering my own cart, strapped in safe and sound.

One Sunday morning, the air conditioning could not ease the heat rising in my apartment. Maybe it was the humidity that reminded me of the summer day when my brother had molested me. I wrote in my journal: "My brother molested me thirty years ago." Although I had spoken about this with Karen a long time ago, and with my stepmother an even longer time ago, I stared at the words as if I'd never seen them before. In fact, I hadn't. I'd never written the words; writing was a form of documentation, and I'd never dared to document the dreadful truth. A significant part of my history was now on paper. I wrote it again but in a different way: "Eric molested me." Those three words were his history, too.

I had spent my teens, twenties, and thirties unable to tell my mother that my father and my brother had sexually abused me, her only daughter. I knew that her emotional equilibrium depended on her not knowing the truth. I needed my mother and I needed her sane. I also needed her approval and acceptance. She'd disapprove of me if she knew the unacceptable truth. That's how we functioned as a family, with an equal measure of acceptance and avoidance; admission of the truth would upset the balance. Now, in my forties, the emotional roller coaster ride took a sharp turn. I could no longer stay on track without telling the truth.

I was sweating even as the ceiling fans circulated air above my head. To cool off, I walked to the grocery store for ingredients for an ice-cold smoothie: bananas, strawberries, and yogurt. I must have forgotten my mission because I walked home with a bunch of sunflowers I'd purchased for a dollar a stem. I arranged those sunflowers repeatedly, putting two in a vase with their heads facing each other and then three in the vase with heads turned away from each other. Four heads in the vase flopped in different directions; the petals made no contact with each other. I snipped the excess foliage that muddied the water, emptied the vase and refilled it again. Sunflower pollen covered the table with a yellow-orange dust.

Although I'd taken a shower earlier that morning, I took another. The shower stream served to cover the sounds of my sobbing, draining me of energy and dirty secrets. I spent the afternoon in my rocking chair, writing my story and studying my sunflowers. A migraine borne of heat and exhaustion kept me company that night.

The next morning, I awoke to a throbbing toothache. My right cheek was swollen and stretched out of proportion. I called the dentist to make an afternoon appointment. Then I called my mother, and hung up before she could answer. The anticipation of disclosure weighed heavy on my mind like canyon boulders. What would my mother say? Would she believe me? Would she blame me?

I envisioned my family members in their Monday morning routines. Dad, Rusty, and Eric would be at their respective jobs. Mom would be in her robe. She'd have on her favorite morning show, *Regis and Kathie Lee*, while doing loads of laundry, eating cookies with tea, taking vitamins and minerals. I felt guilty for making her answer the phone to no one there.

While I was waiting for the gumption to call again, a television advertisement for equal opportunity in education caught my attention. "The mind is a terrible thing to waste," it claimed. The copywriters got it wrong. It is not that the mind is a terrible thing; it is a terrible thing to waste a mind. I'd almost lost my mind under a load of secrets. Now it was time to ferret those secrets out from under.

When my mother answered the phone the second time, I started the conversation slow: "Mom, I have to tell you something."

Perhaps it was my tone of voice that made my mother pause before asking, "What is it?"

I couldn't say the words I'd written. I couldn't make small talk either. Words escaped me.

"Lynnie, are you all right?"

"No, Mom, something is terribly wrong."

"What?"

"Are you sitting down?"

"Yes. What is it?"

"Somebody in the family did something to me."

"Did somebody hurt you?" she asked.

"A long time ago, somebody hurt me bad, and it still hurts."

"Was it your stepfather?"

I paused, wondering why she would assume the worst of him.

"No. It wasn't Dad."

"Then it was your father. There was a time or two that you became so *needy* after seeing him. I wondered if he'd done something to you."

"Yeah, it was him, but he wasn't the only one. I don't want to talk about my father just yet."

"Who else was it?"

"It was Eric."

"You mean your brother?"

"Yes. Eric is my brother."

"Oh, God. What happened?"

"You don't want to know."

"Whatever it is, it's time I know. I'm going to call Dad at work and ask him to come home. When I call you back, will you tell him?"

"Okay."

I wanted to be the one to tell her so that I had some control of the conversation. However, if she was to know the truth, I had to tell it to her through my stepfather, sparing her from hearing it first hand.

Later that morning, my mother called. "Dad's home," she said. "He's on the line. I'm going to hang up now, so you can tell him."

I had no chance to say that I preferred to speak to her alone. But there was no longer a chance that I could hold the words back. When my stepfather asked me to tell him what happened, the words tumbled out like a mudslide after heavy rains.

"Eric locked me in his room…he fondled my breasts…he put his finger in my vagina…"

"I'm sorry that happened," Dad said. "You know, that happens in lots of families."

"It didn't just *happen*. He was *sixteen*. He was *not* a boy. Besides, that doesn't make it right."

"It's good that you told me. Your mother is resting. I'll tell her later and we'll call you back. We'll get through this, okay?"

Having a middleman diminished whatever power I may have had in direct conversation with my mother. I'd given control of my story to my stepfather. Would my stepfather tell it like it is? Or would he tell a second-hand version to ameliorate my mother's anguish?

When my mother called again, she said, "I'm so sorry, sweetheart. I don't doubt you for a second. I knew something was very wrong back then. At first I thought it was all about your father. Then I sensed there was a terrible rift between you and your brother. Had I known for sure what was going on, I would have put a stop to it."

"Do you understand why I felt so unhappy, hateful, and hopeless?"

"Yes, I understand exactly. This explains everything."

Perhaps she could identify with sexual abuse. Perhaps on some parallel universe in some other time zone she'd been hurt in a similar way. After all, she never talked about *her* father or her uncles except as perverts. Her belief in me was a relief during that day of disclosure. She stayed sane and steady as we talked about the reasons and ramifications of abuse. She showed patience of the kind I'd wanted decades before. But I was still feeling the burden of decision: When and how should I confront my brother?

That afternoon, the dentist diagnosed an abscessed tooth that called for an immediate root canal. A molar had rotted at the root and required extraction. A clear yet symbolic coincidence between the body and spirit appeared. The scars of abuse that had festered for life and infected every relationship now called for release.

Over the next couple of weeks, I had subsequent conversations with my mother and stepfather. My mother told me she would be there for whatever was necessary for me to heal. When I felt ready to tell my mother how my father had abused me, she put my stepfather on the phone.

"Your mother has a virus. She's not up to hearing this," Dad explained. "Tell me what happened, and I'll tell her for you."

Again, I was entrusting my stepfather with vital information that I thought was better shared solely between my mother and I. After the conversations with them and before I had a chance to confront my brother, my mother went to Eric's house for a party.

"How could you make nice now that you know?" I asked my mother.

"We were celebrating your grandmother's birthday. I went for the family's sake," she explained. "I was so worried about Frank because his ulcers were acting up under the stress."

"That's the way it's always been and it has nothing to do with me. Eric does not yet know that you know."

"Well," she said, "I don't know how I'm going to deal with this. I can't turn my back on my son."

"I don't expect you to."

"I hope I didn't do anything wrong," she said. "It's hard to know the right thing. By the way, I told Rusty. I thought he had a right to know. After all, he was affected, too."

"You told him already?"

"Yes. He says you have all of his support."

"That's nice, Mom."

"I failed you as a mother, didn't I?"

"No, Mom, I love you."

"I love you, too. What about your father? Maybe if I hadn't divorced him, he wouldn't have done that to you."

Our conversation took a turn as I reassured her that leaving my father, her first husband, was the best thing to do at the time. I thought we'd taken long strides toward understanding in the initial conversation of disclosure, but we were on a treadmill of bad memories and worse mistakes. Speculating on right or wrong, finding fault and placing blame was serving no purpose in healing.

That same summer, I confronted my brother in a letter. Eric responded with contrition for sins he could not remember committing. "I knew there was something between us," he said.

"Do you remember?"

"No, I don't remember the details. But I know. I *know* I am responsible."

"What *do* you remember?" I dared to ask again, still looking for his documentation of the facts.

"All I remember of my childhood is that it was shitty," he said.

He even went to counseling for the first time to request hypnosis but the therapist refused to conduct "regression therapy." In subsequent phone calls, Eric apologized to me. He didn't ask for forgiveness; he said he did not deserve forgiveness.

Long into autumn, I thought about the mixed feelings I had toward Eric. At first I judged him because he avoided accountability by conveniently forgetting his crimes. I couldn't forget how he'd helped to undo my sanity and repressed his memories to maintain an oblivious version of sane. Then I began to understand blocked memory as a method of coping with the incomprehensible. It was as though he had been brainwashed: *you will remember nothing*.

Maybe our father whispered those words in my brother's ear when he played the nighttime games. Maybe if our father had been stopped, my brother would not have been so troubled as to take it out on me. My brother could not take his troubles to our mother; we all sensed her fragile psyche. Maybe the attack on me was an attack on our mother for not protecting him from our father. Maybe it was an attack on the whole family, like my acts of retaliation aimed at my younger brother.

If memories and emotions can be measured, I'd rate my brother's abuse of me with more anguish and anger than my father's. Maybe it's because my father was schizophrenic, alcoholic, addicted. That offers no justification for abusive acts but it gave me pause for empathy, especially since his ultimate act was committing suicide.

I felt forgiveness in the shape of a broken heart mended by compassion. Unseen, unspoken compassion was not enough salve for my mother's wounds. When I told her how much compassion I had not only for my father but also for my brother, she said: "You will never be completely healed unless you fully forgive your brother for what happened."

"Something didn't just happen like an accidental, unforeseen fender-bender on the freeway. Eric used force. You can't force forgiveness on me. But tell me, Mom, exactly how do you want forgiveness to look?"

"I was going through scrapbooks recently. I have pictures of you and Eric holding hands. You two were so close as kids. Maybe you can be that close again. You might need each other in your old age. After all, he apologized to you, didn't he?"

"I don't know if that's enough. Eric betrayed me in the worst possible way. I don't know if…" I hadn't finished the sentence when my mother interrupted: "I never want to hear about your problem again. You can talk to me about anything else, but I don't want to hear about this ever again. I'm hanging up now."

There are many ways to abandon a child, and I felt deserted by her as surely as if she banished me to Siberia. She was forcing me to exclude a chapter that was essential to my story. Neither one of us could call again in compromise. The family façade had finally crumbled under the weight of disclosures and confrontations. We did not speak over the next couple of years, getting information about each other through my grandmother.

"Your mother and Frank sold their house here in the Poconos," Grandma told me. "They moved to Phoenix to be near your brother Rusty and his wife. They have three children now." This news came as a surprise, considering the move had occurred eight months prior. "You didn't know?" my grandmother asked. "Your mother said she speaks to you every week."

"That's not true, Grandma. We haven't spoken in years, ever since I let her know, well, that I was abused."

"I know your mother gets defensive and rude. She's even hung up on me. I wish she and I could have had a better relationship. It's not natural for a mother and daughter to be distant. Put the past behind you. You should call her," my grandmother advised.

I did call her. She told me I gave her the brush-off during our last call, so she was afraid to call me back. We speak about superficial subjects now, such as comparing my cold winters in the Midwest to her warm winters in the Southwest. We talk about her latest virus or flu. Our conversational comfort zone has a small circumference, but I've accepted its limits, not expecting anything deeper than small talk.

I called my brother Rusty, too. I let him know that he could have let me know that he had had a child within the past year. He said that he thought I wanted distance from the whole family. I tried to explain that my relationship with our mother had nothing to do with him, but then I remembered he'd taken on his role of protecting her. For him to call me while she and I were estranged would have been an act of disloyalty to her.

But it's obvious that my family will not be able to build our relationships anew. There is too much strain and pain.

I'm more willing and able to work on my self-improvement by myself. However, I am not alone. The grace of God carried me along on my journey of recovery. I'd inched along a rocky road, even crawled after I'd stumbled and fallen. Now, at last, I see the ultimate destination: a healthy life, a spiritual connection, and emotional and physical well-being.

When we are unable to find tranquility within ourselves, it is useless to seek it elsewhere.

La Rochefoucauld

Epilogue

I'm still here. Although my mind, body, and spirit were affected by my past, there are fewer and fewer times when my past infiltrates my present. I am more able to live in the here and now, and I am optimistic about the future. This is of utmost importance since I am currently facing a life-and-death challenge. About twenty-five years after my suicide attempt, I was diagnosed with Stage II breast cancer. Ironically, in my suicidal mode, I often prayed for a deadly disease that would provide a way out that was acceptable to society. Even more ironic are the measures I've taken to save my life: the devastating bilateral mastectomies and the debilitating chemo are worth it if they improve my chances of living longer. This attitude is a testimony to the therapeutic process and the resiliency of spirit.

Other measures I've taken to counter-act the effects of abuse include activities such as volunteering, yoga, meditation, and massage. (Since I had an aversion to being touched, it took me several sessions to reduce the tension in my body and relax into the beneficial touch.) Although I have attended a non-denominational church that nourishes my spirit, I find as much connection to a Higher Power in long walks. I also find comfort in the company of caring friends. Although there is no magic pill for curing emotional and psychological ills, I've found some respite from migraines in the newer migraine prescriptions and I've gained mood management from the newer anti-depressants. (This is my personal experience, and not intended as a recommendation for any one else. Please consult your doctor.)

While I was writing this book, in my forties, I returned to college to earn a degree in social work and licensing as a therapist. I'd like to help women determine their needs and strengths to enhance their self-esteem and increase their opportunities. I'd also like to advocate for women's rights by providing information and sharing concerns regarding equality, education, and empowerment. I present the benefits of journal writing to groups in spiritual retreats and breast cancer support groups. I am currently writing a non-fiction narrative about my cancer experience. I am still here, and going strong.

About the Author

After her first eighteen years in the Northeast, Lynn Tolson moved to the Southwest where she engaged in careers in real estate and property management. During those years, she survived post-traumatic stress disorder, which manifested in addictions and suicide attempts. Through the therapeutic process, she determined the causes of her dysfunction and was able to ultimately achieve a life that reflects health and happiness. Her memoir, Beyond the Tears, illustrates physical, emotional, and spiritual transformation; her story offers a message of hope. Tolson currently resides in the Midwest where she returned to college to obtain a degree in social work.

18569009R00183

Made in the USA
Middletown, DE
11 March 2015